—— COPPER RED ——

GLAZES

ROBERT TICHANE

Krause Publications,
Iola, Wisconsin

Previously published as *Reds, Reds, Copper Reds*.
Now back in print with an added color section.

Copyright © 1998 by Robert Tichane

Previously published as *Reds, Reds, Copper Reds*,
1985 under ISBN 0-914267-04-3
Now back in print with an added color section.

All Rights Reserved
Published by

Krause Publications

700 East State St.
Iola, Wisconsin 54990-0001
Telephone 715-445-2214
www.krause.com

Please call or write for our free catalog of publications. Our toll-free number
to place an order or obtain a free catalog is 800-258-0929 or please use
our regular business telephone 715-445-2214 for editorial comment and
further information.

Manufactured in the United States of America

Library of Congress Cataloging-in-Publication Data

Tichane, Robert
        Copper red glazes

ISBN: 0-87341-663-5

1. Glaze   2. Pottery   3. Title

                           98-84292
                           CIP

Frontispiece—Ching dynasty peach bloom glazed vase. Courtesy of the
Percival David Foundation of Chinese Art, London. (#579)

CONTENTS

SECTION I - INTRODUCTORY

SECTION II - PRACTICAL

SECTION III - EXPLANATORY

SECTION IV - THE LITERATURE

DEDICATED

TO THE CORNING GLASS WORKS

And To My Friends And Colleagues There

Bruce Adams, Vincent Altemose, Roger Araujo, David Bachman, Rodney Bagley, Raymond Barber, Willis Barney, Roger Bartholemew, George Beall, Frederick Bickford, Linford Bledsoe, Harold Bopp, Nick Borrelli, Robert Brill, Marvin Britton, Ron Burdo, Edward Bush, Gerald Carrier, Kenneth Causer, Harry Clark, Robert Colegrove, James Cowan, Phil Crooker, Lois Crooker, Robert Dalton, Robert Doman, Maude Dunning, Thomas Elmer, A. A. Erickson, Doris Evans, Frank Fehlner, James Flannery, Elton Harris, Hans Holland, Robert Gardner, George Hares, Bob Heitzenrater, Andrew Herczog, Herbert Hoover, Robert Howell, Francis Hultzman, Jack Hutchins III, Clint Janes, Norma Jenkins, Andy Kacyon, Ann Kane, Bob Kerr, Irwin Lachman, John MacDowell, Fran Martin, Robert Maurer, Roger Miller, Dave Morgan, Peter Oberlander, Jim Osgood, Galene Paul, Milt Peterson, Dave Pickles, Leonard Pruden, Jan Schreurs, Joseph Sterlace, S. D. Stookey, Y. S. Su, Paul Tick, Stephen Tong, Brent Wedding, William Whitney, Virginia Wright, and ....

Storeroom for copper red decorated vases at Ching-te-chen (1981).

1   INTRODUCTION

The question of why a whole book should be written on the subject of a single glaze is certainly a valid one. However, I think that I have some good answers: first of all, I like copper red glazes; in addition, I couldn't find a satisfactory explanation of how to make copper red glazes; and finally, by the time I had collected all of the various pieces and had run all of the necessary experiments, the whole amounted to a bookful of instructions. In order that it not be scattered again, I have assembled this information in these covers.

The problems that confront us with regard to copper reds are certainly manyfold, but there are two outstanding features which need to be emphasized. The first one is that good copper red glazes **are** possible. One only has to visit one or two large museums to realize that the Chinese were capable of making good copper red glazes as far back as the fifteenth century. That is the good news about copper reds!

A second feature of copper reds becomes apparent after visiting **several** museums. This feature concerns the variability of color in Chinese copper reds. Practically no two Chinese copper red glazed wares have identical colors. While this complaint is rather common in any manufacturing operation, it is especially noticeable with these glazes. The more involved I became with this glaze the more I found that this was the core problem. All of us can, on occasion, make good copper red glazes, but few of us can do such work regularly.

The aim of this book will be to enable ceramists to make **good** copper red glazes **consistently**. Although I hope that this purpose will meet with 100% success, there may be a few people who will not be able to make copper reds with the help of this book. For them the results should at least afford an understanding of **why** success has not been attained.

Many people have spoken to me about the fact that firing in a test kiln is not like firing in a production kiln. And, I heartily agree with that. They then ask: "Why did you do all of your experiments in a test kiln?" Actually, Lauth and Dutailly have answered this question very effectively, but I'll state it again. Without a test kiln there is no way that you would be able to do the number of experiments that are required in a field like that of the copper reds. Since we only have one lifetime, it is desirable that we use it as effectively as possible, and that is why I have used a test kiln. I have run hundreds of tests, alternately testing and correcting and so forth. And the only way that you can do this in a reasonable length of time is with a test kiln. That is my only excuse. I certainly agree that the actual tests cannot be duplicated in a large kiln, however the information that you learn from a test kiln will apply to a large kiln if you make allowances for the different types of firings.

I would hesitate to recommend that every potter try to make copper red glazes. While it is a fascinating subject, and is worth a quick trial, it may not be practical to pursue this glaze arduously, unless you are a dilettante. The stiff requirements—that you have exceptional control over your kiln; that you be able to make reproducible firings; that you adhere strictly to the required reducing conditions in the kiln; and that the final reduction time in the kiln be duplicated exactly for each firing—all make this a severe test for the potter. If these parameters are met, then one must also be careful about using the same components every time, mixing them and applying them in the same way and adhering to a strict control of thickness. Without such care, copper glazes will not be consistent. It is not that any **one** standard needs to be precise, it is the combination that is difficult.

If you don't want to go to extremes, but still want to make an attempt at copper reds, I would recommend that you try a peach bloom glaze, since this is one of the least strict in its demands. Frankly though, I cannot imagine a potter being able to resist making at least one stab at a bright copper red glaze. Try it, and good luck!

In addition to the people listed on the dedication page (who contributed mightily to the contents of this book), I would like to thank Tom Elmer for the magnificent job of translating Paul Ebell's opus. Also, the many electron micrographs and x-ray analyses performed by Len Pruden were of great assistance in leading to an understanding of copper red glazes.

Jean Lee, at the Philadelphia Museum of Art, furthered this work immeasurably by interpreting their fine collection of Chinese copper reds for me. At the Freer Gallery of Art, Josephine Knapp showed me through their collection. In the way of samples, Margaret Medley was very helpful by contributing sherds of Chinese Chun ware and an early underglaze copper red, while Don and Ursala Farm allowed me to slice up an especially useful Chun sherd.

In the realm of information, kudos must go to: Dean Frasché, for keeping me up to date on Chinese copper reds; to Fance Franck for locating the Ebelmen reference; to the Cornell University History of Science Library staff for the Lauth article; to the Alfred University Ceramics Library staff for permission to replicate the wood cuts from Stanislas Julien's book "History of Chinese Porcelain;" and to the staff of the Ching-te-chen porcelain factories who allowed me to roam through the kiln rooms and shops where Chinese copper reds are made today.

A 13th century Egyptian pottery segment—decorated with copper ruby lustre.

2 HISTORICAL

Copper red glazes and glasses have a long and varied history. Robert Brill (in a paper on "The Chemical Interpretation of Glassmaking," 1970, The Corning Museum of Glass) commented that copper red glasses were made in Egypt at least as early as the Eighteenth Dynasty (ca. 1500 BC). The fact that copper red colors date back this far shouldn't be a surprise though, because both copper metal and glasses were made at that time, and one could expect that they would have been combined by some early Edison. The only additional procedure required for making copper reds is that of firing in reduction; and even this can be explained by the accidental use of a smoky fire, such as might be the case with brush or wood fires in a poor draft.

The early copper reds are unlikely to have been very beautiful, but at least they were reddish, and there aren't many ways to get reds in a glaze. They were probably saturated copper glazes, with several percent of copper oxide present. The normal blue or green copper glaze (fired in oxidation), might only have 2-3% copper present, but the reds, since they weren't subtle, would consist of much higher percentages of copper. Brill, in his article, mentioned glass analyses with 5, 10, or 15% copper oxide present.

After the Egyptians, the next prominent occurrence of copper reds was during the Sung dynasty of China (960-1260 AD). At that time, the famous Chun glazes were often splashed with a red-purple-blue color, due to some copper content. From an examination of Chun ware, it is evident that the glaze was a very high-fired one, and for this reason the copper coloration on the surface was quite variable. Also, there were differences in the composition of the glaze, especially with regard to lime content, and this led to deviations in color too. Some of the copper red splashes on early Chun ware are magnificent, but the colors grade off into plum, purple and blue too. Furthermore, where the copper content has become too high, they also form blacks and greens, when the high concentration of copper is oxidized during the cooling process.

Later Chun ware, that became more "artistic," is noteworthy for its mottled look with combined blue, red, white and purple streaks. This type of coloration may be due to variations in lime and phosphate content. But, in any case, it is not as eye-pleasing as the earlier Chun ware. This is evident in the names given to the ware by the Chinese, such as, "mule's liver" and "horse's lung," which are quite descriptive of the appearances.

Starting in the Yuan dynasty, we find some copper red appearing as an underglaze coloration. It occurs as an accompaniment to cobalt blue underglaze decoration, and as an individual colorant. Unfortunately, copper red in underglazing is rarely successful. The colors tend towards brown or purple, or other "off" hues, and rarely do we see beautiful red underglaze colors. As we shall note in the technical section, this is quite understandable, because the components of bodies are incompatible with good red colors.

Early in the Ming dynasty, particularly during the reign of Hsuan-te, in-glaze copper reds were made by the Chinese. Again, underglaze reds were made too, but still with limited success. In the red glazes which then appeared, the whole ceramic article was sometimes covered with color. One such notable piece is the "monk's cap" jug in the Palace Museum Collection on Taiwan.

From the time of Hsuan-te, until the beginning of the eighteenth century, copper reds were only made occasionally. However, during the long reign of Kang-hsi in the Ching dynasty, the copper red glazed ware of China came into its own, with the production of sang de boeuf, peach bloom, and so-called flambé glazes. It was during the Kang-hsi period that we received the report from Pere d'Entrecolles (in his second letter on ceramics), where he announced that the red color of Chinese glazes was definitely due to copper. Unfortunately the amount of information that he was able to obtain was limited and not much further was discovered until the nineteenth century.

After the Kang-hsi period and up to the present day, copper red glazes have become more common and of better quality. But even at present there is some mystique about them, because there are a number of factors which cause copper red glazes to become either too pale, too dark, or an off-color, hence the contents of this book.

Moving from Chinese to European work, we find an interesting historical sequence. Shortly after Pere d'Entrecolles wrote his first letter, the secret of porcelain making was unraveled by Bottger in Germany, and then it was rapidly disseminated over Europe—though mainly in Germany and France. There the production of hard porcelain coincided with the emergence of the science of chemistry from the shadows of alchemy. The beginnings of porcelain in Europe date from about 1720, and the beginnings of chemistry as a science date from 1789 (at which time Lavoisier's "Elementary Treatise on Chemistry" was published). So the sciences of ceramics and chemistry began to evolve simultaneously. Because of the fact that copper reds are reduction fired, the chemistry of the operation is of great importance. Often, though, porcelain was fired in a slightly reducing atmosphere, since this procedure neutralized the effect of iron contamination on the color of both bodies and glazes. When iron in either location is in the oxidized state, it tends to be yellowish or brownish. When it is in a reduced state, it will tend to be either a pale blue or a pale green color, and then will have the same optical effect on the ceramics that bluing has on laundry. The bluish-white color of reduced porcelain actually looks whiter to the eye than a pure white color. Thus the stage was set for the firing of copper in reduction and its transformation to the red state.

Further help from China resulted when French missionaries and native priests sent additional technical material from Asia to Europe. One of the first of these—after Pere d'Entrecolles—was Father Ly, who collected both samples and information from the Ching-te-chen locale. He sent this material to the French porcelain factory at Sevres at the request of M. Brongniart, the director. There it was analysed and reproduced by Ebelmen and Salvetat. After analysis, some sample copper reds were made and they are now to be found in the Sevres Museum.

Ebelmen and Salvetat gave as the formula for an analysed Chinese glaze, this composition: 73.9% silica; 6.0% alumina; 2.1% ferric oxide; 7.3% lime; 4.6% copper oxide; 3.0% potash; and 3.1% soda. However, the glaze that they made with this composition was said by Vogt to be less than a bright red. Later comments have implied that the copper content was too high, and most workers since that time have recommended the use of less than one percent copper oxide. As we shall see, the final concentration of copper will depend upon the temperature to which the glaze was fired as well as the thickness of the glaze. So, using this particular composition, Ebelmen and Salvetat might have been able to achieve success if the glaze was thin enough and if the firing temperature was high enough.

After this pioneering work by Ebelmen and Salvetat, further research was done by Hermann Seger in Berlin and by Lauth, Dutailly and Vogt at Sevres. In addition to these men, numerous scientists have experimented with copper red glazes, although only a small number of them have reported their results in the literature. With regard to copper red glazes, the most recent, thorough and scientific article was the one in the Journal of the American Ceramic Society in 1959 by Brown and Norton. An annotated bibliography containing remarks on this and other articles will be included in this volume, so no more will be said about them at this time.

It is encouraging to note that as new tools and techniques are perfected, new discoveries continue to be made in the copper red field—witness the recent article by W. D. Kingery and P. Vandiver in the November 1983 issue of the Bulletin of the American Ceramic Society.

The red rose whispers of passion
And the white rose breathes of love;
O, the red rose is a falcon,
And the white rose is a dove.

   John B. O'Reilly—A White Rose

A Chinese copper red vase of the Kang-hsi reign with a "crushed strawberry" appearance.

3   CHINESE COPPER RED GLAZES

Since the history of Chinese glazes is not my forte, and since Hobson has already prepared excellent volumes in this area, some of his remarks on Chinese copper red glazes will be included at this point.

CHINESE POTTERY AND PORCELAIN

R.L. HOBSON

THE HSUAN-TE REIGN (1426-1435)

The honours of the period appear to have been shared by the "blue and white" and red painted wares. Out of twenty examples illustrated in Hsiang's Album, no fewer than twelve are decorated chiefly in red, either covering the whole or a large part of the surface or painted in designs, among which three fishes occur with monotonous frequency. The red in every case is called *chi hung* and it is usually qualified by the illuminating comparison with "ape's blood," and in one case it is even redder than that!

The expression "chi hung" has evidently been handed down by oral traditions, for there is no sort of agreement among Chinese writers on the form of the first character. The *Tao lu* uses the character which means "sacrificial," and Bushell explains this: "as the color of the sacrificial cups which were employed by the Emperor in the worship of the Sun." Hsiang uses the character which means "massed, accumulated." And others use the character which means "sky clearing," and is also applied to blue in the sense of the "blue of the sky after rain." In the oft quoted list of the Yung Cheng porcelains we find the item: "Imitations of Hsuan *chi hung* wares, including two kinds, *hsien hung* (fresh red) and *pao shih hung* (ruby red)." There can be little doubt that both these were shades of underglaze red derived from copper oxide, a color with which we are quite familiar from the eighteenth century and later examples.

For, in another context, we find the *hsien hung* contrasted with *fan hung*, which is the usual term for overglaze iron red, and the description already given of the application of *pao shih hung* leaves no doubt whatever that it was an underglaze colour. The two terms were probably fanciful names for two variations of the same colour, or perhaps for two different applications of it, for we know that it was used as a pigment for brush work as well as in the form of a ground colour incorporated in the glaze. The secret of the colour seems to have been well kept, and the general impression prevailing outside the factories was that its tint and brilliancy were due to powdered rubies, the red precious stone from the West which gave the name to the *pao shih hung*. It is known that in some cases such stones as carnelian (*ma nao*) have been incorporated in the porcelain glazes in China to increase the limpidity of the glaze. This is reputed to have happened in the case of the Ju yao, but neither carnelian nor ruby could serve in any way as a colouring agent, as their colour would be dissipated in the heat of the furnace. The real colouring agent of the *chi hung* is protoxide of copper (cuprous oxide). If there were nothing else to prove this, it would be clear from the fact hinted in the *Po wu yao lan* that the failures came out a brownish or blackish tint. This color has always proved a difficult one to manage, and in the early part of the last dynasty, when it was freely used after the manner of the Hsuan-te potters, the results were most unequal, varying from a fine blood red to maroon and brown and even to a blackish tint.

The peculiar merits of the Hsuan-te red were probably due in some measure to the clay of which the ware was composed, and which contained some natural ingredient favorable to the development of the red. At any rate, we are told that in the Chia Ching period (1522-1566): "the earth used for the *hsien hung* ran short."

Among the favorite designs expressed in the Hsuan-te red were three fishes, three fruits, three funguses, and the character *fu* (happiness) repeated five times. All these are mentioned among the Yung Cheng imitations. A good idea of the fish design is given by a cylindrical vase in the Franks Collection, which is plain except for two fishes in underglaze red of good color, and rising in slight relief in the glaze. The glaze itself is of that faint celadon green which was apparently regarded as a necessary feature of the Hsuan-te copies, and which incidentally seems to be favourable to the development of the copper red. The *sang de boeuf* red of the last dynasty is avowedly a revival of the Hsuan-te red in its use as a glaze colour. Indeed, certain varieties of the *sang de boeuf* class are still distinguished as *chi hung*. The large bowls, "red as the sun and white at the mouth rim," as mentioned in the *Po wu yao lan*, have a counterpart in the large bowl of the last dynasty with *sang de boeuf* glaze, which, flowing downwards, usually left a colourless white band at the mouth.

The Hsuan-te period extended only to ten years, and specimens of Hsuan red are excessively rare today, even in China. It is doubtful if a genuine specimen exists outside the Middle Kingdom, but with the help of the old Chinese descriptions and the clever imitations of a later date, there is no difficulty in imagining the vivid splendours of the "precious stone red" of this brilliant period.

LUNG-CHING (1567-1572)

We read in the "*Tao shuo*" that the Imperial factory was reestablished in the sixth year of this reign (1572), and was placed under the care of the assistant prefects of the district. This would seem to imply that for the greater part of this brief period the Imperial works had been in abeyance. Be this as it may, there was no falling off in the quantity of the porcelain commanded for the Court, and the extravagant and burdensome demands evoked a protest from Hsu Chih, the president of the Censorate, in 1571. It was urged among other things that the secret of the copper red color (*hsien hung*) had been lost, and that the potters should be allowed to use the iron red (*fan hung*) in its place: that the size and form of the large fish bowls which were ordered made their manufacture almost impossible: that the designs for the polychrome (*wu tsai*) painting were too elaborate, and that square boxes made in three tiers were a novelty difficult to construct. Fire and flood had devastated Ching-te-chen, and many of the workmen had fled, and he (the president) begged that a large reduction should be made in the palace orders.

We are not told whether this memorial to the emperor had the desired effect. In the case of the next emperor a similar protest resulted in a large reduction in the demands. But the document discloses several interesting facts, and among other things we learn that the designs for some of the ware and for the coloured decoration were still sent from the palace as in the days of Cheng Hua.

KANG-HSI (1662-1722)

Meanwhile, we pass to the reign of Kang-hsi, the beginning of what is to most European collectors the greatest period of Chinese porcelain, a period which may be roughly dated from 1662-1800. Chinese literary opinion gives the preference to the Sung and Ming dynasties, but if monetary value is any indication, the modern Chinese collector appreciates the finer Ching porcelains as highly as the European connoisseur. These latter wares have, at any rate, the advantage of being easily accessible to the Western student, and they are not difficult to obtain provided one is ready to pay the high price which their excellence commands. It will be no exaggeration to say that three-quarters of the best specimens of Chinese porcelain in our collections belong to this prolific period, and they may be seen in endless variety in the museums and private galleries of Europe and America, nowhere perhaps better than in London itself.

With regard to the porcelains made in the early years of Kang-hsi, there is very little information, and their special excellence has been assumed mainly on the supposition that the viceroy Lang Ting-tso exercised a beneficent influence on the wares of this period. He is reputed to have been sponsor of the Lang yao, which in the ordinary acceptation of the term includes the beautiful *sang de boeuf* red, an apple green crackle, and perhaps a cognate crackled green glaze on which are painted designs in *famille verte* enamels. The explanation of the term *lang yao* is far from clear, and, as was already hinted, the connection of the viceroy Lang Ting-tso with this or any other of the Kang-hsi porcelains is by no means established. Bushell accepted the derivation of Lang yao from the first part of the viceroy's name as representing the best of several Chinese theories...there can be little doubt that the *sang de boeuf* red or red *lang yao* is the special color described in detail by Pere d'Entrecolles in 1722 under the significant name of *yu li hung*, or "red-in-the-glaze." The reader can judge for himself from the description given by d'Entrecolles in his second letter [as contained in the chapter of this book on d'Entrecolles-RMT].

The *lang yao*, then, is the *chi hung* of the Kang-hsi period, the brilliant blood red commonly known by the French name *sang de boeuf*, and today it is one of the most precious monochromes. A choice example shows the changing tints from a brilliant cherry red below the shoulder to the massed blood red where the fluescent glaze has formed thickly above the base. The color flowing down has even left an even white band around the mouth, and has settled in thick coagulations on the flat parts of the shoulders and again above the base; but in spite of its apparent fluidity the glaze has stopped in an even line without overrunning the base. The glaze under the base is a pale buff tone and is crackled, and a careful examination of the surface generally shows that a faint crackle extends over the whole piece. The glaze, moreover, is full of minute bubbles and consequently is much pinholed, and the red color has the appearance of lying on the body in a dust of minute particles which the glaze has dragged downward in its flow and spread out in a continuous mass, but where the colour and the glaze have run thick the particles reappear in the form of a distinct mottling or dappling.

To obtain the best colour from the copper oxide in this glaze it was necessary to regulate the firing to a nicety, the margin between success and failure being exceedingly small. Naturally, too, the results varied widely in quality and tone; but the permanent characteristics of the Kang-hsi *sang de boeuf* are (1) a brilliant red varying in depth and sometimes entirely lost in places, but always red and without any of the grey or grey-blue streaks which emerge on the *flambé* red and the modern imitations of the *sang de boeuf*; (2) the faint crackle of the glaze; (3) the stopping of the glaze at the foot rim. The colour of the glaze under the base and in the interior of vases varied from green or buff crackle to plain white. The secret of this glaze, which Pere d'Entrecolles tells us was carefully guarded, seems to have been lost altogether about the end of the Kang-hsi period. Later attempts to obtain the same effects, though often successful in producing large areas of brilliant red, are usually more or less streaked with alien tints such as grey or bluish grey, and are almost invariably marred by the inability of the later potters to control the flow of the glaze which overruns the foot rim and consequently has to be ground off. But it is highly probable that the modern potter will yet surmount these difficulties, and I have actually seen a large bowl of modern make in which the ox blood red was successfully achieved on the exterior (the interior was relatively poor), and the flow of the glaze has been stopped along the foot rim except in one or two small places where the grinding was cleverly masked. So that it behooves the collector to be on his guard.

Another type of red, also classified as *lang yao*, has the same peculiarities of texture as the *sang de boeuf*, but the color is more of a crushed strawberry tint, and has in a more marked degree that thickly stippled appearance which suggests that the color mixture has been blown on to the ware through gauze. This is probably the *chui hung* or *soufflé* red mentioned by Pere d'Entrecolles in connection with the *yu li hung*. The same glaze is often found on bowls, the color varying much in depth and the base being usually covered with a crackled green glaze beneath. This crackled green is a very distinctive glaze, highly translucent and full of bubbles, like the red *lang yao*, and it is sometimes found covering the entire surface of a vase or bowl and serving as a background for painting in *famille verte* enamels. It seems, in fact, to be the true green *lang yao*, and one is tempted to ask if it was not in reality intended to be a *sang de boeuf* red glaze from which a lack of oxygen or some other accident of the kiln has dispelled all the red, leaving a green which is one of the many hues produced by copper oxide under suitable conditions. These conditions might well be present in such an enclosed place as the foot of a bowl; and if they happened to affect the whole of the piece, what more natural than to trick out the failure with a gay adornment of enamel colours?

KANG-HSI MONOCHROMES

We have already had occasion to discuss a few of the Kang-hsi monochromes in dealing with the question of *lang yao*. But besides the *sang de boeuf* there is another rare and costly red to which the Americans have given the expressive name of "peach bloom." Since their first acquaintance with this color in the last half of the nineteenth century, American collectors have been enamoured of it, and as they have never hesitated to pay vast sums for good specimens, most of the fine "peach blooms" have found their way to the United States, and choice examples are rare in England. "The prevailing shade," to quote from Bushell's description, "is a pale red, becoming pink in some parts, in others mottled with russet spots, displayed upon a background of light green celadon tint. The last colour occasionally comes out more prominently, and deepens into clouds of bright apple green tint." The Chinese, in comparing the colour, have thought of the apple rather than the peach; it is *pin-kuo hung* (apple red), and the markings on it are *pin-kuo ching* (apple green), and *mei kuei tzu* (rose crimson). Another Chinese name for the colour is *chiang-tou hung* (bean red), in allusion to the small Chinese kidney-bean with its variegated pink colour and brown spots.

It is generally supposed that, like the *sang de boeuf*, the "peach bloom" owes its hue to copper oxide, and that all the accessory tints, the russet brown and apple green are due to happy accidents befalling the same colouring medium in the changeful atmosphere of the kiln. This precious glaze is usually found on small objects such as water pots and brushwashers for the writing table, and snuff bottles, and a few small elegantly formed flower vases of bottle shape, with high shoulders and and slender neck, the body sometimes moulded in chrysanthemum petal design, or, again, on vases of slender, graceful, ovoid form, with bodies tapering downwards, and the mouth rim slightly flaring. In every case the bottom of the vessel shows a fine white-glazed porcelain with unctuous paste, and the Kang-hsi mark in six blue characters written in a delicate but very mannered calligraphy, which seems to be peculiar to this type of ware, and to a few choice *clair de lune* and celadon vases of similar form and make.

The colour in the peach bloom glaze, as in the *sang de boeuf* is sometimes fired out and fades into white or leaves a pale olive green surface with only a few spots of brown or pink to bear witness to the original intention of the potter. The glaze is sometimes crackled and occasionally it runs down in a thick crystalline mass at the base of the vessel.

Needless to say this costly porcelain has claimed the earnest attention of the modern imitator. The first real success was achieved by a Japanese potter at the end of the last century. He was able to make admirable copies of the colour, but failed to reproduce adequately the paste and glaze of the originals. I am told that he was persuaded to transfer his secret to China, and with the Chinese body his imitations were completely successful. The latter part of the story is based on hearsay, and is given as such; but it is certain that there are exceedingly clever modern copies of the old peach blooms in the market; otherwise how could an inexpert collector in China bring home half a dozen peach blooms bought at bargain prices?

The copper red used in painting underglaze designs will sometimes develop a peach bloom colour, and there is a vase in the British Museum with parti-coloured glaze in large patches of blue, celadon, and a copper red which has broken into the characteristic tints of the peach bloom glazes.

Another red of copper origin allied to the *sang de boeuf* and the peach bloom, and at times verging on both, is the maroon red, which ranges from crimson to a deep liver colour. There are wine cups of this colour whose glaze, clotted with deep crimson recalls the "dawn red" of the wine cups made by Hao Shih-chiu. Sometimes the red covers only part of the surface, shading off into the white glaze. The finer specimens have either a crimson or a pinkish tinge, but far more often the glaze has issued from the kiln with a dull liver tint.

Naturally the value of the specimen varies widely with the beauty of the colour. The pinker shades approach within measurable distance of the pink of the peach bloom, and they are often classed with the latter by their proud owners; but the colour is usually uniform, and lacks the bursts of russet brown and green which variegate the true peach bloom, and the basis of the maroon is a pure white glaze without the celadon tints which seem to underlie the peach bloom. It may be added that the maroon red glaze is usually uncrackled.

There is a type of glaze which, though variegated with many tints, still belongs to the category of monochromes. This is the *flambé*, to use the suggestive French term which implies a surface shot with flame-like streaks of varying colour. This capricious colouring, the result of some chance action of the fire upon copper oxide in the glaze, had long been known to the Chinese potters. It appeared on the Chun Chou wares of the Sung and Yuan dynasties, and it must have occurred many times on the Ming copper monochromes; but up to the end of the Kang-hsi period it seems to have been still more or less accidental on the Ching-te-chen porcelain, if we can believe the circumstantial account written by Pere d'Entrecolles in the year 1722: "I have been shown one of the porcelains which are called *yao pien*," or transmutation. This transmutation takes place in the kiln, and results from defective or excessive firing, or perhaps from other circumstances which are not easy to guess. This specimen, which, according to the workmen's idea is a failure and the child of pure chance is nonetheless beautiful, and nonetheless valued. The potter had set out to make vases of *soufflé* red. A hundred pieces were entirely spoiled, and the specimen in question came from the kiln with the appearance of a sort of agate. Were they but willing to take the risk and expense of successive experiments, the potters would eventually discover the secret of making with certainty that which chance has produced in this solitary case. This is the way they learnt to make porcelain with the brilliant black glaze called *ou kim*; the caprice of the kiln determined this research, and the result was successful."

It is interesting to read how this specimen of *flambé* resulted from the misfiring of a copper red glaze, no doubt a *sang de boeuf*; for in the most common type of *flambé* red, passages of rich *sang de boeuf* emerge from the welter of mingled grey, blue and purple tints. The last part of d'Entrecolles' note was prophetic, for in the succeeding reigns the potters were able to produce the *flambé* glaze at will.

There are, besides, many other strangely coloured glazes which can only be explained as misfired monochromes of the *grand feu*, those of mulberry colour, slaty purple, and the like, most of which were probably intended for maroon or liver red, but were altered by some caprice of the fire. But it would be useless to enumerate these erratic tints, which are easily recognized by their divergence from the normal ceramic colours.

CHIEN LUNG (1736-1795)

Probably the greatest of T'ang's achievements was the mastery of the *yao pien* or furnace transmutation glazes, which were a matter of chance as late as the end of the Kang-hsi period. These are the variegated or *flambé* glazes in which a deep red of *sang de boeuf* tint is transformed into a mass of streaks and mottlings in which blue, grey, crimson, brown, and green seem to be struggling together for preeminence. All these tints spring from one colouring agent—copper oxide—and they are called into being by a sudden change of the atmosphere of the kiln caused by the admission of wood smoke at the critical moment and the consequent consumption of the oxygen. Without the transformation the glaze would be a *sang de boeuf* red, and in many cases the change is only partial, and large areas of the deep red remain. It will be found that in contrast with the Kang-hsi *sang de boeuf* these later glazes are more fluescent, and the excess of glaze overrunning the base has been removed by grinding.

NINETEENTH CENTURY PORCELAINS

KUANG HSU (1875-1909)

The collector's interest in Kuang Hsu porcelain is of a negative kind. When it is frankly marked he sees it and avoids it. But the Chinese potters towards the close of the century evidently recovered some part of the skill which the ravages of the Taiping rebels seemed to have effectually dissipated; for they succeeded in making many excellent *sang de boeuf* reds and crackled emerald green monochromes which have deceived collectors of experience. Even the best, however, of these wares should be recognized by inferiority of form and material, and in the case of red the fluescent glaze will be found in the modern pieces to have overrun the foot rim, necessitating grinding of the base rim. There are also fair imitations of the Kang-hsi blue and white and the enamelled vases of *famille verte* or on-biscuit colours, and even of the fine black and green grounds. But here again the inferior biscuit, the lack of grace in the form and the stiffness of the designs will be at once observed by the trained eye. When marked, most of these imitations have the *nien hao* of the Kang-hsi, and this is almost invariable on the modern blue and white.

Black spirits and white, red spirits and gray,
Mingle, mingle, mingle, you that mingle may.

Thomas Middleton—The Witch.

4 CHINESE COPPER REDS IN MUSEUMS

This chapter will describe the results of visits to two American museums: The Philadelphia Museum of Art, and the Freer Gallery of Art.

At the Philadelphia Museum of Art—thanks to the kindness of Jean Gordon Lee, curator of Far Eastern Art—I was able to examine a large number of Chinese copper red glazes. Although I didn't count the number of specimens, I am sure that there were between one and two dozen examples of the *sang de boeuf* type and several of peach bloom type that I was able to examine closely by eye and with a hand magnifying lens (10X).

The first comment that should be made—and which will be a relief for the average potter—is that there are many variations in Chinese copper red colors. Some of the reds were deep and dark colored, some were bright, others were brownish, purplish and even bluish red. So that, if one considers his own output, he should not be ashamed of having a variety of shades coming out of each kiln. In addition, one must take into account the fact that all of the pieces which are in museums are obviously the end result of a long selection process. This started with the removal of ware from the Chinese kilns, at which time the best pieces were chosen for selected markets; then, over the years, a further gleaning by connoisseurs took place; and finally, the finest pieces were collected by museums. Hence, the examination of museum pieces today is not equivalent to what one would see if he were looking into a newly opened Kang-hsi kiln.

Because of the fact that some Chinese copper reds are called ox bloods, I had gotten into the habit of using that term, but, as Jean Lee pointed out, the term "crushed strawberries" is much more appropriate for the best colors on Kang-hsi vases. With the small clear spots in a bright red ground, the term "crushed strawberries" is much easier to visualize than ox blood. The dappled surface of the glaze also makes one think of red Delicious apples, where one sees a spotty, streaky effect on a good red color.

There was another type of copper red glaze at the Philadelphia Museum which I had never heard described appropriately, but which is fairly common. It was a glaze with an underfired look. This copper red glaze of the Ching dynasty was quite uniform from top to bottom, with only a thin white band at the top. This uniform glaze also tended to have a strong orange peel appearance, which is one of the reasons that it appears to be underfired. Then too, the uniform glaze, while it is constant in color from top to bottom, is not of an exciting red color; it could be better described as brownish or purplish, and it is definitely not as beautiful as a crushed strawberry piece.

On other pieces, a running effect—which is related to high alkali content—is almost always found when one notes a good red color, and it is noticeable because of the amount of glaze which accumulates at or near the foot. Frequently these drips are ground off, but sometimes the foot of a piece has been so designed that there is a tendency for the glaze to accumulate rather than to stream off. Here, instead of having vertical foot surfaces, there can be flares—either inward or outward—so that the glaze drip at the bottom will collect and not run down and react with the setters and then have to be ground off.

OPALS

Still another variation of the ox blood glaze was one at the Philadelphia Museum which was opalescent and bluish. This type of coloration is usually found all over a piece, but this particular one was educational because it had the opalescent-bluishness more on one side than the other. Because of this you could see that it was derived from a normal copper red. At the time I examined this vase I happened to have a sample piece of copper red to which an excess of limestone had been added. In this test piece the bluishness was very similar to that noted on the Chinese piece. I therefore think that it is likely that some of the bluish-purple opalescent copper reds of China are due to variations in the lime content of the glaze. In coarse mixtures, this circumstance could lead to flambés.

OTHER COPPER REDS

An examination of another one of the vases at the Philadelphia Museum showed a white zone of perhaps 2-3 inches width at the top of the ware, where the glaze had run thin during the firing, and where the red color was lost—either due to volatilization or to reaction with the body. In this area, there was no evidence of any copper at all, either oxidized or reduced. At the foot of this same piece though, where accumulation had occurred, there was a definite, strong greenish hue below the red. But, by eye, it was hard to judge whether the green was due to copper which was oxidized, or whether it was due to iron picked up from the body, forming a green celadon. Unfortunately, lacking a non-destructive analytical technique, we were unable to resolve this question.

Going back up this body, to zones just beneath the white area, or to other vertical surfaces where the glaze had run thin, we usually see the brightest reds. If there is a crushed strawberry effect, it is limited in area and doesn't cover a whole piece. It will be found just below a white region, and in the vertical portions where the glaze has run thinnest. It is apparent, that to get bright reds, the glaze must be overfired. I have yet to see a bright, brilliant red that covers an entire piece. Whenever a ceramic article has been fired to the point where it has a uniform red color, it invariably does not have a **brilliant** color.

TIN

As far as chemistry is concerned, I was left with a feeling that the Chinese did not use tin to obtain their copper red color. If they had used tin, then they might have been able to get even better colors. I suspect that the copper red color in the ox blood glazes was produced by a combination of copper and iron rather than by a combination of copper and tin. Undoubtedly tin was a scarce commodity, and, although it may have been used in small percentages to make coins and bronze articles, it wouldn't have been available in the large quantities that would have been required for glazes. In my work I have found that a weight ratio of two parts tin to one part copper produces the best coloration, so they would have needed a rather large source of tin and this was evidently not available.

Another hint that iron is the co-colorant with copper in these reds, is that often, where the glaze has rolled thick at the foot, it is brownish in color. Although this might be due to copper alone, I think that it makes more sense to believe it to be copper plus iron. Also, along these lines, there is the evidence given by Vogt in his analyses of the Chinese copper red glazes before and after firing. He never reports tin in other than trace quantities. And, since he has found it in traces, I would assume that his analytical techniques would have been able to pick it up in larger amounts. Hence the fact that Vogt doesn't report tin indicates to me that it was not present in significant quantities in the copper red glazes of China. Also, in Vogt's analyses, there is enough iron present to take care of the oxidation-reduction cycle involving the iron-copper couple. Actually, the problem that the Chinese had with the loss of the ability to make good copper red glazes might be related to the iron situation. As time went on they may have gotten better raw materials in which the iron content was lower and lower, until finally they reached a point where they would have had difficulty in obtaining good copper reds. Thus this may have been one of their problems. The only thing that goes against this theory is the knowledge that almost every analysis of Chinese bodies and glazes, from ancient times to the present, has shown one percent or more of iron oxide present. Such a percentage doesn't hurt the red color much and yet it provides enough reduction for the chemical reaction.

MULTIPLE COATINGS

On one or two of the vases in Philadelphia there was evidence that multiple coatings were used to improve the color on the taller shapes that the Chinese made. Others have commented on this, and after close examination of this ware I see no reason to doubt it. One sees not only an accumulation of glaze at the bottom, but also evidence of an accumulation of glaze on the shoulders of "ess" curves on vases. They may have coated the whole vessel uniformly once and then applied a second coat on the upper half to allow for the increased flow and the thinning of the glaze on the top. One often sees a paleness on the vertical sections at the top of a glaze, and an extra coating there would help to neutralize this effect.

Another strange phenomenon on many copper red wares is the grooved appearance at the foot of the piece. When examining the vases, it became obvious to me that something unusual had been done to the base of the pieces; and it appeared that perhaps the vase had been ground off at the foot using a grinding stone with a rough surface. But this didn't seem logical—the mechanics seemed wrong. Finally, after seeing even more of this at the Freer Gallery in Washington, I decided that what might have happened was that instead of the vase being held against a rotating wheel, that the vase was rotated and and a stone was applied to the foot. In this way, with the vase turning and the stone stationary, a groove could be worn in the foot because of a rough stone. In the reverse case, where the stone was turning and the vase was stationary, this wouldn't be the case. I believe, therefore, that this is the explanation for the ringed grooves at the foot of Chinese red glazed ware.

PEACH BLOOM GLAZES

With regard to peach bloom glazes (which appeared during the Kang-hsi reign of the Ching dynasty), my personal experience was that this color could be obtained by adding rather high quantities of alumina to a copper red glaze. Something on the order of 20% clay added to an ox blood glaze would produce a peach bloom effect. The resulting glaze, when examined with a hand lens, would be seen to consist of a very bubbly matrix, due no doubt to gases evolved from the clay and trapped by the glaze. An examination of my glaze in thin section resulted in the observation of many undissolved particles of clay and silica as well as plenty of voids.

One fascinating aspect of Chinese peach blooms is their unevenness. It appears that the glaze was **sprayed** on, even though this wouldn't be absolutely necessary. Nevertheless, a spraying technique would explain some of the irregularities on the peach bloom glazes which give them a lot of their charm. A Chinese peach bloom glaze will frequently have deep red or green specks which are scattered around just as if one had spewed them out of a sprayer. Such a peach bloom glaze often has the same haphazard appearance that one notices after using a spray can with a malfunctioning spray head.

One feature of Chinese peach bloom glazes is that, on examination with a hand lens, even in a relatively uniform region of the glaze, one can see that there are speckles on a larger scale than the gas bubbles. Some of these dark spots seem to be clear of gas bubbles. These may be due either to unmixing of the glaze, or to being the place where a bubble has broken and left a fairly uniform non-bubbly area behind.

TESTS

After returning from Philadelphia, I made some glazes in which copper oxide was used as a colorant instead of my usual copper carbonate. The copper oxide was formed by heating copper metal to 800°C in air and then cooling so that the surface would oxidize. The hot copper was then dipped into cold water where the oxide flaked off and settled out. In this way, I accumulated enough flake copper oxide to do my coloring tests. In the process of making the glaze, I took the copper oxide flakes and ground them with a mortar and pestle. Here the interesting thing was that the flakes did not grind up readily to a fine powder (which was only natural because they tended to form sheets between the mortar and pestle surfaces). It was not like grinding a granular material such as silica, but was more like trying to grind mica, which is also difficult to pulverize in this fashion. There was a great tendency for the flakes to remain unground even though the grinding time was extensive. This resistance to fine grinding could certainly explain why there are some greenish spots (evidence of high copper concentration) on the peach bloom glazes. It may be that the Chinese copper oxide was in the form of flakes. Perhaps they took copper coins, heated them, and then plunged them into water. Pere d'Entrecolles does comment ("Ching-te-chen" p. 119): "Before the liquid copper coagulates and hardens, a small broom is dipped lightly in water and, tapping on the handle, water is sprinkled onto the molten copper. A film forms on the surface, and is lifted off with small iron tweezers, and is plunged into cold water where the particles form piece by piece." If the particles here are copper oxide flakes, then this covers the situation very well. It would be simple to use this procedure in a test fabrication of a peach bloom. The only difficulty would be in getting the same particle size distribution that the Chinese had.

Another effect noted on peach bloom glazes was on a water coupe at the Philadelphia Museum where an engraved design—a dragon I believe—was apparent in the surface. The engraving was done in a line style rather than in the shaded type found in *ching-pai* ware. In areas where the glaze was thick, the engraving was hard to discern, but in thinly glazed portions the glaze was translucent and the lines were full of a deep pink color. This sort of result is surprising because one would expect that any reddish glaze in direct contact with the body would tend to become clear. However, because of a large alumina content in this glaze, it might not react strongly with the body, and there might not be much discoloration at the glaze-body interface.

There are apparently about eight different shapes of ware that were used as foils for peach bloom glazes during the Kang-hsi reign, and of these, only one, a water coupe, is normally found to be inscribed. The Chinese shapes with peach bloom glazes are: a variety of small vases, one or two water coupes, a brush washer, a seal pigment box with cover and possibly snuff bottles.

UNDERGLAZE COLORS

One of the other pieces at the Philadelphia Museum of Art was an underglaze red of Ching vintage that was quite bright in color. It was very smeared and was not distinct and crisp in its design, but it was obviously an underglaze decorated piece with a thin overglaze. My experience with underglaze reds is that the brightness of the color depends to a marked extent on the kind of overglaze that is applied and not too much on the type of underglaze material. Hence, it is quite likely that the high quality of the color on this underglaze piece is due to the fact that the Ching Chinese were using frits in their glazes and this provided a better base for copper red development and gave them a good color with an underglaze red.

Although the next comment is not specifically related to copper reds, I can't help mentioning the fact that I observed and drew some conclusions about bubble structure in various glazes seen at the Philadelphia Museum of Art. First of all, it is obvious that no bubble in a glaze can be bigger in diameter than the thickness of the glaze. So, by external observation of the size of the largest bubble, one can get a good idea of the maximum glaze thickness. With peach bloom glazes this is not very practical, because the bubbles are mostly of a very fine size and there is no thickness information that can be obtained in this case. But, in ox bloods, some of the bubbles are of a large size, so one must assume that the glaze is rather thick. This is also the case when we examine cross sections of copper reds. The ox blood has to be of a certain minimum thickness before the reds can be of high quality. If you go below this optimum thickness then it is difficult to get good copper reds because you literally cannot add enough copper to cause a red color to develop. Therefore, bubble measurement is a potential way to evaluate some glazes.

After the visit to the Philadelphia Museum of Art, a shorter visit was made to the Freer Gallery of Art in Washington, D.C. where Mrs. Josephine Knapp very kindly allowed me to examine some of their copper reds, including both ox bloods and peach blooms. The Freer also had vases with the "crushed strawberry" appearance and they had the same characteristic features seen in the pieces at the Philadelphia Museum of Art. A big benefit of the visit to the Freer Gallery was a confirmation of the similarity of Chinese copper reds, both of the ox blood and the peach bloom varieties. It is nice to know that pieces in different collections show evidence of being from the same source in China.

Courtesy of the Freer Gallery of Art, Smithsonian Institution, Washington, D.C. (43.5)

A Chinese seal pigment box of the Kang-hsi reign with a peach bloom glaze.

5 COLOR AND COPPER RED GLAZES

To understand some of the problems of copper red glazes, it is essential that we have an understanding of the concept of color. While an intensive treatise on color would not be appropriate for a book on glazes, still, a condensed description can be given here. If more information is required, you are referred to your local library or to the nearest encyclopaedia. Either of these will have a color description sufficient for an enquiring mind.

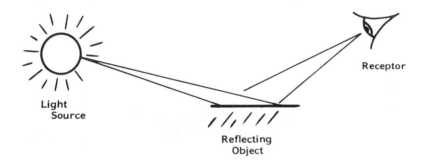

For our work, the essential information is a basic notion of the mechanics of color. The concept of color requires three ingredients: first, there has to be a light source; second, there has to be an object from which the light is reflected, or through which light is transmitted; and finally, there has to be a human eye. Practically, other receptors besides the eye can give information which will allow us to evaluate color, but for the judgement of copper reds, nothing is more useful than the eye as a receptor.

LIGHT SOURCES

First let us consider sources of light and their effect on color as observed by the human eye. The pre-eminent source of light is the sun, which has a spectrum to which we may compare all other light sources (see the following figure). This spectrum is not perfect; it is not even a straight line from one side of the visible spectrum to the other. It is curved and there are blank spots in it, and there is even a higher percentage of blue light than red in sunlight. But, concerning the kind of light which is emitted by the sun, if one takes a prism and allows sunlight to pass through it and be projected on a white screen, the usual "rainbow" of colors will be observed. This "rainbow" represents the total light spectrum emitted by the sun. Notice that I have said **light**! It is not the total amount of **energy** emitted by the sun! The sun also emits energy in the ultraviolet and infra-red portions of the spectrum, but since the eye is not normally sensitive to either of these radiations, the use of these in color work is precluded. We only need to consider the portion of the sun's spectrum between the blue and the red portions, in other words the visible portion of the sun's spectrum which is called light.

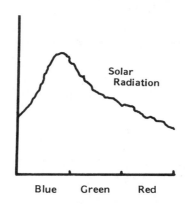

As was mentioned before, and as can be seen in the figure, there is a variation in intensity of the different colors coming from the sun. If we are using daylight as a source, we will find that there is a difference between sunlight and skylight; also there is a difference between morning, noon and evening sunlight—even on a clear day. With the appearance of dust, haze, fog and clouds, the variations in the type of light that we observe during the day will vary markedly.

However, I will let you read all about these differences in an encyclopaedia or in a color manual, where you will obtain a much more detailed description. Let us work with sunlight as if we were dealing with standard noon sunlight on a clear day in Washington, D.C. Such sunlight will have the spectrum illustrated in the figure.

Usually, the observation of a copper red glaze in sunlight is the preferred way to view a glaze if a fairly accurate indication of the color is desired. Once we start observing copper red glazes by illuminants other than sunlight, we get into predicaments which may lead us to distorted conclusions about our colors. Probably the most common distortion will be found when copper reds are viewed in light from a normal fluorescent fixture in which a so-called "cool white" fluorescent bulb is used. Unfortunately, the most common fluorescent lamp in use today is the "cool white."

Although it is a bit out of the realm of the contents of this book, I think that a short description of a fluorescent lamp and its light output should be given in the next section so that the reader may understand why fluorescent lamps are poor light sources for viewing copper red glazes.

Inside a fluorescent lamp, a mercury vapor discharge emits radiation in the ultraviolet and in a few sectors of the visible spectrum, with very little light in the red region. The ultraviolet light of this discharge is used to excite a phosphor inside the lamp. This phosphor is the source of the majority of light coming out of such a lamp. The fluorescence from a phosphor can be depicted by a curve such as the one below. As

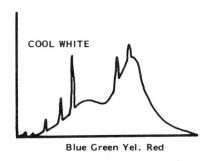

COOL WHITE

Blue Green Yel. Red

you will note, by comparing it to the sun's spectrum (given previously), its emission is strongest in the green and yellow regions, with a sharp fall-off in the red. That is the fact which makes most fluorescent lamps poor sources for the examination of red colors. They do not emit a high percentage of light in the red, therefore trying to view a red object in such a light would be misleading. Since every copper red glaze has some color components in other portions of the spectrum, these will be accentuated by a fluorescent source, to the detriment of the red appearance. Blue and green tints will be enhanced, while reds will be reduced in intensity, and there will be a large distortion of the color. If our copper red color were a pure red with no blue or green in it, there would not be a problem, except for the fact that the color would be less intense than under a red light. In any case, we must always shun evaluation of copper red glazes under fluorescent lights.

Other discharge lamps will provide distorted color also, and these too should be avoided. This category includes lamps such as high and low-pressure sodium lamps and mercury lamps of other kinds. Occasionally, discharge lamps will be acceptable (such as high pressure xenon lamps), but these are exceptions.

The best artificial source of light for viewing copper red glazes is an incandescent light with a tungsten filament. The spectrum from such a lamp is given in the following figure. As you can see, the amount of energy emitted in the red is excessive, so the incandescent light actually gives a better looking red than would be expected from sunlight. Even though it is not perfect, it gives us the best common source for our examinations and comparisons.

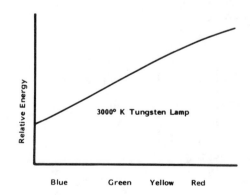

Having dealt with light sources, we can next turn to the **object**. If we have something which reflects only red light, or which transmits only red light, and if we view either of these specimens in an appropriate kind of sunlight, then an average eye will observe that they are red in color. Still, there are a variety of reds. The subject may transmit not only red light, but also some blue or some yellow, in which case it will be a variant of pure red. The same holds true for a reflecting object. It may reflect other colors in addition to red and may appear to be a color variation. **But**, if we have a material which reflects only that portion of the spectrum at about 6500 Angstroms in wavelength, or if it transmits only in this region, then we will view that subject as red via the human eye. Obviously it is assumed that we are talking about a normal human eye and a normal response.

DETECTORS

I will say very little about color detectors, because there is not much we can do about our own (other than viewing the world through rose-colored glasses). Let's merely hope that we are neither color blind nor far away from the average human eye response curve. The mere existence of an **average** response curve implies that we all see colors differently. Fortunately most of us will agree pretty well, but the rest may have to work with black and white glazes!

THE REASON FOR COPPER RED COLOR

Copper reds are not **solution** glazes as are cupric ion, cobalt ion or ferric ion glazes. The copper in a copper red glaze is present in the form of extremely fine particles—probably in the range of 50-200 Angstrom units (that is, about a millionth of a centimeter).

An explanation of the interaction of these minute clumps of copper atoms and the waves of light passing through glass, is entirely beyond the scope of this book (and beyond the ken of this writer). I have not been able to acquire a practical understanding of the cause of the red color, because it is apparently only explicable by a mathematical interpretation of the electromagnetic concept of radiation and its interaction with matter. As matter of fact, the interaction of light with solution colors is also quite "hairy" when considered on a fundamental basis. So much for theory! From now on we will consider only that the red coloration of copper red glazes is due to the presence of tiny copper particles and we will concentrate our efforts on how to obtain these tiny particles and how to recognize them when we have them.

Although we may not understand the concept of the electromagnetic theory of light, we can still understand that small copper particles suspended in glass give good red colors and that larger particles (perhaps from 500 Angstroms on up) will give ugly colors. As the particle size grows from 200 to 500 Angstrom units, the light transmitted through a copper containing glaze is changed from a red to a blue color. And, if the particle size grows even further, the effect will be the same as having metallic particles present and you will get metallic appearing colors. This can be observed in copper red glasses that have been allowed to form large particles. When these glasses are viewed in transmitted light, **blue** colors will be seen. However, when examined in reflected light, the same glass will show a metallic, coppery appearance. These variations in color due to particle size changes are the main reasons for the distortions of copper reds into purples, blues and *flambés*.

In almost every copper red glaze that I have examined in thin section by optical microscopy, I have observed other colors besides pure red. Only occasionally have I found a glaze that contained just a transparent red color. It is much more common to find evidence of blues in glazes, especially near the body. And frequently, metallic colors will be apparent in reflected light when excess copper metal is present, or when excessive growth of copper particles has occurred. Thus, variations from good copper reds are common and are to be expected.

EXPERIMENTING WITH RED COLORS

There are two basic ways to observe colors. One of them is by reflected light and the other is by transmitted light. The first process, reflection, is generally concerned with pigments (i.e. opaque materials). Therefore, since we usually observe copper red glazes on the surface of a non-transmitting body, we can commonly consider copper red colorations as reflective materials, although this is not 100% valid. Let us look at some experiments that can illustrate color variations which occur in the reflection process.

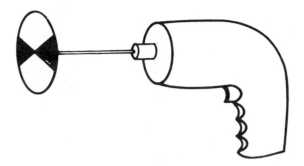

REFLECTION EXPERIMENTS

There are some very simple experiments that we can perform to illustrate a loss in the quality of a good red color. First of all, to do this experiment, you will need some sort of rotating device, which preferably will have a speed of a few hundred revolutions per minute, so that the human eye can be deceived. I have found it convenient to use a single beater on a hand food mixture as the rotator. One need only tape a cardboard disk to the end of the beater to obtain a perfect spinner as shown above. You must next go through a discarded magazine until you find a bright red colored page that will cover the area of the cardboard disk. When this disk is rotated, the color will be the same as when it is motionless. At this point, go back to the magazine and cut out pieces of blue, black and white areas. Now comes the interesting part. First, cut out several pie-segments of the three non-red papers, and alternately paste them to the red disc. Then rotate the disc. With black segments plus red you will observe a darkening effect during rotation; with blue you may end up with a maroon (depending on the shade of blue); and with white, you will find a pink color during rotation. This will give you an idea of why copper colors degrade even when they have a high percentage of red in them. The simultaneous presence of a dark color such as blue or black will cause a distortion of the red. Thus, if you have a bright glaze, but, if deep inside this glaze there is some bluishness, the glaze will not appear as bright as if it were pure red. The experiment with white segments on red to give pink colors, is an example of what happens when bubbles are present in a glaze. This is the result that is noted in peach bloom glazes in the presence of undissolved material and many fine bubbles.

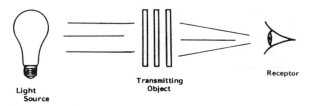

Light
Source

Transmitting
Object

Receptor

TRANSMISSION EXPERIMENTS

In **glasses**, as differentiated from glazes, we are usually dealing with transmission, and we need to look at things a little differently. This time the experiment will require some clear colored plastic sheets. You can take a piece of red plastic and look at an incandescent light through it. Then you can look at a fluorescent light through this same red plastic and see how the color is distorted in the second case.

Looking through the piece of red plastic can be useful to demonstrate other things too. Most importantly it can demonstrate the effect of increasing the thickness of a glaze and the result that this will have on coloration. If you take the piece of red plastic and double it or quadruple it, you will observe an increase in the intensity of the red color. As you continue this process of doubling the thickness, you will observe that the color does not become redder and redder indefinitely. It finally becomes darker instead of just redder. After a while, the absorption of light will result in a blackening, and, with copper reds we have a problem with this phenomenon. The basic copper red color is an intense red, and with the normal thicknesses involved in making copper red glazes, the color is a very deep ruby, even in thin sections. Also, our tendency is to have too thick a glaze rather than too thin a one. As the copper red color thins out it tends to become a brighter red, whereas with thicker sections it becomes much darker and approaches a black. This consequence can be observed by looking through a large number of sheets of red colored plastic.

In another experiment, if the red plastic is backed with a sheet of green plastic, it gives you an indication of the muddying effect of other colors on copper red in transmitted light, just as the addition of blue to the augmented disc in reflected light caused off-colors. From this experiment, we can see the need for keeping red colors in a high state of purity, as well as the need for avoiding the simultaneous presence of blue or green colors—such as might be present from iron or cupric ions.

SUMMARY

Summarizing, I think that one can say, that in order to form a good copper red we have to tread a rather narrow line. We must have a select concentration of copper in a glaze so that we can avoid either the loss or the darkening of the color. Furthermore, the dilution of a good red color with another color can also destroy its purity. Our perfect red glaze must have an optimum thickness and it must not be contaminated with any of the more common coloring agents.

A beautiful Chinese sang de boeuf glazed vase of the Ching dynasty. Note the white area at the mouth and the roll of glaze at the foot.

6 OX BLOOD GLAZES

The ox blood glaze may be considered to be the classic copper red glaze. My concept of an ox blood glaze is: one which has a deep red color and is opaque rather than transparent. But, since copper red glazes are so ephemeral, ox bloods trend off into several variations. For example, ox bloods can be partially or totally transparent in rare cases. They may also go towards the beautiful crushed strawberry color, a deep apple red, or even off-shades like the ugly livery colors. Another offshoot of the ox blood color is the flambé color where blue streaks enter in. For the moment though, let us just consider straight ox blood colors.

Good ox blood reds have been made in quantity since the Kang-hsi reign of the Ching dynasty (1662-1722 AD). Still, there have been ups and downs in the manufacturing process, and times when the glaze has either been better than average or when the glaze has been lost completely. Until 1850, the ox blood color was not made to any extent in places other than China (i.e. Ching-te-chen), even though Pere d'Entrecolles had written in 1722 that the ox blood color was definitely due to copper in the glaze. We must remember though, that porcelain itself was not made in Europe before the early eighteenth century. When, in 1850, Ebelmen and Salvetat received samples from China which they could analyse, then the copper red color began to be sought in European laboratories and factories. Because of difficulties with analytical techniques, the first analyses were not too successful, and although reds were obtained, they were not of high quality. Only in 1880 were the procedures refined and good reds obtained. When Europeans began making use of their gold ruby knowledge and added tin oxide to copper red glazes, they began to get better colors.

Prominent among the early ceramists were Lauth, Dutailly, Vogt and Seger, whose work on copper red glazes will be included in later chapters.

Five glazes which are purported to be successful ones are listed in the following tables I & II (note that each glaze is basically a porcelain glaze with an added frit). Seger adds a soda-baria-boro-silicate frit; Lauth and Dutailly use borax; Vogt adds alkali-lead-silicate frits; and Tichane uses an alkali-boro-silicate frit.

I can vouch for the fact that my composition produced an ox blood red glaze, and I have no reason to doubt that Lauth and Dutailly's, Seger's and Vogt's formulations are also acceptable compositions in combination with appropriate firing conditions. But making ox blood reds from these formulas is not cut and dried. There are certain factors that must be considered and emphasized in order to get good looking glazes using these recipes.

Starting with the basics, these materials **must** be well mixed in order to get good reds. Tin oxide, especially, must be well dispersed in the glaze. Another factor to consider is glaze thickness. I have found it essential that a certain minimum glaze thickness be applied to ware in order to get ox blood colors. This thickness happens to be fairly great. It is desirable to have a glaze which is 0.2-0.3 mm thick or even 0.5 mm so that a good red color can be developed. The result of thin glazes will be very evident in case you make this error, because thin areas will be colorless and red colors may then only be found in areas where the glaze has run and piled up in droplets.

Naturally the firing temperature must be suited to the glaze. In the case of these five glazes with their relatively high alkali contents, it is necessary that the glaze be fired no higher than is essential. I would recommend a close control over the final temperature—as a starter 1250°C might be a good test. This temperature can then be adjusted depending on whether the glaze has flowed too much or too little.

The most important consideration on firing is to perform the firing operation in mild (but completely) reducing conditions, until the glaze has fused and sealed over. At this point, before the glaze has completely matured, it is necessary to switch from a reducing to an oxidizing atmo-

TABLE I

COPPER RED GLAZE COMPOSITIONS

Seger (1883) Copper Red Composition

75% Porcelain Glaze

0.3 moles Potash
0.7 moles Lime
0.5 moles Alumina
4.0 moles Silica

23% Frit

0.5 moles Soda
0.5 moles Baryta
0.5 moles Boric Oxide
2.5 moles Silica

0.5% Copper Oxide
0.5% Ferric Oxide
1.0% Tin Oxide

Lauth & Dutailly (1888) Copper Red Compositions

	I	II
Pegmatite	40	31.2
Sand	40	36.4
Limestone	18	0.0
Fused Borax	12	12.9
Soda Ash	0	4.8
Baryta	0	10.4
Zinc Oxide	0	4.3
Copper Oxide	6	5.0
Tin Oxide	6	2.5

COPPER RED GLAZE COMPOSITIONS (cont.)

Vogt (1899) Copper Red Composition

Lead Frit	20
Copper-Lead-Iron Frit	20
Pegmatite	30
Silica	20
Limestone	13
Kaolin	4
Magnesite	3

Tichane (1983) Copper Red Composition

Custer Feldspar	39
Pulverized Flint	23
Limestone	15
#25 Frit	21
Copper Carbonate	1
Tin Oxide	2

TABLE II

COPPER RED OXIDE COMPOSITIONS

	Seger	L&D I	L&D II	Vogt	Tichane
Silica	62.6	67.0	61.0	61.6	64.1
Alumina	11.2	7.1	5.8	4.4	9.9
Boric Oxide	2.4	8.2	9.5	0.0	3.6
Magnesia	0.0	0.0	0.0	1.7	0.0
Lime	8.5	9.9	0.0	7.4	9.3
Baryta	5.1	0.0	8.4	0.0	0.0
Zinc Oxide	0.0	0.0	4.5	0.0	0.0
Soda	2.1	0.0	0.0	2.9	4.4
KNaO	0.0	7.8	10.7	0.0	0.0
Potash	6.2	0.0	0.0	5.8	5.9
Fluoride	0.0	0.0	0.0	1.8	0.3
Cupric Oxide	0.5	5.0	5.0	0.6	0.5
Tin Oxide	1.0	5.0	2.5	0.0	1.7
Ferric Oxide	0.5	0.0	0.0	0.9	0.0
Lead Oxide	0.0	0.0	0.0	12.7	0.0

sphere. This final firing in oxidation, which may last approximately an hour, is essential for the production of good copper reds. Reds are **possible** if fired completely in reduction, but the quality of the color improves when a final oxidation is used.

Of the firing disasters which can occur in making ox blood glazes, the most common is overfiring. This may be the result of either too high a final temperature, or too extended a firing time. One must remember that copper is volatile and diffusible in our glazes and therefore the firing time should be as brief as is consistent with other requirements. In addition to brevity, the maximum temperature should be no more than is required for the formation of a smooth glaze. The high alkali content in ox blood glazes means that they will have a tendency to run, so extended firings will cause a loss of glaze and the formation of drips. Also, because of volatility there will be a tendency for the glaze to become white, because of the loss of copper. Naturally, running of the glaze will cause a thinness at the top of the ware and this also will result in the loss of color—because of the necessity for a minimum thickness in order to develop a red color.

I sometimes think that never blows so red
The Rose as where some buried Caesar bled;
That every Hyacinth the Garden wears
Dropt in her Lap from some once lovely Head.

Omar Khayyam—Rubaiyat.

A Chinese peach bloom glazed vase of the Kang-hsi reign.

7 PEACH BLOOM GLAZES

Peach bloom copper red glazes seem to have begun during the Kang-hsi reign (1662-1722) of the Ching dynasty. The color description—peach bloom—may or may not be the best description of the color, but it is so ingrained in history that there would be no point in trying to find a substitute now. The color is a pink, which can be either pale or medium red. There are also some other shadings from these pinks into tan, brown and green colors. I have before me a full color picture of eight pieces from the New York Metropolitan Museum of Art, and the colors in this photograph range from tan to yellow to deep green in variations on the basic pale pink and deep pink colors.

Another aspect of peach bloom glazes, which adds to their charm, is the way in which the color varies on a single piece. Only rarely is a piece entirely uniform. Frequently a peach bloom glaze has red spots on it and occasionally these spots become deep green (even black). Wherever the glaze is a little thick, as over an engraved line, the color deepens and becomes darker red.

Hobson stated that Americans had a strong liking for peach bloom glazes and were willing to pay high prices for the best examples; therefore, many of the finer peach bloom glazes are now on display in America (for which we can be grateful). I know that the Philadelphia Museum of Art has a fine collection, as does the New York Metropolitan Museum of Art, the Smithsonian Institution and the Cleveland Museum of Art. Another interesting aspect of peach bloom glazes is that the number of body shapes is quite limited. Most of the Kang-hsi pieces seem to have been destined for the writing table. There are brush washers, water droppers, seal stamp ink holders and in addition a few varieties of small vases. Hobson comments that peach bloom glazes can also be found on snuff bottles. All of these articles are fairly small, which is in keeping with the nature of the color. These subtle, delicate glazes would definitely not be appropriate on large vases or pots.

Looking at photographs of peach bloom articles, one is struck by the evidence of highly reflecting surfaces—as is apparent in the reflections of incident light on the pieces. They all appear to be fully fired, with no visible matteness.

We are fortunate that making replicas of peach bloom glazes meets with more success than making ox bloods. Since the colors are not brilliant, it isn't even necessary to add auxiliary agents, and therefore I put no tin or iron oxide in my peach blooms (although the Chinese may have used iron oxide in theirs). In any case, the addition of iron oxide can be left to the discretion of the potter.

My conclusion, after making a number of test glazes, and after looking at the Chinese pieces at the Philadelphia Museum of Art, has led me to the feeling that this glaze is a feldspathic one with added clay (the clay initiates devitrification in the glaze). I have also come to the conclusion that the pink color results from the fact that the copper red color has been diluted—that is, it has been washed out by the simultaneous occurrence of many bubbles and many fine, undissolved crystalline particles in the glaze.

The batch that I used to make a first attempt at peach bloom glazes was one which contained: 5 parts Custer feldspar; 3 parts Supersil silica; 2 parts calcium carbonate; two parts #25 Pemco frit; 2 parts calcined kaolin; and 0.1 part copper carbonate.

In experimenting with the peach bloom glaze, results showed that feldspars made a greater difference in the end product than did the clays that were used—as long as the clay concentration was constant. When potash and soda feldspars were compared, I found that potash feldspars gave a lighter pink color and soda feldspars gave a darker pink. This may be entirely due to the lower melting temperatures of the soda spars and their greater fluxing ability. Probably the soda spar dissolved more of the clay in the glaze and therefore gave more clarity to it and made it appear a darker red. It also could be seen that the potash spar glazes became paler in color as they became harder (i.e. with lower potash content). If this assumption is correct, a glaze batch with a smaller quantity of soda spar might approach the potash spar in its lighter color quality.

One thing that discouraged me in these tests was the fact that very uniform colors were the usual result and my pieces didn't have any of the irregularities which showed up in the Chinese glazes. For this reason I wonder if the Chinese glazes were applied by spraying (which could give less uniform results than dipping).

Another question that arose from early experiments was in regard to the lack of red, green or black spots on replica glazes. The spot defects were probably attributable to the way in which copper was added to the glaze. And, although I tried several ways of adding coarser particles of copper, only one of them was successful. This course was the addition of **flaked** copper oxide as the colorant in the glaze. The flake copper oxide was made by heating scrap copper tubing in my kiln (at 800°C) in air so that cupric oxide formed on the metal and flaked off when the tubing was quenched in water. The resulting black flakes were difficult to grind up to a uniform powder, hence this may explain the irregularities in some of the Chinese ware. Perhaps they oxidized copper coins and used the oxide flakes as a glaze colorant.

The fact that these are flaky particles, since they come from flat surfaces, means that when one tries to grind them between the faces of a mortar and pestle, they merely slip between the two grinding surfaces and are not pulverized as are chunky granules.

An examination of a genuine peach bloom glaze shows it to be filled with many tiny bubbles and to be littered with undissolved fragments of batch. Evidently a high alumina content makes the glass more viscous, so there is less of a tendency for silica and clay particles to dissolve in the glassy batch. It is unfortunate that I don't have any fragments of genuine Chinese peach bloom ware that could be used for analytical purposes. It would be interesting to find out if a high alumina content **is** present in the glaze. Still, the results from test glazes show that the peach bloom effect can be obtained by adding large amounts of clay to a glaze batch, and when simulated glazes are held up against a genuine Kang-hsi peach bloom, the agreement is striking.

Courtesy of the Metropolitan Museum of Art, Rogers Fund, 1917. (18.56.35)

A Chinese Ming dynasty bowl painted in underglaze copper red.

8 UNDERGLAZE REDS

You can't beat learning from the masters, so let's take a look at the genuine article. Thanks to Margaret Medley I have at my disposal a sherd of fourteenth century Chinese underglaze copper red ceramic. I was able to take this sherd and make a thin section of it and also a polished cross section. Even when these were examined visually a number of interesting things were observed. For example, on the inside surface of the sherd, the coloration was a definite greyish-black, with no red tint in it. However, on the outside surface, the grey underglaze design had a reddish color associated with it. In cross section the physical appearance of the inside glaze showed that it was much thinner than the outside glaze. But, both of them had a layering effect that is observed in many Chinese glazes. Observation at low magnification with a microscope showed an insoluble material which is present in higher concentrations in some layers than in others. As I have commented in previous work, I believe that this layering is due to the application of material of greatly different fusion points, either at one time, or after different firings. When these undissolved materials are observed at high magnification, there is no definite crystal structure in them, so I am led to the conclusion that they are areas where high concentrations of refractory (aluminous?) materials are found. Perhaps these areas are rich in kaolin.

On further examination of these cross sections in reflected light, it was noted that on the outer, thicker layer (the red colored layer), one could see a reddish tint in the glaze. This tint was not very evident when examining the glaze under transmitted light. On the inside surface there was practically no reddish tint with reflected light.

In addition to the hazy crystalline areas in the glaze, it is also jam-packed with quartz relicts. In fact, an examination of the glaze shows it to be about one-half undissolved material. It is one of the **least** glassy glazes that I have ever observed. It is even more un-melted than a Kuan glaze.

This un-melted aspect of the glaze is one of the reasons that the red is not any brighter than it is. If it is examined with a hand lens at 10X, it appears to be hazy to the eye—which is only natural with all this undissolved material.

When a cross section of this glaze and body was examined by Leonard Pruden using a scanning electron microscope and x-ray analysis, he found that the glaze composition was not markedly different from the body composition, except for the presence of some extra calcium oxide. One of the analyses of the glaze on the inside surface also showed it to have an alumina content that was higher than that of the body. Thus the glaze composition for this particular sample may be merely a body mixture with added limestone as a flux.

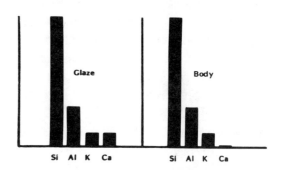

A further examination of the underglaze sample brought other details to light. Although the compositions of the glaze and the body were not exceptional, it was found that some droplets of a shiny, metallic-appearing material were present at the interface between the glaze and the body. When I saw this with the optical microscope, I assumed that the droplets were either a brassy material or some pure copper. However, Len Pruden's x-ray examination showed that the droplets were composed of copper and sulfur with small amounts of arsenic present (as one would expect in a native ore). Thus, the Chinese, rather than using copper oxide or copper metal, were using copper sulfide as a colorant in this fourteenth century specimen.

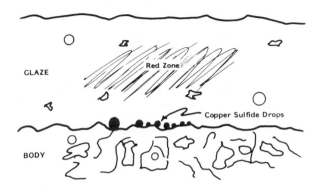

An examination of the sherd with a hand lens at 10X showed that in cross section the black appearing material on the inside surface was a layer which was next to the body. Above this layer was a colorless layer of glaze, so the black that one sees is observed by looking through a transparent (actually hazy) glaze. One fascinating aspect is that, for the black decoration, all of the design edges are sharp. On the opposite (outer) side, where a red color is showing, an examination with a hand lens shows that here too, there is a black layer next to the body. This is covered by a **thicker** hazy glaze layer, and in this case the glaze has a reddish hue. There could be a reddish hue on the inside surface too, but because the glaze is so thin it is not readily observable there, and the only thing normally seen is the black color. (By looking very, very carefully at the inside surface, a slight amount of pinkish color can be seen occasionally, but it is quite scarce.)

Returning to the outside surface, the outlines of the leaves and other patterns are blurry in the pink areas because the copper is diffusing from the black sulfide layer into the glaze. Although this copper diffusion causes the red color, there is also an **outward** diffusion which results in a blurring of the sharp lines of the designs in copper sulfide which were painted on the body.

These observations bring us back to considerations which we had when we were talking about ox blood colors; namely, that a certain thickness of glaze is required before a copper red color can be obtained. When a glaze is too thin, it is either not possible or it is difficult to get a copper red because red coloration tends to be destroyed close to the body. On the inside of this underglaze red specimen, where the glaze is extremely thin, even though there is plenty of copper present no red color appears. However, on the outside, where the glaze is two or three times as thick, the copper can diffuse from the body into the glaze and enter parts of the glaze where it has a composition different enough from the body so that a red color can develop.

Going from the examination of a Chinese underglaze copper red to my own experiments with underglaze copper red, the most interesting result that I found was that the critical part of successful underglaze reds is not the underglaze material, but rather the covering glaze. I ran a number of experiments where the underglaze component was varied to a great extent, trying in turn: copper nitrate, copper sulfate, cupric oxide, cuprous oxide, copper sulfide, copper carbonate and even copper metal. Simultaneously, variations in the overglaze were tested too (using a grid pattern). The surprising result was that the effect from the underglaze component was almost insignificant. If the copper was present in a nonvolatile form, then the result would be satisfactory. However, if the covering glaze did not have an appropriate composition, then a variety of red colors would result. Not too surprisingly, many of the previous observations made on ox blood colors were confirmed here. In fact, the best overglaze for making copper red underglaze colors was a material that was the same as an ox blood glaze, only lacking a copper compound.

It was also found in these tests (in line with the observations made on the Chinese piece), that the reds only appeared under thick regions of the overglaze. Where the glaze was about a half millimeter thick, a good red appeared. Where the glaze was too thin, there was no red at all, even though the same amount of copper oxide had been painted on the body. These observations mean that the best colors are going to be obtained from the thickest glazes. Unfortunately, the sharpest images are going to be found in areas where the color is poorest and vice versa.

I can think of only one way to get around this problem and that would be to have a cloisonné-type arrangement. Then the copper material could be hemmed in physically in some way and a thick glaze could be applied over the copper containing area only. On horizontal, flat surfaces (such as the inside of plates) it might even be possible to get sharp patterns using inlays. One might also try extra splashes of glaze **over** the copper patterned areas.

It would be nice to believe that there is some kind of underglaze slip like silica that could be applied to the body to help things along. Then one could put down an underglaze copper red and over that a glaze which would be compatible with a good red. However, I don't know of such a slip. It might also be possible to form a glaze sequentially in situ, by first applying copper oxide in a pattern ; next spraying on silica; then spraying on feldspar; and finally spraying on calcium carbonate. It would be worth a trial.

In trying to make an underglaze copper red, the same constraints are in play as were found in making a standard copper red glaze. It is apparent that both the good and bad effects of copper diffusion are still functioning and that the alumina enigma is still present. In fact, alumina is probably the major dilemma to be faced in making good underglaze copper reds. It **has** to be present in the body, and there it is adjacent to the underglaze copper—the worst place for it to be.

As a way out, it is possible to make "underglaze" reds by putting the copper compound **over** a raw glaze. And, while this can give a good color, the outline of the design may not be sharp because of copper diffusion and glaze running.

Another technique which produces fine red colors was shown to me by Linda Bain-Woods of Kingston, Ontario. She took a Chun glazed piece and splashed it with an ox blood glaze. This produced some beautiful red colors, and over a viscous glaze like the Chun it might even be possible to keep the red color within boundries.

9 LOW TEMPERATURE GLAZES

Yes, I have made low temperature copper glazes. And yes, those glazes did become red when reduced. The problem though, is that I would not call any of them **good** reds. A bright fire engine red or an apple red has never developed from one of these low temperature tests.

One of the techniques that I used to make low temperature glazes was to take a high temperature glaze and to add large amounts of either lead silicate or boric oxide to it. Invariably, the addition of extra lead gave glazes that had an orange tint. So I assumed that all lead glazes would have this "off" color. Probably, if one spent the necessary time, a low temperature copper red glaze could be obtained (i.e. one that would have the desired bright red color). I can only state that in the course of a few dozen experimental melts, I have never been able to get a hint that good reds could be obtained in this way.

In addition to altering some of my high temperature glazes, I have also tried some of the glazes described in the literature. And again, while they are red, I certainly would not define them as **fine** red colors. My feeling about low temperature reds is that they will probably never be comparable to the high temperature colors. One of the reasons that I have for saying this is the collection of copper red glaze recipes that is to be found in Volume 8 of "Studio Potter" magazine that contains several articles on copper red glazes. There are many recipes given in this edition, but none of them are for low temperature copper red glazes. I would assume, that if someone had found a good low temperature color, it would have been included in this volume.

One of the most widely repeated recipes for a low temperature copper red glaze is that given by Harder and repeated by Brown and Norton. However, when I tried it I got a rather poor red, and I have never seen it recommended by contemporary potters. Therefore, I assume that ceramists have probably had the same problems that I had. While it may give a red color, it is not a bright red.

Naturally there are some basic problems with low temperature glazes. One of these is tied up with the fact that a rather thick glaze is required to give the layering which allows a good red to develop in the center of a glaze. Most low temperature glazes are not meant to be used as thick glazes since they don't have the proper viscosity characteristics to be used in this fashion. One would assume that these glazes could be altered to give proper viscosities, but again, I have not seen evidence in the literature of such a solution.

Similarly, the two components most commonly used for making low temperature glazes, namely lead oxide and boric oxide, do not seem to be amenable to producing good reds. In the high temperature range, neither of them is desirable in high concentrations. So we might extrapolate from that and assume that they are not going to be acceptable for low temperature copper red colors either.

Still another problem concerns the temperature range where many processes take place in copper reds. The mere formation of a low temperature glaze requires that several important reactions have to be placed in a limited portion of the temperature spectrum. The diffusion of hydrogen, oxygen, copper and alkalies all have to take place at lower temperatures and in cramped thermal regions, because of the abbreviated firing span. Likewise, the postulated reaction between cuprous oxide and stannous oxide may not be feasible at these lower temperatures.

In any case, I have a strong feeling that the work required for the development of a beautiful, low temperature copper red glaze might be as difficult as the total accumulated work that has been done over the centuries on **high** temperature copper reds. The least that might be required could be a redox agent other than tin oxide. Some agent that reacts at a lower temperature, but which would still convert copper oxide to copper metal would be desirable, and I don't know if such an element exists.

Another comparison might be made to the celadon situation, where low temperature celadons are not famous either. Undoubtedly the reaction can occur, but the mere fact that one does not run into a number of low temperature glaze recipes for celadons makes me wonder about the quality of such glazes. Similarly the fact that over the years no one has made a **commercial** copper red that fires at low temperatures leads one to believe that this too is not a likely event to expect.

What do I advise? If you are adventurous, give it a try, but at least be bold in your attempts. The fact that many ordinary experiments have failed means that some new avenues need to be pursued.

The wild fire dances on the fen,
The red star sheds its ray;
Uprouse you then, my merry men!
It is our op'ning day.

Joanna Baillie—The Outlaw's Song.

A Chinese Chun-type flower pot of the Ming dynasty with a variegated copper red glaze.

10 HARE'S FUR GLAZE FORMATION

Hare's fur type glazes are those glazes which have a delicate texture formed by a glaze mixture flowing and intertwining as it moves from the top to the bottom of a ceramic piece. This type of glaze appearance is most notable on certain brown temmoku glazes, but it is also seen on blue Chun glazes and copper reds of the flambé variety. The mechanism for formation of hare's fur type glazes becomes especially apparent after working with copper reds. These glazes have a very accentuated layer structure and, while layering is found to some degree in all glazes, it is quite marked in copper reds. Therefore, a thorough investigation of copper reds requires an examination of layering to explain the hare's fur effect.

LAYERING

Let us now take a look at layering as it occurs in copper reds, and consider the situation closely. The first step is to determine the number of layers. Mellor commented on five in his article, but for simplicity's sake, we will discuss only the three major ones.

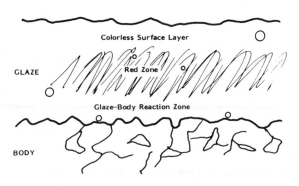

The first layer, next to the body, is the reaction zone between the glaze and the body. The highly alkaline glaze has reacted strongly with the body in this stratum and has formed a sub-layer that is high in alumina. The aluminous layer is incompatible with copper red because it does not promote the phase separation which is necessary for color formation. So, in a copper red glaze, the layer near the body is clear, or at least not red.

The second layer, which is more or less pure glaze, is the red one. And, in a copper red glaze this layer is frequently found to be strongly opalescent on the side adjacent to the body. If the copper red layer is of any thickness, and of any intensity, it becomes a livery color and is not a good looking red when viewed from the body side of the glaze.

The glaze then goes through a transition to the surface and this is the third layer that I will discuss. The interesting thing about this layer is the transition. It changes very gradually from the red central zone into a clear layer that is present at the surface. The reason for the clear layer here is manyfold. For one thing there is some small penetration of oxygen (or loss of hydrogen) and this oxidizes the copper so that the red is lost. In addition, there is volatilization of copper from the surface, and this happens very noticeably in reduction. There is an actual absence of copper in the gradation from the surface down to the red layer, and this is why the cross section is always clear at the top. You can try all sorts of tricks to get a red precipitate there, but none will form; there is simply not enough copper in the upper layer. The copper concentration increases gradually going from the outer to the central red zone and in between the two there is formed a beautiful red color. This is the most desirable red. If one could make the central layer thin enough, the glaze would have this beautiful color, and crushed strawberry-appearing glazes are of this type.

Summing up, this is the situation: in the glaze close to the body a clear layer exists; then a copper red layer is found in the center, grading into a bright red; and finally, another clear layer is noted at the surface. The next question is: what are the events that happen to these layers during glaze development?

In every glaze there is a great deal of bubble formation. When a powdered substance melts, it traps gases from the environment—mainly nitrogen, oxygen, carbon dioxide and water vapor; in addition, as the components of the glaze decompose, they evolve gases—such as carbon dioxide from carbonates and water from clays; finally, as the porous body heats up, it generates bubbles from the expanding gases in its pores. All of these must find their way through the glaze or else they will be trapped in it.

During glaze formation, a great many bubbles are formed at the glaze-body interface. This is just as true here as it is in a glass of beer, where bubbles form at the glass-liquid interface. Now, consider what the color effects of this bubble formation will be. If it were possible to make a perfectly clear copper red glaze, with no bubbles at all, you could look in at the top and see a beautiful red, because this would be the first layer to be seen. However, the situation is as follows: gases bubble up **through** the sandwich—first passing through the clear bottom layer, then the red middle layer and finally the clear top layer, promoting a complex mixing action. At the end, when the bubble breaks, a relict in the form of a circle is left and the surface has a mottled appearance as can be seen in the following figure:

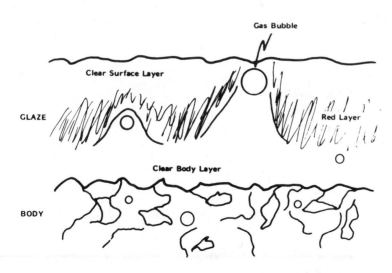

This relict is definitely not of the same composition as the surface, so the net effect is that a circular segment of liver colored glaze has been brought up and overlaid in a good-looking red glaze. On further heating, the glaze continues its process of running down the side of the piece. Because of these two actions, the glaze is left with the track of a bubble on the surface as the flow continues. Since the circle contains some dark colored material, one gets a streak running through the beautiful red color, and this is part of the hare's fur effect. There will be a good red color mixed up with other colors in a streaky set of tracks down the article. The less liver color present, the better looking the ox blood is, while a thick brown central layer will produce a poorer looking color. This is why there are many varieties of ox bloods. There are no two alike any more than there are two snowflakes alike, and it is all because of the welling up of bubbles through the multiple glaze layers.

In the formation of copper reds, there are two conceivable ways to get rid of the hare's fur effect. First of all you could get rid of the bubbles. If you had a glaze with no bubbles, then you would have a glaze which was perfectly uniform in color (though layered). Or, if you had a glaze with no layering that too would do the job. However, it is just about as easy to obtain a bubble-free, unlayered copper red as it is to find peace in Lebanon. You can approach this situation of course, and that is what we try to do, through slow firing and the use of a hard biscuit. Unfortunately volatilization of copper reduces the usefulness of this recourse. Another solution is to use a fritted glaze to minimize bubbling, but this technique deals only with some of the gases. Let's face it, bubbles and layering are here to stay.

In conclusion, the welling up of bubbles through a multicolored, multilayered glaze and the subsequent flow of this glaze down the sides of ware leads to the often noted hare's fur effect.

11 BASE GLAZE EFFECTS

There are obviously some base glazes which are best for copper red effects. And, in order for us to gain an insight as to what elements or materials are to be preferred, let us look at the glazes which have been recommended by Seger and Vogt, as shown in Table I; and in addition, let us look at some more recent glazes which are given in Table II. To make the recipes comparable, they have all been converted to weight percentages of oxides.

In Table I there is: first, Vogt's analysis of a raw Chinese red glaze obtained in 1882; next, Vogt's analysis of a drop of a fired Chinese red glaze; third, Seger's analysis of a piece of Chinese copper red glaze; fourth, the oxide composition of Vogt's glaze made to duplicate the Chinese red; fifth, one made by Seger which represents his best copper red glaze; and finally a glaze which I have arrived at by trial and error, which represents my best ox blood composition.

The first four of these glazes have been made with added lead oxide to soften the glaze, while the last two have been fluxed with boric oxide. The obvious volatility of lead oxide at the necessary firing temperature seems reason enough to avoid this material today, although we might find some loss of boric oxide too, if we analysed the last two glazes. One other change between the last two and the first four glazes is the change from iron oxide to tin oxide as the auxiliary reducing agent. This use of tin probably had its origin in the European knowledge that tin oxide was desirable for the production of **gold** ruby glasses.

TABLE I

COPPER RED GLAZE ANALYSES AND COMPOSITIONS

Oxides	Vogt Chinese Batch Analysis	Vogt Chinese Glaze Analysis	Seger Chinese Glaze Analysis	Vogt Glaze Replica	Seger Glaze	Tichane Glaze
Silica	62	70	71	64	62	65
Alumina	4	7	3	5	11	10
Boric Oxide	0	0	0	0	3	4
Lime	7	8	9	7	8	9
Magnesia	2	2	2	1	0	0
Barium Oxide	0	0	0	0	6	0
Potash	6	5	5	5	6	6
Soda	3	3	3	5	2	5
Iron Oxide	1	1	1	0.4	0.5	0
Lead Oxide	13	4	4	12	0	0
Copper Oxide	0.6	0.5	0.9	0.3	0.5	0.7
Tin Oxide	0	0	0	0	1	1.5

TABLE II

CONTEMPORARY COPPER RED GLAZE COMPOSITIONS

Oxides	Kring	Grebanier	Ball	Nelson	Tichane
Silica	65	60	64	59	65
Alumina	15	14	9	5	10
Boric Oxide	0	7	4	9	4
Lime	13	10	9	0	9
Barium Oxide	0	0	4	8	0
Magnesia	0	0	1	0	0
Potash	6	4	4	2	6
Soda	1	5	1	8	5
Zinc Oxide	0	0	1	5	0
Iron Oxide	0	0	0	0	0
Copper Oxide	0.5	0.3	1	2	0.7
Tin Oxide	1	1	1	2	1.0
CONE	**10**	**9**	**10**	**8**	**8**

TABLE III

COPPER RED GLASS ANALYSES

Oxides	Williams Glass	Ebell Glass
Silica	71	40
Boric Oxide	6	—
Potash	14	10
Soda	2	—
Lead Oxide	—	47
Copper Oxide	2	1
Tin Oxide	4	2

If we consider in turn each of the common elements used in copper red glazes, we can get an idea of the influence of each material.

SILICA

First of course is silica. There are numerous references in the literature on the desirability of high percentages of silica in copper red glazes. The experiment which demonstrated the importance of silica to me was the one concerning the reaction zone between a copper red glaze and two different body materials. the fact that a copper red glaze maintains its color while in direct contact with a silica surface, while losing its color in contact with porcelain, demonstrated to me the desirability of silica as a glaze component. Naturally, there are reasons why silica cannot be used in extremely high quantities even though this might seem to be desirable. The problem is that silica, in high percentages, causes the firing temperature of a glaze to increase greatly. As we go above 70% silica we find that higher and higher firing temperatures are required. Therefore, because of the problem of the loss of copper by volatility, we must place an upper limit (of about 70%) on the quantities of silica that we include in a copper red glaze. Otherwise, we would probably like to have up to 80% silica in a base for copper reds.

ALUMINA

Alumina, the material which causes glazes to be different from glasses, is a problem in copper red glazes. While normally we like to have alumina in a glaze because it increases the viscosity and hence decreases the tendency of a glaze to run and devitrify, in copper red glazes it is not a desirable element above certain low concentrations—at least insofar as ox blood reds are concerned. The peach bloom colors are another matter, as they seem to need large proportions of alumina. In an experiment to determine the optimum concentration of alumina in a glaze, tests using either aluminum oxide or clay showed that while the quality of the glaze texture improves, the color definitely is degraded from a deep red (at low alumina levels) to pinker tones whenever the alumina concentrations rise much above 10%. The change is not obvious until glazes are placed side-by-side, at which time the gradual pinkening can be seen. Personally, I think that the best rule for the use of alumina is to avoid it whenever possible, and never intentionally add any material containing alumina when it can be omitted. The addition of clay therefore, would not be advisable as far as my experiments would indicate. Naturally, when feldspar is used in a glaze, there has to be some alumina content, and this plus any alumina which comes from the frit is the only addition which I would accept as a glaze ingredient.

BORON

An element which is found only in more recent copper red glaze compositions is boron. And, although boron is not particularly desirable as far as copper red color is concerned, it is quite useful as an ingredient which will lower the fusion temperature of a high firing glaze. Therefore, we can accept the presence of boron (in the range of 5-10%) as an additive which will lower the maximum firing temperature by about 2 or 3 cones. Although boron can be added by using materials such as borax or colemanite, I prefer to add it in the form of a frit, so that there is the least possible solubility of boron in the glaze slip, and so that there will be less of it moving into the body when it is applied to the ware. In excessive amounts, boron will   encourage phase separation and bluish opalescence, which can give a flambé effect to copper red glazes. I personally do not like flambé reds, but if they are desired, boron additions are one means of obtaining them. The addition of high amounts of boron should be approached with care though, because phase separation will also degrade the durability of glazes.

ALKALINE EARTHS

As for the alkaline earths, calcium is normally used in copper red glazes and functions as a major fluxing material. It is obviously possible to substitute for calcium and in Table II we see that Nelson's glaze has substituted barium oxide for calcium oxide—apparently successfully. Nevertheless, since calcium is perfectly acceptable, I have used it because of a desire to avoid the toxicity associated with barium compounds. As for magnesium oxide, it can be used to advantage in small percentages. A 1-3% magnesium oxide addition will assist in the fluxing of glazes without affecting the color to any degree. I have avoided magnesium merely because I try to keep my glazes as simple as possible, so that there is less confusion about what elements are causing problems in wayward glazes. However, in one experiment where I added 5% magnesia to my best glaze, there was no observable change in the color. A touch of magnesia would be acceptable in a completely developed glaze batch.

As far as the bad points of alkaline earths are concerned, one has to be careful with additions of calcium oxide, because a slight excess (over 10%) can result in opalization due to phase separation. This opalization will give bluish colors, and if the mixing is not thorough, a flambé effect will be seen. I believe that the flambé effects in Chinese glazes were due to high calcium oxide content. On the other hand, excessive amounts of magnesia or baria will lead to glaze crystallization and matte effects. These will result in a paling of the ox blood color and, although you might want to try making a peach bloom by this technique, it should be avoided in attempts to make ox bloods.

ALKALIES

Alkali metals seem to be desirable elements in copper reds. The paper by Norton and Brown comments that they found it very easy to obtain copper reds in a sodium silicate glass. It is too bad that such a glass has poor durability and has no practical use. Our normal problem with alkalies is the fact that it is difficult to get enough of them in a batch using ordinary insoluble raw materials. Therefore, we usually do not have excess soda or potash in a glaze. We need to try to get as much alkali in as practicable, either by using feldspars or frits.

A look at Table II shows that some wide variations of soda:potash ratios are possible in successful copper red glazes. My experience has been that a glaze which is high in soda but low in potash does not give as good a color as one with the reverse ratio. For this reason I use only as much soda as is necessary to make use of raw materials which are convenient. For example, I chose my frit because of its high boron content and low alumina content and accepted the soda level that went along with it.

Lithium has been recommended by some writers, but I have not found it to be essential for good reds. Looking at the glazes in the tables, it can be seen that the combined alkali content hovers around 10% in various ratios. The choice between these ratios does not seem to be critical.

With regard to other additives to copper red glazes, you can see in Tables I & II that lead is sometimes added and so is zinc. But, the problem with both of these is volatility. We have enough problems with the loss of copper, without having to worry about the volatility of other glaze components. In addition, both zinc and lead are noted for their effect on glaze colors and I have found them undesirable from this standpoint when they are used in sizable quantities. Additions of 5-10% lead oxide to my best ox bloods resulted in a paling of the color; and the same was true of zinc. Rather than adding any lead or zinc to a glaze, I would prefer to add a small amount of magnesia if fluxing is the goal.

Today, iron oxide is a strange element for copper red glazes, because in our modern materials we can control iron at a very low level and thus can almost ignore it. In early raw materials potters suffered from iron oxide as a contaminant and it was probably rare when a glaze had less than one half of one percent of iron oxide in it (prior to the twentieth century). In early copper red glazes, iron oxide was performing the role that tin oxide does in our glazes. Vogt adds no tin oxide to his glaze because iron oxide was performing the necessary oxidation and reduction. Naturally it is to be preferred that iron oxide be absent, because it adds a little "off" color; and although some of the Chinese glazes were quite brilliant, the capability of making even brighter reds is apparent if tin oxide is substituted for iron oxide.

The objective of providing a table such as Table II is not to prove that the glazes are identical, or that one glaze is superior to all the others. The point is to show that there are certain limits within which you can create copper red glazes and this collection gives you an idea of some of the limits. Perhaps the most practical application of this table would be to compare these glazes with one of your own; and then, if you have a favorite glaze which approximates one of these, the solution would be to adjust your own glaze slightly and add copper oxide and tin oxide to produce a good copper red.

The reason for presenting the two copper red **glass** formulas of Table III is to point up the fact that good glass compositions are definitely **not** good glaze compositions. Neither of the two glasses would stay on the side of a ceramic vessel. In addition, they would be quite prone to dissolve a ceramic body. Another interesting fact about these glasses is the total absence of alumina in them even though both scientists knew of the desirability of alumina in glass to improve the durability.

As a final note, it can be mentioned that all of these glazes were fired in reduction in the temperature range of cones 8-10 (i.e. in the neighborhood of 1250°C).

The Pobble who has no toes
Swam across the Bristol Channel;
But before he set out he wrapped his nose
In a piece of scarlet flannel.

Edward Lear—The Pobble Who Has No Toes

12 EXPERIMENTAL TECHNIQUES

The optimum conditions that one could imagine for making copper red glazes would be to have at one's disposal a great variety of materials which could be tested in the glaze; then, having these materials, to be able to apply them in several ways; and finally, to have facilities available that would allow one to fire them under any practical circumstance.

Obtaining raw materials is not too difficult a task, especially after one has been working in the ceramic field for a while, since one tends to accumulate many kinds of staples. So, if you have available two or three feldspars, a couple of kinds of silica, several types of clay, a few frits, several copper compounds and some miscellaneous materials such as tin, arsenic, antimony, and iron, in the form of their oxides, then it would be possible to test most of the glaze batches that have been used in the past as well as some that might be useful in the future. I do not think that it is necessary to go into the exotic elements (such as the rare earth series), but a good palette of materials is desirable. Fortunately in an experimental case such as the development of a good copper red, it is not necessary to have hundred pound sacks of each of these materials. In the usual tests, quite small quantities will be perfectly satisfactory. If one is fortunate enough to have a neighbor who is active in ceramics, this is even better, for it is quite practical to swap back and forth.

The appliances necessary to mix the raw materials and to apply them to the bodies are even less of a problem. One can work very satisfactorily with a large mortar and pestle, and if necessary, a small ball mill. These will allow for adequate mixing of ingredients. As for application, any of the normal spraying, dipping or brushing techniques would be appropriate. I have found that by adjusting the consistency of the slip and by painting glazes on bodies, I can evaluate copper red colors and compare them to one another in an effective way.

FIRING CONDITIONS

However, the firing operation, which is touchy even for an average glaze becomes a very critical proposition in the case of copper reds. It is fortunate that at the present time oxygen sensors are coming on the market. These should make mastering of copper red glazes a lot easier than it has been in the past. The best circumstances that one could imagine for firing would be having a furnace in which one could control and monitor the temperature and its rate of climb. Then, if one could also evaluate and adjust the gas composition, life would be perfect.

People in the past have (in most cases) lacked the desired, controlled firing conditions. When reading the literature of a century ago, one sees that the problem of making copper reds was intimately tied up with the problems of firing. The best experimental conditions which have been reported until now have been those of Brown and Norton in their laboratory work at MIT. And, although we may envy people who have such things available as tanks of hydrogen and carbon monoxide, and tightly sealed combustion chambers, we can recognize that the results of such experiments may not have too much application in the real world. We, after all, have to deal with kilns in which there are varying mixtures of gases such as hydrogen, water vapor, carbon monoxide, carbon dioxide, air and a number of incompletely burned hydrocarbons. Therefore, although the laboratory conditions may give some hints as to what mechanisms may be involved in the formation of copper reds, when we work in ordinary conditions, we may have to make adjustments for circumstances which are never encountered in the laboratory.

The conditions under which I ran my experiments, while not perfect, were satisfactory, and, I think, a useful intermediate step between a large production kiln and a small laboratory furnace. My test furnace consisted of a small kiln, just large enough for one four inch diameter bowl. It could be heated either rapidly or slowly as desired. In most cases the firings were much quicker (normally 1-2 hours) than in a large kiln. The cooling rate was also rapid (1-2 hours), but in any case it was slow enough to develop copper reds. This kiln was fired with natural gas and forced air, and could be adjusted quickly to give either an oxidizing or a reducing atmosphere. The prime advantage of this kiln though, was that (because of the positive pressure of the fire gases) it was always either 100% oxidizing or 100% reducing. There was no problem with leakage or incompletely mixed gases.

Until now I have used the technique of observing the condition of the flame as it leaves the kiln to determine whether oxidation or reduction was prevailing. If a blue tongue of gases was emitted, then I considered that reduction was underway. When the blue tongue disappeared, then I felt that oxidation was occurring. Obviously, the results verified these suppositions. The sole drawback of this kiln was that there was a slight thermal variation from front to side, but this was not a gross effect.

The most important requirement in firing is the ability to understand what it is that has caused a certain glaze result. If it is possible to repeat glazing and firing conditions and to obtain identical results, then one feels that the process is under control. Presumably, if the circumstances of firing are understood well enough, then one can translate techniques from one kiln to another. Therefore, the proof of the success of my experimental firings will lie in whether or not I can provide directions for glazing, which will allow another potter to make fine copper reds in his own environment. This is the test which is critical to the evaluation of any work.

Obviously, some modifications will have to be made to make the transition from a small test kiln to a large production kiln. For example, because of the extended period of firing in a production kiln, it may be necessary to add extra copper to the batch; or, to place the glazed article in a copper washed sagger, so that the extended time of gas impingement will not vaporize so much copper that a good red cannot result.

OXIDATION AND REDUCTION

Some of the wildest conditions reported in the literature are those which concern the timing of oxidation and reduction in a copper red firing. In general, most ceramists recommend a reduction firing during the middle temperatures. But, except for that, the conditions vary widely. For example, Seger, who was a noted experimentalist, recommended that alternate oxidation and reduction firing be used. This would imitate the type of firing that would be encountered in a wood kiln. There the addition of fuel might initiate reduction and then, after its consumption, lead to oxidation as the fire burned low. And, if the net result of this was a slight reduction, then it is quite logical to arrange for alternate redox firing in a gas kiln. I can imagine though, that the original wood firing process went from mildly reducing to heavily reducing and back again, and never actually passed through an oxidation state.

Other authors have their own special techniques for firing copper reds, so that they can get certain body and glaze effects. These people have given recommendations for all sorts of complicated firing schedules.

Still, there is one theme which runs through many procedures and this is the frequently recurring comment that a final oxidation firing should be used. This procedure is almost as common as the use of reduction in the mid-temperature ranges. For myself, I didn't believe **any** of these complicated procedures, and for a long time I performed all of my firing in steady, mild reducing conditions. I simply turned the furnace on, adjusted it to light reduction, and then continued the firing to the end in this mode. Some of the glazes were good and some of them were bad, but because it was possible to get some good reds, I felt that an incursion into oxidation was unnecessary.

Nevertheless, since I saw so many recommendations for alternating firing conditions, I did do some experiments. The first one I did was an alternate redox firing with reduction for 10 minutes alternating with oxidation for 10 minutes. In addition to being tedious, this procedure also appeared to be unsuccessful. Yet I had the feeling that some oxidation might be all right at the end of the firing, even though I didn't believe that oxygen could penetrate the glaze (because of my previous work on celadons). I therefore ran a firing (as previously described in the redox chapter) which answered all of my questions. I used a cut-up piece of copper red glazed ware as a final experiment. One piece was kept for a standard of color, a second piece was refired entirely in reduction, and a third piece was refired to the top temperature in oxidation. Much to my surprise, the one that was refired in oxidation had a superior red color when compared to either the original or the one refired in reduction. After this experiment I became a convert to the concept of doing a final oxidation fire on copper red glazes. I was so convinced, that from that time on I have always fired my copper reds in reduction until they are sealed over; then I have finished them in oxidation until the desired top temperature was reached.

The oxidized glazes not only look good from the outside, but, when examined in cross section (using a microscope), they also appear to have a brighter red layer. Hence, I have considered that a final oxidation step is a good technique to use for copper reds, even though I am not certain that I fully understand the mechanism of the reaction.

A possible explanation for the confusion in the literature may be the fact that many large kilns, which are slow to cool, would give this kind of treatment to glazes even if no intentional final oxidation fire were used. A large kiln, which cooled slowly, would perform its oxidation after the firing ceased, and would not need a special terminal oxidation step, because it would have the same kind of conditions at the end of the firing. The mechanism of what occurs during this final oxidation step has already been discussed in the Oxidation and Reduction chapter, so it will not be repeated here.

When clay has such red mouths to kiss,
Firm hands to grasp, it is enough:
How can I take it aught amiss
We are not made of rarer stuff.

Edward V. Lucas—Clay

13 THINGS THAT GO WRONG

This could easily be the longest chapter of the book, because, as we know, for every correct way of making glazes there are probably a dozen incorrect ways. However, in this chapter we will limit ourselves to discussing the particular ills that plague copper red glazes, with the emphasis on color variations.

LOSS OF COLOR

Color loss is probably the most common defect seen in copper red glazes and can be due to a number of causes. The usual place to notice the lack of color in a copper red is at the top of a tall piece. With this defect the first thing to consider is volatilization of copper from the glaze which can occur either because the firing was prolonged or because the firing reached too high a temperature. Another turn of events which will lead to clear glazes is the application of too thin a glaze or the generation of too thin a glaze through running. This also is noted at the top of pieces, where the thickness of any glaze is a minimum due to the action of gravity. Theoretically one could compensate for this lack of color at the top by adding more copper and tin, by applying a thicker glaze or even by adjusting the viscosity so that there is less tendency for the glaze to run. However, the problem is that some of these cures result in poor colors in other portions of the ware. While you may succeed in obtaining a red color at the very top of a piece, the conditions that you have used can result in poor colors in the main portion of the glaze. So it is a trade-off and you have to decide which is preferable, a white-appearing zone at the top and a good color below that, or a completely red object with not as bright a red color.

Still another defect which results in the loss of color in copper red glazes is the absence of an auxiliary reducing agent. If you make a glaze containing copper alone, you will have to add much more copper to get a red than you would if tin or iron were present.

One would like to imagine that by increasing the copper content that it would be possible to use a thinner glaze, but unfortunately the mechanics of copper color formation do not allow this to happen. Copper reds are sandwich glazes, which normally have a clear layer on top and a clear layer beneath the red zone. One is faced with the problem of making sure that there is enough thickness of the glaze to allow the existence of a red zone in the center. If the total glaze thickness is less than that required, then the mere addition of extra copper oxide will not allow red formation.

Probably the best technique to use for avoiding transparent zones is the design of a glaze that will fire at the lowest temperature commensurate with good color. This requires the adroit use of boric oxide, since it is the principal means that we have for lowering the final firing temperature without ruining the color of the glaze. Another possibility is a decrease in the firing time for the glaze. But this will lead to glazes with higher bubble counts and may distort the copper red color. Thus we have to work on the various trade-offs until an acceptable color is obtained.

POOR COLORS

By **poor** colors I mean **ugly** colors. In general, poor coloration is due to too much copper in the glaze or copper that has formed particles of too large a size. These large particles result in a livery or a dark glaze appearance.

The blending of blue and red colors on a rapidly rotating color wheel is the best way of demonstrating what it is that causes ugly colors in copper reds. The presence of blue really destroys the bright red appearance which we like so much. The reasons for poor color can be: too much copper; too thick a glaze; too much iron; or a cooling rate that encourages large copper particle formation. Frequently, the appearance of a bad color means that we have gone too far in our attempts to avoid clear colorless glazes. We normally have too much copper in the glaze when bad colors form. The result is, that instead of the very tiny (20-100 Angstrom) particles which provide us with red transmitted light, we have large clumps of copper which diffract, refract, and reflect light to give blue components which are detrimental to a pure red. Similarly, when we try to make reds without tin, it is common to get bad colors, because then we do not get the subtle reaction between stannous oxide and cuprous oxide to form very fine copper crystals. When iron is used as a reducing agent in place of tin, the occurrence of yellow, blue or green colors from excess iron also tends to distort the copper red color.

The main solution for ugly color formation is obtaining a good balance between copper and tin. One can then back off on the concentration until there is only slightly more than enough copper present to give a red color.

PINK COLORATION

Although I list pink glazes among the defects, they may not always be undesirable. When we try to make a peach bloom glaze, we want a pink glaze rather than an apple red. In any event, the effects that cause pink glazes to appear will be the same, whether we are doing it intentionally or accidentally.

The usual cause for the generation of pink colors is the dilution of copper reds by a white background blended with the red. Anytime that we have a matte glaze with reduced copper in it we will tend to get pink rather than red colors. The crystals which dilute the red color and cause reflection, refraction and diffraction of light, can be of many varieties. One type of glaze that I use for the generation of peach bloom is a high alumina one in which the crystals are either undissolved clay or newly formed mullite, wollastonite, or anorthite. Similar defects can be obtained by using excess silica, which remains undissolved. It won't matter much whether the crystals have been newly formed or whether they are undissolved batch materials, although one would expect that newly formed crystals would be of smaller size and would have a larger effect on light diffusion.

Yet another type of diffusion is noted in bubble opals. If we have an extremely bubbly glaze, it will appear pink, for the same reasons as before—diffusion diffraction and refraction of light. The formation of a

good pink solely from bubbles is difficult merely because the bubbles must be present in high concentrations. Usually one finds bubbles acting in conjunction with crystals, as when we have a glaze with too much clay in it. In this case there would be a lot of undissolved clay as well as many bubbles trapped because of the high viscosity.

In general, when a pink glaze occurs, you can consider it to be underfired. As noted before, when a 1250°C maturing glaze is pulled from the furnace at 1150°C, it gives a good illustration of some of the mechanisms which are occurring during glaze fusion. One of the effects noted was that this glaze, which normally was a good ox blood, became a speckled pink matte glaze. Hence, we must suspect underfiring whenever pinkness occurs in a glaze which would normally give a good color.

All in all, pink glazes are not major problems in the copper system. They can be avoided by the proper choice of glaze and appropriate firing conditions.

BLUISH COLORS

Sometimes, when a copper red is expected, there will be a bluish tint in the glaze, particularly in limited areas. This, in its most pervasive state, is called the **flambé** effect and may be caused by many different factors, one of which is related to the pink coloration. The bluishness is often due to phase separation of one liquid in droplet form dispersed in another liquid. Instead of the dispersion of crystals, as in the pink situation, this dispersion of one glass in another consists of tiny droplets instead of tiny crystals. Because of the optical consequences, we get an opalescence and a distortion of color rather than a mere dilution.

The most common cause for blue coloration (in my experience) is the presence of a little too much lime. The mere addition of 2-5% calcium oxide to an ox blood glaze will frequently give this bluish tint. Not surprisingly, there is a strong resemblance between the appearance of this blue and the appearance of the flambés of the Kang-hsi period.

Also, as in the case of the pink glazes, this may be desirable. If it is, then just the addition of lime to an ox blood glaze can produce it. However, I consider it to be a defect and I wouldn't normally try to make either a bluish or a flambé type of glaze.

Another material which will cause a blue color of this kind is boric oxide in excess. This too will cause a liquid-liquid phase separation and because of optical effects will give a bluish coloration. Since the addition of excess boric oxide can also lead to poor durability in glazes, I would recommend lime as an additive in preference to boric oxide if this type of appearance is desired.

As for curing an opal blue defect, I think that a slight adjustment of the glaze composition will succeed without the need for going into a firing modification. Backing off on either the lime or the borate content should cure the problem.

GREEN COLORATIONS

I have observed two types of green coloration. One of them is a celadon color and the other is a cupric oxide color. These two can be distinguished only when the color is very deep, because at low concentrations, when the colors are pale, it is difficult to differentiate between a celadon and a copper green, especially since the two may coexist.

The celadon color, caused by iron, is most frequently noted where the glaze has run thin at the top of a piece or where it has dripped near the bottom. This coloration is due either to contamination of the glaze from its batch materials or contamination of the glaze by reaction with a body containing sizable amounts of iron.

A pale green celadon color is not too objectionable, because it is a light tint. However, if it is desirable to avoid it, this can be done by using purer batch materials, by avoiding strong reactions between the glaze and the body, and by any other technique that we have mentioned in the first section on clear glazes. In other words, any procedure which will improve the red color will make the pale green celadon color less noticeable. In the old Chinese glazes, where iron was used as an auxiliary agent instead of tin, there was an appreciable celadon color, because it was a necessary part of the glaze batch.

The other kind of green is the one due to high concentrations of cupric ion in the glaze. When these are mixed in with a red color, they may not be observed as such unless the concentration is high. The time that copper green is noticeable in a glaze is when copper is not well dispersed and there are specks. This is commonly seen in the Chinese Kang-hsi peach bloom glazes where the copper oxide has evidently been used in a poorly dispersed form. Then, where there were specks of copper oxide, one finds specks of green in the final glaze.

It seems strange that a copper green color would persist under highly reducing conditions, but my feeling is that the green color forms after the reduction firing has been completed and that it is a complex reaction between oxygen of the air and high concentrations of copper in the glaze. At low concentrations, it is not much of a problem, but at high concentrations, oxygen from the air can form excess cupric oxide. Then, it becomes a strong fluxing agent and encourages more oxidation by further exposing copper to the air; in this way the reaction feeds on itself. One of the reasons that this rings true is because strong green copper spots in a red copper glaze are found to be much thinner than the red portions of the glaze. Evidently strong fluxing has occurred there.

To avoid this situation, one should back off on the total concentration of copper and make sure that the copper is well dispersed in order that no fragments of copper oxide will be present to give local high concentrations.

Another time that copper green will occur is when a glaze has been fired in alternate oxidation and reduction and has not sealed over before the final oxidation period. This can be quite embarrassing when you expect good ox blood reds from a kiln and instead find only strongly colored greens. Obviously you have to know your glaze and you have to be sure of the firing conditions, so that when the final oxidation is performed there is no chance that copper in the glaze will not be sealed off.

GLAZE BLACKENING

One source of blackness would be from using lead in the base glaze and then overreducing it, allowing lead to be reduced to the metallic state. However, in most high fired glazes, lead will be volatilized, and in the usual glaze, reduction will not be carried to such an extreme, so this is not a severe problem.

Another cause of blackening or greying of a copper red glaze is trapped carbon. If a glaze is fired in extremely heavy reduction (which is recommended by some authors) then there is a chance that carbon will be deposited in the raw glaze and will not be oxidized at any later time. In this state, when the glaze fuses over, small carbon particles will be trapped. This defect can be recognized by the appearance of black spots and a greyness rather than a jet black color. The obvious remedy is to avoid such severe reduction and also allow for a burn-out time if such a severe reduction does take place.

A more frequent cause of blackness in glazes is a high concentration of copper, especially in conjunction with the green coloration which we have just discussed. If there are local areas where copper concentrations are extremely high, then, during the oxidation of this copper in the cooling process, it can be converted to the cupric oxide form which is a dull jet black. This black will have a dull matte appearance and will be noticed on the very surface of the glaze. It will almost always be associated with some deep green coloration as it blends off from the **very** high concentration which gives the black. At the lower concentrations, which give a green, there may be a further change into copper red. This color sequence is seen in the Kang-hsi peach bloom glazes where specks of copper oxide have been present and where they have been oxidized on cooling to give the matte black cupric oxide. The obvious solution is to use well-dispersed copper compounds and to use them in low concentrations.

GLAZE RUNOFF

A major problem with copper red glazes is excessive flow. This is because some fluid glazes (with high alkali content) promote red colors. These glazes will then run off the ware. Also, there is a tendency to overfire copper red glazes in attempts to get clear colors, and this also will lead to runoff, especially on tall forms. The difficulty can be so severe that copper reds have to be treated as one treats crystalline glazes, namely by placing them on soft ceramic setters that can be ground off easily after firing has been completed. In fact, the Chinese today normally grind off the entire bottom of their copper red pieces, because flow has usually taken the glaze well over the base. A means of controlling this problem is the selection of glazes with high viscosities; and yet this runs counter to the needs of good reds. Therefore it can only be carried so far.

A technique which the Chinese used during the Kang-hsi reign was the use of an appropriately designed foot. A vase could be designed so that it turned either in or out and this allowed the drip at the bottom to collect just before it ran off. Also, in some of the current production in North China, a rather large unglazed section is left at the base of vases and thus the glaze never reaches the foot.

I think that the best solution for the drip problem is careful firing to just the correct temperature. Other than that, design would seem to be the next best solution for excessive flowing.

STREAKS AND OTHER TEXTURES

Copper red glazes commonly have mottling of various sorts. The usual variation from a perfectly uniform glaze seems to be caused by bubbling. Knowing the processes that occur during glaze formation, it is not at all surprising that textures appear frequently. Normally a copper red glaze is layered, with clear zones above and below a central red region and this is a major cause of color variation. Another factor is the occurrence of bubbling (as in any glaze). Then, with these two situations combined, we have bubbles welling up from the glaze-body interface, through a clear layer, into the red layer, and again into a clear layer. Due to this process the glaze goes through variations in color from pale to deep red and we have a texturing effect known as hare's fur.

Another aspect of mottling is the frequent occurrence of blue particles of copper on the body side of the red layer. Thus, as the bubbles well up through the glaze, they drag along bluish, reddish and clear layers, and again we have a variegated effect.

Not to be ignored either, is the previously mentioned fluidity of the glaze. Because the glaze is fluid and is streaming off the ware, it will provide another dimension of mixing and we will get further striating effects. If the glaze were rather viscous when the bubbles welled up, then we would get circular distortions, but, as the glaze is flowing, these spheres become elongated and streaks appear.

The question of whether one **wants** to avoid all streaking is a hard decision to make. I personally feel that texture adds interest to copper reds, and if we had a perfectly uniform red color, it would not be pleasing to the eye. However, if you want to minimize streaking, you will have to minimize layering, bubbling and flow. It would be possible to minimize some of the running; and the bubble formation could be decreased by fritting the glaze; but to get a perfectly uniform red color, it might be necessary to glaze only horizontal surfaces. I believe that any vertical surface will contain some texture.

Sorrow and the scarlet leaf,
Sad thoughts and sunny weather:
Ah me, this glory and this grief
Agree not well together!

Thomas W. Parsons—A Song for September

14 COPPER REDS—METAL OR OXIDE?

Throughout the history of copper red glasses and glazes, there has been a question of whether the red coloration is due to cuprous oxide or copper metal. Perhaps the most scientific explanation is the one which uses the electromagnetic theory of light to explain the color as a function of the properties of copper metal particles of very fine size, suspended in a glassy matrix. This type of theoretical work was performed by Mie in 1908 and then was refined by later workers. Unfortunately this does not offer much satisfaction for those of us who are non-mathematical in outlook and who desire a "hands-on" explanation of how copper reds are formed.

Some people have worked from analogs such as comparisons with the gold red coloration in glasses. Others have hypothesized from logic, reasoning and experiments. We will not try to assess blame or give kudos to those on one side or the other, for they were all honorable men who were reacting to information of varying quality.

Basically, the confusion is brought about by two factors. One is that the color of cuprous oxide is definitely reddish when examined in bulk. So it seems logical that a red could be obtained by the precipitation of cuprous oxide in a glass. From a similar line of reasoning one might imagine that the color could be due to copper metal, because it too has a reddish hue.

Actually, neither one of these thoughts is too appropriate, because neither of those colors is even close to the beautiful copper ruby exhibited in the best copper reds. Furthermore, such logic is misplaced because the copper ruby is not a solution color, but is a colloidal color. And, there may be no more relation between the bulk material and the final color than there is between the color of a butterfly's wings and ground-up butterfly wings.

Rather than keeping you in suspense as to my opinion, I will acknowledge from the start that I feel strongly that the copper red color is due to copper metal in colloidal dispersion in glass. With that out of the way, I will continue with my discussion as if it were certain that the color was due to copper metal. Towards the end, I will furnish some explanations which I think will convince you that cuprous oxide could not be the coloring agent in copper reds.

The colloidal metal concept seems plausible when one considers the circumstance of a continuous transition in particle size, from bits of atomic dimensions to some which are resolvable optically. For instance, if we look at thin sections of copper red glazes which have "gone bad," we find that there are transitions, going from homogeneous areas where copper ruby exists, to those places where very tiny particles can be resolved, and finally, to those sections where much larger particles can be observed. In this case one feels that he is watching a continuous transition of particle sizes and that once one gets below the optically resolvable size—which is the region where beautiful ruby colors appear—that it is quite believable that the red color is as much a function of particle size as it is of material composition.

On the other hand, one can also recognize that there is no fundamental reason why undissolved cuprous oxide particles might not be functioning in this same way (if they did not dissolve at this concentration). So there is still a case for the beautiful red color being a product of fine cuprous oxide particles also.

Some work in the last 50 years has been done using x-ray diffraction and electron microscopy as well as electron diffraction, to determine if the red element in glass is copper metal or cuprous oxide. This work has been useful, but only to a point. The problem is this: there is a possibility that both colorants are present at the same time. Thus, although one may find copper metal in the glaze, this does not eliminate the possibility that some cuprous oxide may be present simultaneously. But what if, (heaven forbid) copper metal particles were present but were covered with an extremely thin layer of cuprous oxide? This always leaves us with a small question, because electron microscopy cannot recognize color as such. It can only recognize small particles and then identify them as copper metal, copper oxide, or copper silicate. Yet, in recent work on the red regions of glazes, copper metal **has** been identified by use of electron microscopy and electron diffraction. Also, copper metal has been found by means of x-ray diffraction on fractured surfaces of copper red glazes.

A big point in favor of the presence of copper metal in reduced glazes is the fact that copper metal can be formed by hydrogen or carbon monoxide reduction at very low temperatures. It is stated in chemistry texts that copper oxide can be reduced to the metal at temperatures as low as 120°C. Thus, during the firing process it is feasible for copper metal to be formed. One experiment that is fascinating in this regard is one in which a copper-containing glaze is fired in reduction to the maximum temperature of a kiln (say 1250°C), and at the highest point of the firing, is taken out of the kiln and is plunged into a bucket of water to quench the glaze. When this is done, the glaze remains a transparent pale color. Now, if one examines this quenched clear glaze, it can be noted that there are copper metal droplets in some areas. These copper droplets may be small—perhaps 0.1 mm in diameter—but they can easily be seen with a hand lens at ten power. My conclusion from this observation is: during glaze operations, it is to be expected that cupric oxide will be reduced all the way to copper metal. Although copper is seen in relatively large droplets, one could extrapolate and conclude that **fine** droplets might be even easier to reduce to copper metal. In any event, when this quenched glaze is reheated to 600-800°C in air, a red color forms in the former clear zones. In regions where the small copper droplets were found, some dark spots are present which presumably are due to black cupric oxide.

Another observation which helps me to believe that copper metal is the colorant of copper red glazes is that a continuous gradation of particle sizes is found in the colored areas. When the particle sizes are large, off-colors result—like the livery hues. As particles become finer and finer, they finally reach the point where their interaction with light yields a transparent ruby red color. My observation of this was by optical microscopy, where a look in cross section at a glaze, using transmitted light, showed first a transparent red glaze near the surface, then an opalescent reddish hue, and finally a grey-blue color towards the body region. The bluish area definitely appears to be made up of particles that are resolvable by optical microscopy. However, the interesting part of this experiment is that when the light is changed from transmitted to incident (reflecting light), the bluish color is no longer apparent, but instead, in that area, a coppery metallic color appears. This color, one feels, is due to large flakes of copper, and it seems that it is a part of a logical progression from invisible (red producing regions) to larger, visible copper particles. The latter give various colors in transmitted light, but produce metallic, coppery colors in reflected light.

One more account, which makes it appear that elemental copper is the colorant, is an observation of the copper staining process. As we have noticed previously, it is possible to get cuprous ions to migrate into glass using thermal or electrical potentials. Mr. Leibig of Corning Glass Works, in two US patents (2,075,446 and 2,198,733), described placing soda-lime glass bulbs in a bath of molten **cuprous** chloride. He then tells of the formation of a yellow layer on the surface of the glass which is in contact with the cuprous chloride. The point of interest is the circumstance of formation of this yellow color and what happens to it on further treatments. Evidently, on heat treatment alone, nothing further happens to the yellow color. One gets a further reaction of the cuprous ion-containing glass only by heating it in an atmosphere containing hydrogen. Hydrogen is well known for its ability to penetrate glass (because of its small size), so one finds that after suitable heat treatment in hydrogen, the yellow turns to a beautiful ruby red. One can only ask then: if the red color is not due to copper metal, then how else can the action of hydrogen be explained? The cuprous state, which exists between the oxidized cupric and the reduced copper metal, can **only** be changed by reduction into copper metal.

A further comment about this yellow color can be made in reference to Rawson's work on copper staining. He did electron microscopy on both the yellow stain and the ruby color in glass, and found particles in the ruby red regions of a copper stained glass which were identified as copper metal. Of further interest was the fact that when he examined the yellow stained area by electron microscopy, he was able to find **no** evidence of particles. It would appear from this work that the yellow color is due to cuprous ions in glass and that it is dissolved in some way (possibly as a silicate) and is not present as discrete particles. Furthermore, this same yellow glass, after being treated with hydrogen at an elevated temperature, can be reduced to give a red color.

Additional staining experiments which would seem useful in explaining the copper red color are those described in the patent by Helen Williams (2,428,600). Mrs. Williams describes a technique for making copper stained glass by heating it in the presence of copper chloride vapors at temperatures of about 600°C. The extra fillips that one gets from her experiments are that a variety of effects can be obtained, depending on how strongly one reduces the yellow stained result of her first reaction and on how concentrated the copper content is. According to her patent, if one reduces a high concentration of copper in a rapid fashion, at a high temperature, then a copper metal mirror will be obtained. If the reduction takes place more slowly, at lower temperatures and with lower concentrations of copper ion, then good ruby colors are obtained. Again, one sees the transition between a ruby and a metallic appearance with nothing more than a slight change in thermal conditions causing the difference. Hence, I feel that we are observing a transition process, and that both the red color and the copper mirror are due to the same phenomenon, namely a deposition of copper metal in glass.

An experiment that was interesting, though, was one that occurred accidentally. On reading an account about cuprous oxide in Partington's book "Inorganic Chemistry," I noted a statement that cuprous oxide crystals consist of small **transparent** reddish particles. Having never looked at cuprous oxide powder through the microscope before, I immediately took a sample, dispersed it in immersion oil, and examined it at 100X magnification using bright transmitted light. Using this technique, it could be noted that the particle color was a garnet or deep amber hue. A more exact description of the hue would be a deep, brownish, orange-red color. It was certainly not a deep ruby color. Since I had just been examining some thin sections of copper ruby glazes before this, the thought immediately occurred that this cuprous oxide color was certainly not deep enough in intensity to account for ruby red glazes and glasses. The deep red thin-sections of copper ruby glazes had only one percent copper oxide in them, and yet they were of the same depth of color as the pure cuprous oxide particles (of approximately the same thickness). Therefore, it was apparent that if that garnet color was the maximum depth of color that could be obtained from cuprous oxide, then there was no way in which it could give the depth of hue that was observed in a 1% copper red glaze. After this observation there was no longer any doubt in my mind that copper ruby coloration in glass had to be due to copper metal.

One last experiment will describe another negative aspect of the copper red problem. This experiment involved melting a **glass** containing cuprous oxide. My intent was to see what the color might be in a glass which was melted in neutral conditions and which contained cuprous oxide. To this end, I asked Elton Harris, Andy Kacyon and the melting group at Corning Glass Works to melt a batch in an electric furnace. This glass was placed in a covered silica crucible and then was put in a furnace which was running at 1550°C. After melting for approximately four hours, the crucible was removed and the glass was poured on a steel slab in order to quench it.

Although the melt took place in air, the fact that the heating was done rapidly ensured that little air was able to penetrate the melt. In fact, the presence of calcium carbonate in the batch probably caused a "washing-out" of the air through evolution of carbon dioxide.

The only reducing material in the batch was the cuprous oxide itself. If it had been oxidized during melting, a green or blue glass should have been the result. If, on the other hand, the cuprous oxide color was the red colorant, then the final glass should have been red or it should have been convertible to red after further heat treatment. A thermal decomposition of cuprous oxide would not be expected, since this is only reported to occur at 1800°C.

None of these things occurred. The color of the quenched glass was a yellowish hue. It was not as bright as a stained copper yellow (since the melt only had 1% cuprous oxide present), but it certainly was not a green or red. Furthermore, when heat treated it did not change hue, but remained yellow. Only when heat treated in the presence of hydrogen did it turn red, and that only occurred near the surface where the hydrogen was able to penetrate. Thus, once more I felt that the only possible interpretation of these results was that the copper ruby color was due to the presence of finely divided metallic copper.

15 OXIDATION AND REDUCTION

Reduction is the key chemical process for the formation of copper red glazes, and although reduction is not a difficult condition to maintain in a fuel-fired kiln, an **appropriate** level of reduction may be hard to attain. This chapter will consider some of the nuances of oxidation and reduction in the formation of copper red glazes.

COPPER REDUCTION

Copper metal formation from either the cupric or cuprous state occurs readily at moderate (600-800°C) temperatures when one is using an atmosphere that contains hydrogen and/or carbon monoxide. This can be observed by putting **excess** copper carbonate in a glaze, reducing it, and finally quenching it from a high temperature. After this treatment, the formation of copper metal droplets can easily be observed with a hand lens, or even with the naked eye. There can be no doubt then that complete reduction has occurred.

Another experiment which shows the ease of reduction of copper ions is the refiring of a green copper glaze in a reducing atmosphere. In this case, if a bright green copper glaze were refired at about 600-800°C in a heavily reducing atmosphere, it would be found that the copper silicate in the glaze had been converted to copper metal—as indicated by either a red color in the glaze or a red, metallic-looking surface. The fact that this is just a surface phenomenon indicates the difficulty that gases have in penetrating glass.

REDUCING GASES

At this point a note should be taken of the "water gas" reaction. When an organic material such as natural gas (methane) is fired, it is found that reaction (1) occurs:

$$(1) \quad CH_4 + 2 O_2 = CO_2 + 2 H_2O.$$

Or, methane burning in air produces carbon **dioxide** and water vapor.

If, however, firing takes place with an **excess** of methane, then equation (2) results:

$$(2) \quad 2 CH_4 + 3 O_2 = 2 CO + 4 H_2O.$$

In this case excess methane burning in air produces carbon **monoxide** and water vapor. In addition, an important thing to remember is that the end products of this reaction, carbon monoxide and water, can react further at the temperature of the kiln so that a third reaction, the "water gas" reaction results (3):

$$(3) \quad H_2O + CO = CO_2 + H_2.$$

This means that carbon monoxide and water vapor interact to form carbon dioxide and **hydrogen**. This reaction is in near-equilibrium at temperatures of around 1000-1200°C. Therefore, if equivalent amounts of water and carbon monoxide are present, these will react until there are nearly equivalent amounts of water, hydrogen, carbon monoxide and carbon dioxide. Thus, any time that there is reduction firing it can be expected that all four of these products will be present (unless there is an extreme excess of one of the components).

If there is an extreme excess of methane, then there may be another reaction (4):

$$(4) \quad xs\ CH_4 + O_2 = xs\ C + xs\ H_2 + 2 CO.$$

This reaction represents the thermal cracking of methane to give carbon soot and hydrogen. This reaction is the reason for problems with carbon deposition and black discolorations in glazes. If the glaze is porous, and if carbon is being formed through thermal decomposition of fuel, then it is possible that carbon would be trapped in the glaze, and it would be difficult to remove once the glaze sealed over. The reason for this is that oxygen does not penetrate a molten glaze very readily.

Carbon is also dangerous for another reason. It may cause reduction of tin from the oxide to the metal. Tin metal can then alloy with copper metal and form droplets which are too big to give color effects and which are not soluble in a glaze. Therefore, it is sensible to keep only a mild state of reduction in our copper red kiln. We are in the red glaze business and not in the metal smelting profession.

If a black color does appear in a copper containing glaze, it may be due to an assortment of things: perhaps carbon black; possibly cupric oxide; or even small metal droplets. Your knowledge of how the kiln was fired will indicate which of these is most probable.

NONMIXING OF KILN GASES

We sometimes have the mistaken idea that the gas content of a kiln is perfectly uniform throughout its volume. But this notion should be put aside as quickly as possible. When splashed areas are found on celadons or other reduced ware, it is obvious that some local oxidation has occurred. This should be a warning that kiln atmospheres are not uniform. They are probably **never** uniform! The mixing of fluids (and the gases inside the kiln are fluids) is always difficult to achieve in a perfect manner. In automobile engines, for example, it is hard to mix gasoline vapor and the combustion air to get a homogeneous mixture, so poor combustion processes result and it is necessary to use catalytic converters to clean up the mess. In kilns this is also true. There are even problems from leakage through cracks in the kiln brickwork; thus when a positive internal pressure is not maintained air can leak in from the outside. Furthermore, there is a serious problem to be considered in the case of secondary air input to the kiln. If only the primary air (the air that is entering the burner and mixing immediately with the gas) is considered, there is probably a fair degree of mixing of air with the combustible gas. However, if there is a burner port which allows secondary air to enter along with the combustion gases, then there certainly is not perfect mixing of the cold secondary air with the very hot combustion gases. This is due in part to the temperature and density differences, but to a great degree it is also the result of the small amount of time that the gases have to dwell in the kiln. In this time span between the entrance and exit of the gases, it could hardly be expected that the secondary air would mix thoroughly with the combustion gases. If you will read Seger's investigation made on the gas composition of a kiln, you will observe that he frequently found both oxygen and carbon monoxide in kiln gases. Though it is known that in **equilibrium** carbon monoxide would burn with oxygen, the fact is that equilibrium does not exist, due to the rapid movement of gases through the kiln.

The remedies for this situation could be several. One would be: to avoid the use of secondary air in kilns and have only air entering the kiln which is going through the burner. Another answer is: to try using a large excess of fuel so that the oxygen will have a higher probability of encountering fuel molecules. The problem here is that the thermal cracking of methane or other fuel to carbon will lead to deposition of carbon in the porous glaze. Yet another solution would be: to keep the gases in the kiln for longer periods so that there would be better mixing, and of course this is one of the benefits of a down-draft kiln.

OVER-REDUCTION

This situation involves the early reduction of copper and tin to their metallic form while the glaze is open. This might lead to copper-tin alloys and large droplet formation. The droplets would be inimicable to copper red formation and one would find that the alloy was not appropriate for good copper red colors. On the other hand, if a mild reduction were to take place, copper oxide would be reduced to copper metal, but tin oxide would only be reduced to stannous oxide. Then, in the final formation of copper reds, the possibility of an alloy would not be likely. Such an alloy formation could be the reason for some of the dark colors we find which cannot be refired to form reds. One melt was made of copper and tin containing **glass** in which cornstarch was used as the reducing agent and no decent copper red was formed. When the glass was examined microscopically it appeared that many fine metal droplets were formed, and these could have been either copper or a copper-tin alloy.

SILICON CARBIDE REDUCTION

There has been experimental work by Baggs and Littlefield on the use of internal reducing agents for the formation of copper reds, enabling them to be made in electric kilns. The agent that they found to be most useful was silicon carbide, because it tends to remain stable at higher temperatures than other reducing agents. The first requirement is to obtain silicon carbide in a finely divided form, so that it can give a uniform color in the glaze and not a spotty color. There is also the need to get the silicon carbide to do its job correctly, and for that the glaze has to be quick fluxing, in order that silicon carbide will not be exposed to air for an extended period of time. In addition to quick fluxing, one would also prefer to have a rapid firing cycle to prevent external oxidation.

I have tried silicon carbide as an internal reducing agent, but have never had remarkable success with it. Copper reds were obtained, but they were not good colors and they were not uniform. My feeling toward the use of silicon carbide is this: there are enough difficulties in making a good copper red glaze; by including one additional problem the situation has just been complicated and one more stone has been hung around our necks. If you are restricted to firing in an electric kiln, simply use cadmium selenide as a red colorant.

CUPROUS OXIDE DISPROPORTIONATION

The question of whether cuprous materials will disproportionate in glazes is a serious consideration in experiments on copper reds. It seemed quite logical to imagine that cuprous materials in glazes—at high temperatures—**could** disproportionate into cupric ions and copper metal. However, some experiments have led me to believe that this is not a common occurrence. The most impressive experiment was that of making a cuprous oxide containing glass. This glass was made in an air atmosphere using a batch containing 1% cuprous oxide. After four hours of heating at a temperature of 1500°C the glass was primarily yellow with just a few streaks of red in it. Thus it seems that cuprous oxide, when dissolved in glass, is thermally stable. The streaks of red color that did occur were so light and so fine, that it did not seem that this was a significant reaction in the glass and that it probably occurred because of contamination of one sort or another. Perhaps the red was caused by a trace of carbon or iron oxide in the crucible.

Another observation which indicated the unlikelihood of disproportionation of cuprous compounds in glazes, was the examination of Margaret Medley's 14th century copper red from China. The sample, which had been fired at about 1200-1300°C, was found to have droplets of a material at the glaze-body interface which was undoubtedly cuprous sulfide. Since there was some red coloration also, this glaze must have been fired in a reducing atmosphere. So, one is left with the surprising result that cuprous sulfide is stable at these temperatures in a reducing atmosphere. Undoubtedly some cuprous sulfide was reduced to copper metal, because there is a pinkish color in the glaze above the pigment, but, the copper in the overlying glaze can only be present in a small amount. It is evident then that cuprous sulfide does not disproportionate at elevated temperatures.

Apparently cuprous oxide and cuprous sulfide (in low concentrations) are stable at the temperatures found in feldspathic glaze formation. Thus, while there may be some disproportionation, it is not a major factor in such compositions.

The reaction which **seemed** to indicate disproportionation, i.e. the occurrence of green patches at the surface of some copper red glazes, is probably evidence of sample oxidation. The formation of this green color in close proximity to copper reds is associated with **high concentrations** of copper. If one sprinkles copper oxide in parts of a glaze, then these areas will produce copper greens during the firing operation. Also, the fact that these greens form near the surface is a clue as to how they are formed. They are probably formed by oxidation as the glaze cools, rather than by disproportionation. In my tests the greens are almost always formed at surfaces. It is very reminiscent of cobalt blue underglaze blue colors, where, in places over which the glaze has broken, underglaze cobalt has come into contact with the air and a black oxide of cobalt has formed.

GREENS AND BLACKS IN COPPER RED GLAZES

Some experiments were done to try to determine why a copper green color will often result after a copper red glaze has cooled down. This action is particularly noticeable in the case of peach bloom glazes (although it may only be more apparent there because of the light color).

After numerous experiments, I have drawn the conclusion that the green coloration in copper red glazes (at least the dark green color) is closely associated with excessive amounts of copper. One is merely faced with the question of how these excess quantities of copper oxide in the glaze are being converted to either black copper oxide or green copper silicate.

Taking a clue from the thermodynamics of the reactions involved, it is obvious that there is more than enough reducing agent—either hydrogen or carbon monoxide— to reduce all of the copper in a copper red glaze to copper metal if the reduction can occur before the glaze seals over. Starting from this point, and assuming that all of the copper is in the form of metal after reduction, it can be postulated that copper metal droplets form and may become rather large in size if there is excess copper oxide in the glaze. This copper metal will be the starting point for whatever reaction will occur to give us black copper oxide or green cupric silicate. A theory that seems reasonable is: that some copper metal droplets—because of their large size—would be close to the surface of the glaze and could thus react with oxygen after the reduction firing was completed. If the amount of copper present was large, then one would expect that both copper silicate and copper oxide would form. Since copper oxide is black, it would mask any green copper silicate that was formed simultaneously. On the other hand, if the droplets were small, then, during cooling, they could be oxidized by air and could react with the silicate glaze. In this case, since cupric oxide would act as a flux, it would have a thinning effect—which is noted in some

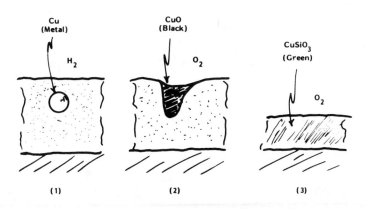

**Stepwise Conversion of Copper Metal
to Green Copper Glass during
the Cooling Process**

experiments. For example, if a large amount of copper oxide is placed in a round spot on top of a copper oxide-free glaze, and then is reduced, oxidized and cooled, it will be found that there is an indentation in the center of the spot where the copper oxide was deposited. This indentation is a green (copper silicate) glass, which is much thinner than the rest of the glaze. It can be surmised that the cooling glaze has been fluxed by cupric oxide, and has formed a green glaze. In cross section the green color and the thinning is very apparent as can be seen in the figure.

An experiment that was done which seems to confirm these thoughts was the following: two samples were made up, one of them to be quenched, the other to be allowed to cool at the furnace rate. On one side of each sample, copper nitrate was applied as an underglaze colorant. Then a glaze of the ox blood type (lacking only copper) was applied. On the other side of the test piece, two spots of copper carbonate were applied **over** the same glaze. These samples were fired in reduction to 1300°C and then the kiln was opened and one specimen was removed and quenched quickly. The other sample was allowed to cool at the normal furnace cooling rate down to room temperature.

Examination of the quenched sample showed that small droplets of copper metal could be observed in the regions where the copper carbonate was applied over the glaze. On the side where copper nitrate was place under the glaze, the copper droplets were not noticed. This latter occurrence may have been due to the fact that the copper nitrate penetrated the body more than the glaze. However, in the two spots on the opposite side of the test sample, it was easy to note 0.1 mm diameter drops of copper embedded in the glaze. On the sample that was not quenched, but was furnace cooled, a deep red color was found in place of the washed out spots which were found in the quenched sample. And, in the center of the deep red color, there were some green patches. In one of the green patches it was possible to observe a black spot in the very center of the nonglassy area. This was rather rough and coarse-surfaced and was very black in color.

After reheating the quenched sample to about 800-900°C (which was not high enough to make the glaze fluid) it was found that the copper droplets were no longer visible. Instead, in areas where the copper droplets had been located, there were black areas on top of the glaze. It appears that the copper metal had oxidized and copper oxide had spread out over the surface in the region where the surface was a dull black.

It seems reasonable that the mechanism for green spot formation is: first, the reaction of aerial oxygen with copper metal droplets in an over-doped region; next, its conversion to black copper oxide; and finally, a transition to a green copper silicate, dissolved in the glaze.

In a large kiln, where the cooling process would be very slow and where the glaze would be in contact with air for a long time at a high temperature, it is to be expected that these green areas would form more readily than they would in a fast-fired kiln (although a final 100°C in oxidation in a fast kiln would accomplish the same purpose).

This is one explanation for green spot formation in areas of copper red glazes where there are local high concentrations of copper. It also is an explanation for the formation of black spots on copper red glazes where there are even higher concentrations of copper which cause the formation of copper oxide rather than copper silicate.

THERMAL REDUCTION

I have doubts about the occurrence of thermal reduction in normal copper red glaze formation, even though cupric oxide is supposed to decompose thermally to give cuprous oxide at 1000°C or 1100°C. The reason for the doubts is that I haven't seen any evidence of this occurring during normal copper red glaze formation. To test for thermal reduction, it might be interesting to make glazes with a neutral background (some that had been fired to different temperatures in a neutral atmosphere) to see if, at low temperatures, cupric blue colors would be formed. And conversely, if, at high temperatures, cupric blues plus cuprous yellows (or greens) would be formed.

MELTING COPPER REDS IN AIR

Previously, some glaze batches were melted as glasses in crucibles at the Corning Glass Works. These batches were melted in one pound quantities in covered silica crucibles. The colorants in the glazes were: cuprous oxide; cuprous oxide plus stannous oxide; and cuprous oxide plus stannic oxide. In all three, the base glaze came out a yellow color on quenching. In the case of the second glass, with stannous oxide and cuprous oxide, a feathery red color appeared too. This glaze could be struck to a dense red on reheating to 700°C.

The next experiment was designed to find out whether these same materials and some others could be used to make cuprous **glazes** on a substrate rather than in a one pound glass batch. This time a sodium-boro-silicate frit was used and to it was added 1% of cuprous oxide to be used as a color batch. To seven different portions of the color batch various reducing agents were added. These reducing agents were: lead monoxide; arsenious oxide; antimony trioxide; bismuth trioxide; a control; silicon carbide; and potassium tartrate. These samples were placed in little piles on a silica crucible cover, then the cover was inserted rapidly in an electric furnace at 1550°C. The batches were allowed to cool in air at a relatively slow rate. The net result was that almost all of the material, instead of appearing yellow as it did in the bulk amounts, appeared as greenish colors. The thinness of the glaze in comparison to the bulk glass evidently led to oxidation, either through atmospheric action or through gases diffusing out of the silica body.

There were two samples out of the seven tested that showed some redness. One of these was the potassium tartrate reduced layer and the other was the silicon carbide reduced glaze. The latter just had some faint pink areas in it. The tartrated glaze showed some red patches that at first appeared black, but on closer inspection seemed to be a very deep ruby red. These spots were scattered around the edges of the glaze. In the centers, all of the glazes appeared greenish.

It is apparent that it is one thing to melt a **glass** and quite another to make a thin **glaze** on a ceramic surface in contact with the atmosphere, where there is a strong reaction of the glaze with both the substrate and the atmosphere. Glazes are definitely more prone to atmospheric oxidation than are bulk glasses.

CARBON VERSUS CARBON MONOXIDE REDUCTION

At one time a copper red batch was melted in which the glass was to be reduced by cornstarch mixed in with the other ingredients. The idea was to cause reduction from the decomposition of this cornstarch. After the melt was completed, the glass did not strike to a red on pouring and didn't even strike to a red after further heat treatment, even though this was normally a good copper red batch. I think that the reason for this result was that the cornstarch had decomposed to carbon during the fast firing that it was subjected to. This carbon then caused a different kind of reduction than we would normally have seen with a milder, gaseous reduction by carbon monoxide. Examination of the non-red glass showed a multitude of fine droplets. Presumably what happened was that both tin and copper were reduced simultaneously by the carbon from the cornstarch and that these metals then alloyed to form a bronze which segregated and hence was not available to give the very fine particles necessary for coloration. In addition, the fact that both the tin and the copper had been reduced completely to the metal left no opportunity for a further gentle reduction to occur, such as we have noted between cuprous oxide and stannous oxide, and which seems to be the mixture of choice when one wants to obtain beautiful red colors. Hence, it is preferred that carbon monoxide be used as the reducing agent for copper reds in preference to carbon which is too strong in its action.

ALTERNATE OXIDATION AND REDUCTION

When I first read Seger's recommendation that alternate oxidation and reduction should be used in the firing of copper reds, I was very skeptical. And, as I heard more about this technique I grew even more skeptical. After making a number of copper red glazes which were quite acceptable in color—using a steady reduction—I came to the conclusion that it wasn't necessary to alternate oxidation and reduction. However, several other references also remarked that this action was advisable, so the problem was intriguing. Finally, after a good friend had complained that one of my red colors was too orange, I decided to take the plunge and run some tests.

The most informative experiments that were done involved the use of a reduced red mug which was cut into quarters. One of these pieces was refired in reduction to 1260°C. The effect here was a slight diminution of the color due to volatilization and running. Another section of the same piece was refired in **oxidation** to the same temperature. This time, much to my surprise and chagrin, the piece turned a deeper red, and was much more like the type known as ox blood.

A sequence of alternating oxidations and reductions of copper red glazes had been tried previously and the result was that not much difference could be noted. However, this last experiment seemed to show that a final firing in oxidation was helpful in producing good copper ruby colors. Therefore, while I don't have the facts to recommend a series of oxidation and reduction steps, I can recommend that at least one oxidation cycle at the end of the firing be used to improve copper red coloring.

A MECHANISM

For an explanation of what the final oxidation is doing to the glaze, and also as an explanation of the preceding steps, consider the following mechanism:

(1)   When a porous, copper oxide and tin oxide containing glaze is treated in a lightly reducing atmosphere of carbon monoxide, hydrogen and water, the copper oxide is reduced completely to copper metal, which is dispersed in the porous glaze in the same manner as the original oxide. The tin oxide, however, is not reduced completely to tin metal because of the presence of moisture in the gases, and is only reduced to stannous oxide.

(2)   With increasing temperature, the porous glaze finally seals over and a glaze results which contains dissolved stannous oxide and undissolved copper metal in the form of very fine particles. These may increase in size to larger droplets depending on the dispersion of the original copper oxide and also upon the particle size of the original copper oxide.

(3)   After the final temperature is reached and the furnace is turned off, the molten glaze is immediately exposed to an oxidizing atmosphere, at which time it cools down slowly in the presence of oxygen. Since hydrogen is not appreciably soluble in the glaze, it diffuses out to the surface where it reacts with oxygen to form water, and in this process the glaze is gradually brought to a more oxidized state.

(4)   Finally, when all of the hydrogen has left the glaze, the glaze itself assumes the role of an oxidizing agent. Whether the glaze is a strong oxidizer or a weak oxidizer will depend on its composition, and this is why highly

alkaline glazes are conducive to the formation of good copper reds.

(5)   In the next step, an alkaline glaze will favor oxidation of the undissolved copper metal. As this happens very slowly, the first material formed will be cuprous oxide, which can be dissolved in the glaze as cuprous silicate. Obviously, if the glaze were strongly oxidizing, it would take cuprous oxide up to cupric oxide and would also oxidize stannous ions to stannic ions. However, since the oxidation is a gentle affair, the first occurrence is the oxidation of copper metal to cuprous oxide.

(6)   Since cooling is going on simultaneously with gentle oxidation, a point will be reached where further oxidation by the glass itself will not be possible. At this stage, another type of redox reaction can be expected and this is the interaction between stannous and cuprous oxide to give copper metal and stannic oxide. This reaction only occurs at relatively low temperatures, because at higher temperatures nucleation is unable to occur. At low temperatures (the striking temperatures) this reaction takes place and gives the desired copper red color.

One of the necessities for the appearance of the final color is not only a redox mechanism, but a physical mechanism. In order for copper metal to precipitate in glass, nuclei must be formed and these nuclei can only form at a specific low temperature where the curve for nuclei formation and the curve for crystal growth overlap. If the concentration of copper is too high, or if the cooling rate is much too slow, or if there is some combination of these two effects, ugly colors will result rather than beautiful reds. Such events as livery colors are due to excessively large particle sizes.

ANALYSIS

An analysis of the copper red formation mechanism shows that there are several sensitive areas that must be controlled in glaze work. In the first place, a glaze must be chosen which will provide the appropriate oxidation mechanism during high temperature cooling. It is necessary to reoxidize the copper metal back to cuprous oxide. On the other hand, if the glaze is overoxidized, cupric oxide and green colors will result (which sometimes happens). Unfortunately if it is not oxidized enough, then coppers red will never form.

Similarly with the phase separation and nucleation steps: if nucleation doesn't occur at the right temperature or if nucleation occurs to the wrong extent, trouble ensues. This is because, with too few nuclei, a good red will not be formed and with too many nuclei, no color may form.

The worst part of all this is that it is almost impossible to evaluate each of the steps separately. They are all combined and intertwined and it is only with difficulty that they can be evaluated. It is possible to make adjustments to the glaze composition—for example the glaze can be made more alkaline. This would seem to be useful as far as providing the right oxidation state is concerned; however, this alkalinity may make the glaze excessively fluid, and the phase separation stage would then be inoperative. Therefore it is necessary to hunt around delicately and by the crudest of cut-and-try techniques make attempts at getting good copper red glazes. It is obvious that it is not possible to excise the oxidation-reduction mechanism and separate it completely from the nucleation and crystal growth mechanism for forming copper reds.

OXIDATION THROUGH DEHYDROGENATION

As an alternative step in the final conversion of copper metal to cuprous oxide, it may be that oxidation is not necessary. For example, it would seem entirely possible that the escape of hydrogen from a glaze could provide the necessary oxidation mechanism for transformation of copper metal to cuprous oxide. Although this may seem to be merely a question of semantics, it is not, because of the fact that hydrogen moves much more easily in glass than oxygen does and thus, while oxygen may not penetrate a glaze readily, we find that hydrogen can escape from a glaze and the net result is the same. We would have **dehydrogenation** occurring, which is exactly the same chemically as an oxidation—merely the loss of hydrogen at a high temperature and its removal from the surface. Then, any glaze penetration by oxygen or even a reaction of the base glaze as an oxygen donor would be unnecessary. The loss of hydrogen could have this effect.

16 THE ROLE OF TIN OXIDE

It has been noted by many authors and experimenters that the addition of tin oxide to copper containing glasses and glazes has a beneficial effect on the color of copper reds. But the question must be raised: what is the cause of this effect?

There are several possible answers, only a few of which are credible. One of them is that tin oxide may participate in an oxidation-reduction reaction with copper, and may cause the reduction of copper ions to copper metal. Another option is that there is a structural aspect to the function of tin oxide (i.e., that tin oxide alters the silica lattice in some way and thus affects the copper red color). Other possibilities are: a tin-copper alloy formation; some other kind of chemical coupling of tin and copper in the glass; or a combination of effects.

Other materials seem to have an influence which is similar to that of tin, and for this reason we may draw some conclusions about tin from the effects and properties of these other materials. For example, the first successful copper reds that were made by the Chinese were undoubtedly Chun ware glazes. These glazes did not have any tin in them, but had a sizable iron content, as they were celadons (containing 1-2% iron oxide). The iron content very definitely had an effect on the copper red color. In the absence of iron, a reddish blush is not nearly as evident. Furthermore, one can always get a better copper red **stain** on a celadon than on a plain glaze. If the two elements, iron and tin, are compared, it is evident that they both have the possibility of entering into oxidation-reduction reactions. Other than that they are fairly dissimilar elements.

Still another important clue about the function of tin oxide in copper reds is the fact that the preferred ratio of tin to copper is about 1:1 on a molecular basis (2:1 on a weight basis).

Although the evidence points strongly to the probability that tin oxide is acting in a redox role, I felt that some additional experiments were called for. To elucidate the mechanism, some glasses were melted and the following section will explain these experiments and outline the conclusions that were drawn from them.

EXPERIMENTAL

The base glaze used for all of these experiments was an alkali-lime-boro-silicate made from Custer feldspar, #3185 frit, and calcium carbonate. The resulting glass had a composition of approximately: soda-5%; potash-6%; boric oxide-18%; alumina-8%; and silica 58%. This composition was chosen to give a fluid glass at the melting temperature used (1500°C). All of the experimental melts were made at the Corning Glass Works with the help of Elton Harris, Andy Kacyon, and their co-workers in the experimental melting department. The glasses were melted in covered silica crucibles in an electric furnace at 1500°C for four hours in an air atmosphere. After melting, they were poured on a steel plate, so that they would be quenched rapidly.

Although these glasses were melted in air, the fact that one of the batch ingredients was calcium carbonate, coupled with the fact that the crucibles were covered, and that heating was rapid, led me to feel that there was not much interaction between the glass and the oxygen of the air. It was felt that the active evolution of gas from the batch, caused by the insertion of the cold crucible into a 1500°C furnace, followed by speedy fusion of the batch (with rapid decomposition of carbonate and evolution of carbon dioxide) would lead to a glass which was saturated with carbon dioxide rather than air. In any case, the results seemed to confirm this conclusion.

EXPERIMENT 1

The first glass melted in this program was one in which 1% **cuprous** oxide was mixed thoroughly with the base glass. After this glass was melted and was poured on the steel plate, it formed a patty which had a yellow color at room temperature. When the glass was further heat treated at 700°C (to see if a red would strike in) no color change was noted. If, however, a piece of this glass was heated in a hydrogen-containing atmosphere (as with a hand torch), it would turn red in a thin surface layer, and often could be made to have a metallic, coppery look after such treatment. These various reactions and colors indicated to me that there was copper left in the glass and that it had not been volatilized in the 1500° firing. Furthermore, I felt that disproportionation had not occurred with this concentration of cuprous oxide, since there was no evidence of copper red or copper green color after the melting and quenching operation. The fact that copper red color could be produced in a later reduction firing implied that copper was still in the glass. And the evidence that it was a yellow-appearing glass rather than a blue, green or red color, meant that it was in some intermediate state of oxidation (presumably the +1 or cuprous state). I felt, after this experiment, that cuprous oxide was stable at a concentration of 1% in a glass melt. This experiment may be considered as the control experiment to be compared to later results.

EXPERIMENT 2

The next glass was melted under the same physical conditions, but the composition of the glass was changed to include 2% **stannic** oxide and 1% **cuprous** oxide. After melting and quenching , it was found that the result was the same as in experiment 1. The glass was a yellow color. It also reacted similarly to heating and reducing; that is, a heat treatment at 700°C in air did not change the yellow color, but firing in reduction did cause its surface to turn red and metallic looking. I felt that stannic oxide did not have an effect on the copper color merely by virtue of its presence in the glass. I also felt that this experiment showed that **stannic** ion (acting as a glass structure modifier, or as a nucleating agent) was not affecting copper red color in the glass. It seemed to be inert as far as influencing copper red formation was concerned.

EXPERIMENT 3

This test was made with the same base glass and the same melting and quenching procedure as before. The addition to the base glass this time was 1% **cuprous** oxide and 2% **stannous** oxide. The melting and pouring were done as before. However, these patties began to strike to a red color after pouring, even in contact with the cold steel plate. They formed some very beautiful wisps of red color in the otherwise clear glass. Approximately 25% of the glass was red colored after pouring. If this glass was then heat treated at 700°C for an hour, it became completely red, and was a beautiful ruby color, especially in transmitted light. The only difficulty with this glass was that because of the depth of the ruby color, it appeared to be almost black in reflected light, and had to be viewed with a very intense transmitted light, or through a very thin section in order to demonstrate the ruby red coloration. My conclusion about the results of this experiment was that the function of tin oxide was as a reducing agent, since the red color could be produced without a reduction firing treatment. I think that the reaction between cuprous oxide and stannous oxide is:

$$Cu_2O + SnO = 2\ Cu + SnO_2$$

During the cooling process this reaction gives copper in the finely divided state necessary for the production of a gorgeous ruby color.

EXPERIMENT 4

To determine if a redox reaction was important for the formation of copper reds, an additional experiment was performed. This experiment was identical to number 3 except that instead of stannous oxide, some ferrous oxide (in the form of ferrous oxalate) was added to the glass. The melting and pouring conditions were duplicates of experiment number 3. The result of this melt was even more striking than in experiment 3. In this case, the glass, although poured on a cold steel slab, was found to strike immediately to a beautiful red color during quenching. Again, the red color was so intense that it appeared black in reflected light. However, when viewed in thin section or when viewed with an intense light source, it was observed that the glass was a ruby of a beautiful hue. The amount of ferrous oxalate added to the glass produced only one percent ferrous oxide, so the color from the iron dissolved in the glass was not enough to distort the red color very badly. A reduction treatment was not necessary to form a red color with this glass, just a thermal process would do the job. The reaction in this case would be:

$$Cu_2O + 2\ FeO = 2\ Cu + Fe_2O_3$$

In a test to see if other reducing agents could cause a copper red to form, the previous case was duplicated, but with antimony trioxide instead of iron oxide. Again, the base glass and the melting conditions were the same. After the test was over, the product was a yellow glass, almost identical to the one in experiment 1. When this antimony and copper containing glass was heated to 700°C for an hour in air, it was found that no color striking occurred—there was no red formation. Only when it was heat treated in a hot reducing atmosphere at 700°C was a red formed. Thus my conclusion was that for some thermodynamic or kinetic reason, antimony trioxide was not a suitable reducing agent for the formation of copper reds (at least under the conditions of this experiment). It is not surprising that people have settled on either iron oxide or tin oxide as the auxiliary agent to be used in copper red glaze formation. If one examines the thermodynamic data, it is obvious that not all reducing agents are appropriate for the reduction of cuprous oxide to copper metal. And, even if the thermodynamics are favorable, sometimes for a mechanistic reason a copper red will not form. The case of antimony may be the result of the fact that antimony pentoxide is not stable thermally above 400°C.

Summarizing the results of these five experiments: I feel strongly that cuprous oxide can be maintained in a glass at a concentration of about 1% without the occurrence of disproportionation. At higher concentrations disproportionation may be a problem. As a comment at this point, let me state that the yellow color, due to cuprous oxide at a concentration of 1%, is rather pale, so it may be overlooked on some occasions, especially in the presence of other tints (from cupric ions or copper metal). In the thin layers that we are apt to find in glazes, cuprous oxide yellow will not be a very noticeable color. A further conclusion at this point is that yellow cuprous oxide (or silicate) in glass can be reduced by hydrogen to give copper reds, which presumably are due to copper metal. Also, in the presence of suitable reducing agents, such as stannous or ferrous oxides, the cuprous oxide can be reduced internally by appropriate heat treatments to give copper red glasses or glazes.

REDUCTION OF STANNOUS OXIDE

In Mantell's book "Tin," he states that it is possible to reduce stannic oxide to tin metal with either hydrogen or carbon monoxide. However, there are limitations to this reaction which seem to show that it will not happen in our glazing operation. In the first place, tin oxide is reduced to metal in hydrogen only if there is little water present. Since the combustion gases in a normal ceramic kiln contain high concentrations of water vapor, it is likely that there will be no reduction of stannic oxide to tin metal because of this factor.

Another comment by Mantell is that if one wants to reduce tin oxide with gases, the reduction depends for its success on the absence of all "slagging phenomena." Thus, since our glass making operations are **completely** "slagged," we are obviously operating under the wrong conditions for the gaseous reduction of stannic oxide to tin metal.

I have tried to make tin metal intentionally by adding large amounts of stannic oxide to a glaze and then firing it in heavy reduction, but there has been little or no evidence that stannic oxide has been reduced to tin in the process. One still sees large masses of white, opaque material in the glaze, where high concentrations of tin oxide were present. And, there is no evidence (when observing it with a hand lens) that any droplets of tin metal have formed. In these same circumstances, if a highly concentrated copper containing glaze is fired in heavy reduction and then is quenched, one finds many droplets of copper. Thus, my feeling is that tin oxide, although it may be reduced to **stannous** oxide in the glaze reduction process, is probably not reduced to tin metal by our firing conditions.

COPPER-TIN ALLOYS

Before examining the published data, it seemed possible that an alloy of tin and copper might be producing the superior red color that is found in tin-containing copper red glazes. However, there are some data and some experiments that seem to refute the possibility that a tin-copper alloy, if present in glass, would give a red color that is similar to the copper red color.

One of the experiments that seems to have a relationship to ours is Rawson's work on copper, silver and combined copper-silver staining in glasses. When Rawson made a copper stain that contained silver, and fired it in reduction, he obtained a brown color that he attributed to the presence of alloy droplets in the glass rather than a combination of copper droplets and silver droplets. The reasoning behind his thought was that the optical absorption spectrum of the combined stain was not equivalent to the separate addition of a copper stain plus a silver stain.

If this is compared to the copper-tin glaze situation, it is found to be possible to get copper red colors either with or without tin present. Apparently the addition of tin to a copper red glaze does not basically alter the hue of the red color. I would think that if copper and tin were alloyed, there would be a marked change in the color of the glaze.

In an experiment along these lines, I tried melting copper and tin together just to see what a 1:1 alloy looked like on a massive scale (I had always assumed that a sample of bronze would be a reddish color). However, when a copper-tin alloy with approximately equal weights of copper and tin was made, the result was an alloy that was silvery with no brassy appearance. It looked just like a silver bead rather than a gold bead. From looking at these massive samples I feel that if a copper-tin alloy of near 1:1 ratio was found in a glass, it would not give a color that was similar to the copper red color.

CONCLUSIONS

Although these experiments have not been exhaustive, and although I am aware of other experiments that could be run (indeed in scientific work there are **always** more experiments that could be run), nevertheless I feel that these experiments support the belief that copper red glazes are assisted in their formation by stannous oxide through the functioning of a redox mechanism that depends on the reaction between stannous oxide and cuprous oxide to give copper metal and stannic oxide. This conclusion is further supported by the role that a final oxidation has on the production of superior copper red glazes. One feels that the final oxidation tends to produce cuprous oxide, which, in the presence of stannous oxide will produce the very fine particles of copper metal that are desirable for forming copper rubies.

17 THE QUENCHING OF COPPER REDS

One of the oddities of copper red glasses and glazes is that they may be cooled rapidly from high temperatures to give clear glasses. These clear glassy materials may later be reheated to modest temperatures (perhaps 500-800°C) to form copper reds. This process is called "warming-in" in the glass industry.

The possibility of quenching a copper red **glass** and then reheating it to get color is one of the advantages that glasses have over glazes. The difficulty in quenching a ceramic piece without running into body weakening is almost insurmountable, while the same procedure with glass is quite feasible.

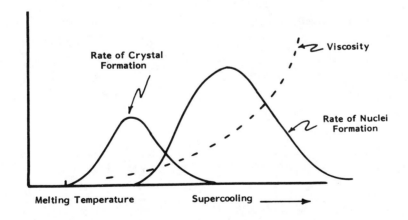

The advantage of rapid cooling followed by reheating, to form a copper red, is shown by the curves in the above figure. This diagram indicates that in many circumstances the **nucleation** temperature of a cooling **glass** is lower than the crystal **growth** temperature in the cooling glass. In other words, as the glass is cooled, it would prefer to grow into a few crystals (on nuclei that were already present) rather than to form nuclei first and then grow crystals. Therefore, if we want to control the number and size of nuclei, we would prefer to approach the desired temperature from a lower point rather than from a higher point. There is also the possibility that the crystal growth curve will overlap the nucleation curve at some point, and then if we cool from a high temperature slowly to a low temperature, there is a real risk of growing large crystals. This is one of the main problems that we have in producing copper red glazes, because fine crystals of copper produce the best red colors.

If a copper red **glass** is quenched to room temperature (and thus is in a clear state), and if it is then reheated slowly to a point where nuclei will form, we can adjust the temperature so that crystal growth may be stopped at any appropriate point for a good color. Since a **glaze** will be difficult to quench, the normal procedure here is to cool from a high temperature slowly through moderate temperatures, so that we won't get into dunting difficulties. Below 500°C the cooling process may be accelerated somewhat. The problem is that the red color in the **glaze** will already have formed at temperatures above 500°C, so we are at the mercy of our glaze composition as far as good copper red colors are concerned.

It would be desirable to be able to select a perfect glaze composition (as far as the base glaze and as far as the copper-tin concentration are concerned); in this way we could get appropriate glazes for appropriate cooling processes. The problems result from the fact that glazes are very non-uniform. As noted in the chapter on the hare's fur effect, it is common for glazes to vary in composition from the outside surface to the body surface. Therefore, though we may start out with an ideal glaze composition, after firing is complete there will only be a thin zone having the desired composition. The layering situation leads to the common observation in copper reds that they are sandwich glazes, with the red zone only occurring at the center, with the zones near the surface and near the body having lost their red color due to changes in glaze composition.

No more need be said at this point about quenching, because it is impractical for copper red **glazes** . The only reason for mentioning it is because of its obvious desirability and because of its usefulness in **glass** formation when copper reds are desired.

Obviously, if you could make a ceramic body which could withstand severe physical shock and which could have a moderate coefficient of expansion (such as a raku-type body), and if this body could be fired to a high enough temperature to produce a good copper red, then it would be possible to quench the glaze and reheat it to form a very desirable color. The problem is that raku bodies are not meant to be fired to a high density, and most copper red glazes require firing to a fairly high temperature. Thus, many bodies would be densified by such a firing. There is some possibility that an open body could be prepared which could be fired to cone 8 and could withstand the thermal shock necessary to quench the glaze, but I don't know if this would result in a desirable piece of ceramics.

A Chinese Ming dynasty (Cheng-te, 1506-21) copper red monochrome glazed bowl.

18 DIFFUSION IN COPPER RED GLAZES

The question of copper diffusion in the formation of copper red glazes takes us to the heart of the process. It also takes us into some complex areas. I don't think that it will be possible to explain everything that occurs during the formation of a copper red glaze, but we can discuss some possible mechanisms as well as some unlikely ones

For a start, let us consider what the diffusing species of copper could be in solid glass. First, the cupric(II) ion is unlikely to move far in our glazes since divalent ions in general do not diffuse readily in glasses.

Neither is it likely that copper metal is the diffusing species in a glaze or glass. For example, it has been noted by experimenters (notably Kubaschewski) that a silver film would not diffuse into glass unless oxygen was present. In a vacuum, he could find no silver diffusing into a glass. We must conclude from this experiment that copper metal also will not move into glass unless oxygen is present. There does seem to be one drawback to the statement that copper metal will not diffuse into glass, and that is the observation of the mobility of metals on the surface of glass. Thin film techniques using the electron microscope have shown that atoms such as gold, copper and silver will move readily on the surface of glass substrates to form nuclei and then larger crystals as they move around under the influence of heat. I think therefore, that at least some short range movement of metal atoms is possible through the "holey" structure to be found in glasses. I feel that this may be the mechanism by which nuclei increase in size after forming inside a glass, giving rise to the copper red formation mechanism. Also, while copper metal atoms may not move as much as one micron, they may move a few tens of Angstroms in glass—which would be all that is necessary for the formation of copper groupings.

Thus, even if we had no experiments that showed that cuprous ion(I) were the diffusing ion, we could assume it by default.

COPPER STAINING

An examination of the copper staining process is probably one of the best ways to get at the mechanism of color formation in copper red glasses and glazes. The normal procedure for staining with copper is to take a glass surface (in preference to a glaze surface), and treat it with a cuprous compound. The treatment may either be a vapor state procedure, as when cuprous chloride is used, or it may be from the solid state when copper oxide in a sulfur dioxide atmosphere produces cuprous ions in proximity to the glass surface. The result of the penetration of cuprous ions into the glass surface is a yellow stained layer. This layer has been reported by Rawson to show no evidence of particles down to a size of 10-20 Angstroms. Thus we may confidently feel that the yellow color resulting from such a mechanism is due to cuprous ions (possibly as the silicate or the oxide), formed in the glass surface. The subsequent treatment of this yellow surface tells us even more. With an appropriate hydrogen treatment (at 600°C) the yellow surface layer can be converted to a copper red colored layer. This red displays the normal transmission curve for copper reds.

Such glass staining experiments tell us one thing in particular, and that is that the copper ions in the plus one state will diffuse into glasses such as soda-lime types. This should not be a surprise, because the cuprous(I) ion has approximately the same size and charge as the sodium(I) ion which is found in the glass. This means that there should be the possibility of an ion exchange and a substitution of copper for sodium in the glass. And, no doubt this is what occurs. Leibig, in his patents, reports on the nearly complete removal of alkali from a glass and the substitution of percentage quantities of copper in its place.

The formation of a red color from the yellow copper-containing glass is possible because of the ability of hydrogen to diffuse into glass at elevated temperatures. We can surmise that hydrogen is reducing cuprous ions to copper metal, since there are no other likely reactions. It is not possible to reduce copper metal to a hydride(-1) at the temperatures that we are talking about, so the reaction must stop at the copper metal stage. This is one of the points in favor of our considering copper red colors to be due to copper metal and not cuprous oxide or some other cuprous compound.

COPPER STAINING OF GLAZES

The procedure for staining **glass** is relatively straightforward and is described in two patents which are included in the chapter on staining. The main object of staining is to produce copper in the plus one state on the surface of glass and then have some way of absorbing sodium ions there during the exchange process, so that one can get movement of cuprous ions **into** the glass and sodium ions **out** of the glass. This procedure in glass is fairly straightforward (although it is not the easiest process in the world); however, when one tries to stain a **glaze**, difficulties occur. The staining procedure is nowhere near as easy with a glaze as it is with a glass. The reason for this seems to be that a **glaze surface** is vastly different from the interior of a glaze, principally because of volatilization of alkalies from the surface. With such a low alkali surface, cuprous ions have little chance of exchanging and hence not much staining can occur.

When we look at the cross section of a copper red glaze, we almost always see a clear layer near the surface, a red layer in the middle, and another clear layer next to the body. This indicates that many reactions are taking place in this relatively thin glaze. The reactions taking place near the surface are diffusion and evaporation of material; and one of the elements that is removed by volatilization is sodium, which is the needed element for ion exchange in the copper red staining process. So, with a relatively sodium-free surface, we have difficulty in getting enough copper metal diffused in to give a good color. An amusing result of this type of reaction is found when one tries to stain a sample which has a crackled glaze. In such a case, you will find that the surfaces in the crazing will be stained to a much greater extent than the ordinary glaze surface, because in these areas a normal glass composition is exposed to the staining process and will give better results than the surface layer.

Another interesting experiment that I have noted is one which shows how diffusion can occur in copper red glaze making. The experiment in question involves taking a drop of copper nitrate, placing it on the inside surface of a bisqued cup, covering this cup with a celadon glaze, and then firing it. One notes that in the area where the copper nitrate drop was placed there is a red coloration in the glaze on the inside of the cup. Also, red appears on the outside glaze on the cup in the same region. Therefore we can tell that copper has diffused from the body, into the inside glaze, and also that it has diffused through the body and through the outside glaze. This movement is probably aided by the fact that some of the diffusion may have taken place before the droplet dried, or before the glaze sealed over; but still it is impressive. Another case, which is puzzling, is the one where a droplet of copper nitrate is placed on the outside of the cup and then is covered with a glaze. In this experiment a copper red color is found in the glaze, but **only** on the outside, with no copper red coloration on the inside of the cup. Thus the mechanism and/or the driving forces are different in these two experiments. The results may be related to the firing (in that the outside of the cup is always hotter) or it may be just a case of the overriding influence of gravity.

Horizontal diffusion of copper in glazes is also readily observed. If a speck of copper oxide is placed on a body, then, in the glaze, it will be noted that the area of copper red formation has expanded markedly in a horizontal direction on the glaze surface.

VISCOSITY

One can conclude, from the example of silica, that the role of viscosity is much smaller than the role of "openness" with regard to diffusion in glass and glazes. Since fused silica is highly viscous at glaze forming temperatures, one can assume (since silica is quite an "open" glass for the diffusion of hydrogen and helium) that the viscosity has only a secondary role to play compared to the "openness" of the glaze. If one could make a glaze containing only feldspar, then one might have an "open" glaze in which cuprous ion could move readily. Since it is normal to add lime to feldspar to make a lower maturing glaze, lime would tend to make the glaze less open and less susceptible to copper movement.

TIN IN COPPER REDS

In addition to copper, let us also consider the possibility of tin diffusion in a glaze since tin has been found to aid markedly in the production of good copper reds. Copper reds containing tin definitely have a red color which is superior to the glazes without tin, so we must examine the case of tin and decide whether it too will diffuse. Tin, however, has no ions or forms which have the ability to diffuse in a glass or glaze. Its ions only exist in the (II) and (IV) valence states, so there is not much possibility that these highly charged ions would be able to diffuse very far. Also, tin metal as a neutral atom wouldn't diffuse much in a glass either. Hence, for any copper-tin interactions, it will be necessary for copper to move to the site of the tin with no expectation of the reverse movement.

QUENCHING

One of the comments which is heard with regard to copper red glazes is that, if they are quenched, then no copper red color will appear until they are reheated. I have performed this experiment and it is true—if the quenching is carried out fast enough. However, one remarkable observation can also be made on these quenched glazes, and that is: if there is enough copper present, it can be observed in the clear, quenched glaze as tiny copper droplets (less than a millimeter in diameter). The droplets are observable with difficulty by the naked eye, but can be seen easily using a ten power hand lens. The fact that the quenched copper-containing glaze is relatively colorless and does not have a green or yellow color, leads one to believe that the copper (which will subsequently form a red on heat treatment) must be present in the glaze as copper metal in very fine aggregates—perhaps atomic copper in some cases. An explanation of what happens next revolves around two possibilities. First there is the option that copper is present in atomic form and that it agglomerates in larger and larger clumps as cooling occurs, until finally aggregates are large enough to cause a red color to appear. This scenario is frowned upon by physicist-type people who cite the example of the appearance of deep colors whenever even the slightest amounts of free atoms are present in solids. This is a legitimate complaint, but we also note that Helen Williams comments (in her patent) that it is possible to have low concentrations of copper present in a colorless glass even after treatment with hydrogen.

A second option is that copper metal atoms are immediately oxidized to cuprous ions by either the base glass itself (after all, it is a sea of oxygen ions) or by a component of the glass such as iron oxide or tin oxide. This case is favored by the usefulness of tin and iron in preparing copper reds.

Pinning down either of these two mechanisms is complicated by the fact that cupric and cuprous ions are undoubtedly always present together in glass. In addition there is confusion offered by a possible disproportionation reaction in which cuprous oxide can decompose to furnish both copper metal and cupric ions. As you will see in the chapter on oxidation and reduction, I tend to favor an oxidation of copper metal to cuprous oxide, but with little more than an intuitive feeling to go on.

A comment should also be made with regard to the fact that copper metal and glasses are incompatible in another way. When copper films are evaporated on glass surfaces, there is not much adherence. Metallic copper and oxide glasses are not the type of system that one would expect to be tightly bonded on an atomic scale unless intermediate oxide layers are present.

OXIDATION OF COPPER IN GLAZES

Another problem which we face is that of explaining the oxidation of copper metal inside a glaze. We can find by reading textbooks that there is not much possibility of oxygen migrating through glass, therefore it is difficult to think of a mechanism by which copper metal in glass would be oxidized. However, it is possible that a surface layer containing copper could be oxidized by the atmospheric oxygen, and that this surface cuprous ion could then migrate into the glass. But, this would not be a continuing process. Once the surface layer had been depleted of copper, the movement would be over. The answer, I think, is an oxidation mechanism that could be called **dehydrogenation** (as was described in the chapter on Oxidation and Reduction). Instead of considering that oxygen moves into glass, you could get the same chemical (or electrical) effect by having hydrogen moving in the opposite direction. Since hydrogen—because of its small size—can get around easily either as a gas or as an ion, this is a logical reaction mechanism as compared to the unlikely movement of oxygen in glass.

We can imagine this reaction:

$$2\ Cu\ +\ 2\ H^+\ =\ 2\ Cu^+\ +\ H_2.$$

The hydrogen gas could then diffuse to the surface where it could react with oxygen in the atmosphere and be released, leaving the potential for more hydrogen to be moved to the surface. In this way, oxygen at the surface could encourage the oxidation of copper metal to cuprous ion without the problem of our having to explain oxygen movement into the glaze. A fault of this mechanism is that one would expect cuprous ion to be mobile also, and whether cuprous ion would have a greater tendency to move than hydrogen, I don't know.

CONCLUSION

I can imagine a mechanism for the formation of copper red glazes as follows: first, there is a glass with sufficient cuprous and stannous ions in it, so that by thermal agitation the copper ions would encounter stannous ions and could be reduced to copper metal. The copper metal would initially be in the form of atoms, but under the influence of thermal agitation, and because of the fact that copper has a low binding energy in the glass, the copper ions would continue to oscillate until they encountered other copper atoms, at which time they would coalesce and form nuclei. These nuclei would also be thermally agitated, but because of their mass would be less mobile than single atoms, so their movement would be restricted. Then, more atoms would accumulate on the nuclei and there would be larger islands of copper formed. If the copper concentration were high, this would be an overwhelming tendency. Also, if copper were able to move freely in the glass (i.e. if the glass were quite holey), copper would be able to aggregate more and there would be more tendency to form large flakes, which would tend to give off-colors to our copper reds.

If one wanted to go as far as an aventurine glass, it would be desirable to concentrate on getting a glass that was as full of holes as possible, so that the copper particles could move around more freely and could aggregate to aventurine-sized flakes.

126   On the other hand, if one wanted to get as beautiful a red as possible, one might want to abort the movement of copper particles quickly. Therefore one would want to cool the glaze rapidly, or better yet quench it and then reheat it to a minimum temperature for nuclei formation and limited crystal growth.

No day has ever failed me quite:
Before the grayest day is done
I find some misty purple bloom,
Or a late line of crimson sun.

Grace Noll—The Day

19 VOLATILITY OF COPPER

INTRODUCTION

A severe problem in making copper red glazes is the loss of red color near the top rim of pieces, especially tall forms. This loss of red color has been attributed to either volatilization of copper from the glaze, oxidation of copper by the atmosphere during cooling or to the fact that the glaze thins at the top and reacts strongly with the body. Probably all three effects have some influence on the loss of color at the top of a piece. An examination of a glaze in cross section will normally show a three layered structure, where there is a clear layer next to the body, a copper red layer in the center (if the glaze is thick enough), and another clear layer near the surface. The clear layer next to the body is due to some form of glaze-body interaction, and will be discussed in a later chapter. The top clear layer, though, is related to volatilization and oxidation effects, and will be the subject of this chapter.

Although I have noted in a previous book (Those Celadon Blues) that there is not much tendency for oxygen to penetrate a glaze, oxygen has more influence in copper reds than in ordinary glazes. However, if oxidation were the main cause for the loss of color at the top edge of copper red glazes, then we should find that re-reduction of a sample would result in a reappearance of the red color at the top. When this experiment was tried however, no evidence of re-reduction was found by looking at either the gross sample, or at cross sections. Because of this lack of re-reduction, I feel that volatilization is a greater cause for the surface loss of red color than is the oxidation reaction.

Along these same lines, the question arises: when **is** copper lost from the glaze? Is it lost during oxidation firing stages? Or, is it lost during reduction firing? Here experiments come to our assistance. In the reduction firing of copper reds in my small test kiln, I normally find that there is a green flame (from copper) appearing at the gas exit from the kiln, so it is obvious that some copper is volatilized during reduction firing.

Another experiment which helps us in deciding when copper loss by volatilization is occurring, is the following trial. In this procedure I have taken a single glaze and placed it on two different cups. One was fired in strong oxidation and the other was fired in strong reduction. The cup fired in oxidation came out with a glaze which was green in color, and this color was evident from the top rim to the bottom of the cup. Furthermore, when this cup was refired again and again, even though there was some change in coloration—possibly due to the flow of the glaze—there was still a fairly strong green color to be noted from the top to the bottom. On the other hand, if the copper glaze (made of the same composition, but fired in reduction) is given a normal firing, it will have some loss of color at the top rim. Then if a further reduction firing is made at a high temperature, even more whitening of the cup rim will occur. And finally, if one fires a copper red cup for an extended period of time, you will find that the red has vanished from the cup in all areas. My conclusion from these experiments is that copper is lost mainly during the reduction firing period.

Another test of this process is to take the oxidation-fired cup and submit it to a low temperature reduction—at 600-800°C—in a heavily reducing atmosphere. Upon examination after cooling, one will find that this cup has either a red or a metallic, coppery look to it, from top to bottom. Also, there is no evidence of a lack of copper at the top rim. Thus I am convinced that most of the volatilization of copper from glazes is taking place during the reduction cycle. Because of these observations, I think that it behooves us to keep the reduction firing period as short as possible in order to avoid loss of copper red color. In order to keep total firing as short as possible, it is desirable to keep the final temperature low and the reduction time short.

PHYSICAL CONSTANTS

The following list is a short collection of some of the melting, boiling and decomposition points of copper compounds:

MATERIAL	MELTING POINT	BOILING POINT
Copper Metal	1083°C.	2595°C
Cuprous Bromide	492	1345
Copper Carbonate	200 dec.	——
Cupric Chloride	620	993 dec.
Cuprous Chloride	430	1490
Cuprous Iodide	605	1290
Cuprous Oxide	1235	1800 dec.
Cupric Oxide	1326	——
Cupric Sulfate	650 dec.	——

Other common salts of copper, such as the nitrate, acetate, etc. have not been reported because they decompose to copper oxide at rather low temperatures and thus become equivalent to the oxide. For example, if copper nitrate is used as a colorant, one would find that at a few hundred degrees Celsius it would decompose to cupric oxide plus oxides of nitrogen, and from that point on, it would act as copper oxide (just as copper carbonate would).

The form in which we add copper to a glaze will often be chosen because of the physical characteristics of the compound (such as solubility or powderiness). Most copper compounds will decompose to an oxide before firing is completed. The further reaction of copper oxide with hydrogen or carbon monoxide then occurs and we have reduction of copper oxide to copper metal. Furthermore, it doesn't matter whether cuprous or cupric oxide is present, because either will produce the metal in reduction firing.

Copper is classified chemically with a group containing silver and gold; and all three of these metals are easily formed by reduction, so it is certain that in a reducing fire we can get copper metal.

While a freshly formed surface of copper is an orange-red color, if the copper is made thin enough, it will appear green in transmitted light. On the other hand, the formation of a colloidal copper suspension in water by chemical means is reported to give a dark red hue. The oxide of copper formed by heating the metal in air is "black" cupric oxide, although where cupric oxide is in contact with copper metal, a layer of red cuprous oxide will be found.

The addition of rather small amounts of other metals to copper results in a large increase in its strength. An addition of 5-10% tin is all that is necessary to form a very hard alloy. If one adds larger amounts of tin (25-50%) to copper, the alloy loses its golden color and becomes silvery in appearance.

At a temperature of 1250°C the element copper has a vapor pressure of one one-hundred thousandth of an atmosphere. From this information we can see that copper metal does not have an extraordinarily high vapor pressure at the temperature used in the fabrication of copper red glazes. Thus, we will have to ask ourselves: if these materials don't have high vapor pressures, then how is copper escaping from the glaze surface?

VOLATILITY OF COPPER HALIDES

As we work more and more with copper red glazes, we find that it is desirable to have an optimum concentration of copper in a glaze in order to get a good color. If there is much less copper than the optimum, then the color will disappear entirely. On the other hand if excess copper is added, then poor colors result. So we tend to have close to the minimum amount of copper in our red glazes. Because of this tendency volatilization is going to be troublesome since it will only take a small loss of copper to cause us to lose the red color. Even so, the low volatility of copper metal causes us to wonder what the mechanism may be for copper loss. If we examine the melting point table which I have given above, we can see that there is one class of compounds that is extremely volatile and which is also rather common. This is the halide series, of which the most common member is the chloride. I have the feeling that copper chloride is the culprit when we have problems with the loss of copper from a glaze.

Chlorine is the twelfth most abundant element in the earth's crust, and is rather ubiquitous in its occurrence. We find certain modest levels in ground water, we find it also in the earth around us, and, it is even present in the atmosphere (the soil receives 10-100 pounds a year per acre from rainfall and dust). Naturally, chlorides are present in trace quantities in wood and other plant life, because of their evolution from earth, water and air. Furthermore, we now live in a society where chlorides have become very common. For example, household water is almost invariably treated with chlorine and often it contains chlorides from softening processes. Even ground water is laced with chloride, because most chlorides are readily soluble and are not ion exchanged with soil particles. One common source—in the Northern United States—is from the air because of the use of halides as road clearing materials in the winter. In the course of time, what with spume from storms at sea and from man's own spume, there is a pretty healthy distribution of chloride across the earth; coastal areas are of course the most heavily laden.

The reason that I am emphasizing the role of chloride in copper red glazes is because of an observation that I made this past summer at a State University which has a number of ceramic kilns spread around one large kiln room. One person was making a celadon glazed bowl in a kiln and next to that bowl there was a small test piece where another person was checking a copper red glaze. The result at the end of the reduction firing was that copper volatilized from the test piece and was fumed on the celadon bowl. This volatility seemed fascinating to me, so I tried to duplicate the result by placing a dish of copper oxide next to a celadon glaze in my small test kiln. However, I was startled to find that there was no volatilization in a short firing, even though copper oxide was extremely close to a celadon glaze. While puzzling over this, the thought occurred that chloride might be the active agent in volatilization of copper. The reason for this was: in the University's collection of kilns they had a salt kiln, and the salt was widely tracked all over the kiln room. Therefore, I thought that in the process of a long firing, sufficient chloride dust would be swept up in the combustion air to convert some of the copper to volatile copper chloride, which would then be fumed on the celadon glaze. Giving this theory a test in my own short-fire kiln, I mixed some sodium chloride with copper oxide and placed this near the same celadon glaze. This time I got a strong copper red splash on my celadon, because the climate was now perfect for copper volatilization.

Using this experiment as a base, I feel that we should be aware of the action of the halogens in copper red glazing kilns. If we are firing with wood, we will need to be extra suspicious, since the presence of chloride in wood ash is going to be an additional source of chloride.

Obviously, the best fuels would be natural gas or liquified petroleum gas (propane or butane). But, even the use of the purest fuel would be insufficient if our air is contaminated. So, it is imperative for us to try to get as clean an air intake location as possible. We should also realize that there is a possibility that chloride may be found in our water supply.

NEUTRALIZATION OF VOLATILITY

A couple of experiments have convinced me that it is possible to neutralize the volatility effect in copper red glazes. This will be true no matter what the mechanism is—whether from the halide effect, or some other process. The theory is, that if one fires copper red ware in saggers, and if the saggers have an interior coating of copper oxide, then either one of two things can happen: first, if there is some contaminant such a chloride getting in and causing the loss of copper, then the large excess of copper on the sagger interior will react with this substance before it gets to the ware, and it will use it up before it can have a harmful effect; on the other hand, if there is merely a volatile atmosphere of some copper material coming off the glaze, then there should be a nearly equivalent atmosphere of some copper material coming off the sagger, and this should neutralize the loss from the glaze.

The reason that I feel that copper coating of saggers is a desirable action is due to two observations. The first is that copper red colors will generally be better on the inside of a container than on the outside (all other parameters being equal). Obviously if there is a different coating thickness from the outside to the inside there will be some confusion. But, if the glaze thickness is the same inside and out, I have noticed that the interior glaze usually suffers less from volatilization effects than the outside. This comes about because the interior of a vessel will not only be emitting, but will also be receiving volatile copper materials as is shown schematically in the figure. On the outside of the container there will be mostly a loss of copper—unless one has a whole kiln full of copper red glazes that are stacked close together. In general then, the

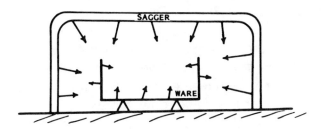

tendency will be for more copper to be lost on the outside than on the inside of a container, and I feel that the use of a copper oxide coated sagger would ensure that the ware is maintained in a vapor of copper that will minimize volatilization losses.

Still another way to minimize the loss of copper from glazes is to diminish firing temperatures and times. There is obviously a point of temperature above which one does not want to go, because of a greatly increased volatility of copper. This desirable maximum firing temperature appears to be approximately 1250°C. I feel that if one fires a copper red glaze to a temperature of 1350°C in an average kiln, that this will lead to excessive volatilization and therefore to poor colors. In order to minimize the temperature required, I have found it useful to add frits to glazes. This was the technique that was used by Seger in the 1880's. We also know that Vogt found that the Chinese were using frits in 1882. I think that the use of frits may have been the contribution made during the Kang-hsi reign of the Ching dynasty which allowed the Chinese to have a renaissance in the copper red field.

Unfortunately there has to be a trade-off for this lowering of the maximum temperature. I have not been able to get good copper reds at temperatures as low as 1100°C. You can only lower the temperature so far. It seems that the problem is that the copper-tin interaction—which is essential for good copper red formation—does not take place unless there has been a certain maximum temperature. If this point has not been reached, then really good colors cannot be obtained. Of course, some sort of red may be obtained at low temperatures, but I have found my low temperature glazes to be more of a brick red than a bright apple red.

MAKING USE OF VOLATILIZATION

Whenever we find a result that counteracts our wishes, it is possible to try and turn things around so that we can use the negative result to get some positive benefit. With regard to volatilization, the thought immediately occurs: if copper is volatile, how can we use this attribute to **improve** some of our glazes. One might try to fume copper vapors on a glaze and form a good red color. This is certainly possible and will be discussed at length in our chapter on staining, but for the most part it may be said that, while this **can** be done, a nonuniform coloration is the usual result.

DIFFUSIVITY AND VOLATILITY

The fact that copper diffuses readily in both body and glaze, gives us another reason to be cautious about copper's volatility. The high diffusivity of cuprous ions in glass will continually bring fresh copper ions to the surface of a glaze, therefore there will be a continual loss of copper. If the diffusion rate were low, then we might be better off in our copper red glaze attempts (except for the fact that it is needed in order to get the groups of copper atoms formed), but usually high diffusivity is working against us.

Since volatility will occur more readily in the open state of a glaze, we should fire as quickly as we can from a temperature of about 500°C up to about 1100°C or wherever our glaze seals over. This should help the volatility problem, and it may be a reason why the alternating oxidation and reduction was so highly recommended by Seger and others. It could be that during the oxidation portion of firing no volatilization was occurring, so that by using alternate oxidation and reduction you could cut the loss down by a factor of about 50%. The only thing that I would worry about would be having the atmosphere in an oxidizing condition just as the glaze was sealing over.

CONCLUSION

As a final comment in this chapter on volatilization, here are some numbers that I have collected and calculated:

If we consider that one molecule of propane reacts with five molecules of oxygen to give three molecules of carbon dioxide and four molecules of water, according to equation (1):

(1) $C_3H_8 + 5 O_2 = 3 CO_2 + 4 H_2O,$

then from stoichiometric calculations we can see that 44 grams of propane react with 160 grams of oxygen to give us the equilibrium products. If we next consider that one part of oxygen is found in five parts of air, then to get the weight of air that would react with 44 grams of propane, we have to multiply 160 by 5. This would give us 800 grams of air. Converting to pounds and rounding off, we get approximately one pound of propane reacting with 20 pounds of air. If we consider a firing where we use 100 pounds of propane, then we find that 2000 pounds of air (roughly) have passed through our kiln.

Now, let us consider the possible contamination of air with chloride. If there was only 0.01% (100 ppm) of chloride in the ambient air, this would result in 90 grams of chloride passing through the kiln. While 90 grams is not much, still, if there is only 1/2% of copper in the glaze, this 90 grams of chloride would go a long way towards reacting with whatever weight of copper we had in our copper red glazes. These are not numbers to be neglected. Even though there may be only a tiny amount of salt dust floating around in air, it is real and it could cause us big problems.

Art thou the topmost apple
The gatherers could not reach,
Reddening on the bough?

Sappho—To Atthis.

A Bohemian glass beaker (ca. 1840) engraved through an outer copper red glass layer.

20 STAINS AND REDUCED COPPER

A good way to start this chapter is to give some examples. If we keep in mind that a **glaze** is different from a piece of **glass**, we can learn something from the excerpts from the two patents which I shall include at this point. Just remember at all times that **glaze** surfaces are depleted in alkali as compared to an average **glass** surface. If more information is desired on these two patents, one may refer to the originals.

METHOD OF COLORING GLASS AND RESULTING ARTICLE

US Patent #2,701,215 (1955)

William H. Kroeck, Corning, NY

This invention relates to the treatment of glass to produce a coloration in its surface with copper, which procedure is commonly known as copper staining.

As conventionally practiced, such process generally includes initially heating a glass containing an alkali-metal oxide at a temperature somewhat below its softening point while in contact with a copper-staining composition comprising a paste or liquid containing a salt or compound of copper to produce in the glass a yellow or greenish-yellow surface coloration and subsequently heating the glass in a reducing atmosphere to convert such yellow color to red. During such treatment, copper ions from the copper-staining composition in contact with the glass migrate into its surface in exchange for alkali metal ions from the glass, the reaction being facilitated or accelerated by an increase in the temperature. The red coloration is caused by reduction of such copper ions to metallic copper.

In the utilization of such process for the production of red light-directing lenses or cover glasses for lamps of the type known as "sealed beam" lamps, it is difficult to introduce enough copper into the glass surface to provide the desired special characteristics, that is, a sufficient absorption of blue and green wavelengths together with a high enough transmission of the red. While the amount of migrated copper in the surface of the glass can to some extent be increased by increasing the time and temperature of firing, this also increases the tendency of the glass article to warp. Repeated or additional applications of the staining composition to the glass in order to avoid the use of excessive temperature and the resulting deformation of the ware result in a non-uniform coloration and the development of haziness in the glass. Alterations in the staining composition including the use of a variety of copper compounds and an increase in the copper content of the composition are likewise ineffective. The use of copper sulfides and of free sulfur in the staining composition, although sometimes recommended for improving the color, does not increase the migration of copper into the glass sufficiently for the present purpose.

I have now discovered that such migration of copper into the glass can be enhanced and that copper stained glass of uniform color having the indicated spectral characteristics and free of haziness can be produced at temperatures low enough to avoid distortion by initially heating the glass while in contact with a copper-staining composition in an atmosphere containing a substantial amount of sulfur dioxide, preferably an atmosphere resulting from controllably burning sulfur in air to develop a yellow color therein and thereafter heating the glass in a reducing atmosphere desirably substantially free of sulfur dioxide until the color due to copper in the glass is red.

Staining compositions suitable for the practice of this invention comprise generally one or more copper components such as cupric oxide, cuprous oxide, cupric sulfide, cuprous sulfide, cupric sulfate or cuprous chloride, the equivalent copper content usually amounting to about 40% or more by weight of the total solids of the composition, the balance of the solids comprising an inert material or materials such as clay, ochre or barium carbonate. These solids are dispersed or suspended in a vehicle such as lavender oil or other essential oil, turpentine, or water to form a paste or liquid which is applied to the glass by brushing, spraying, or dipping. The vehicle is then evaporated slowly enough to avoid bubbling, and the coated glass is placed in a suitably heated kiln.

To facilitate and increase the migration of copper ions into the glass, an atmosphere containing a substantial amount of sulfur dioxide is created in the kiln in accordance with this invention. This may be done by introducing gaseous sulfur dioxide from an external source, such as bottled sulfur dioxide or elemental sulfur controllably burned in air, into the kiln but may also be accomplished by burning flowers of sulfur in the kiln adjacent to the coated ware. During such treatment the door of the kiln is kept closed to prevent substantial ingress of air. Sulfur, burned in air in the kiln, combines with the oxygen and produces a mixture consisting primarily of sulfur dioxide and nitrogen. While relatively small amounts of sulfur dioxide are to some extent effective, an appreciable staining improvement requires at least about 25% sulfur dioxide by volume. When sulfur dioxide is introduced into the kiln from an external source to displace the air from the kiln however, at least about 75% of sulfur dioxide by volume is required for the optimum staining improvement. Desirably not all of the air is displaced by sulfur dioxide since I have found that an atmosphere consisting of sulfur dioxide alone tends to reduce the copper ions, which at this stage of the process results in nonuniformity of color and a tendency to precipitate metallic copper in the staining composition. The sulfur dioxide should accordingly preferably comprise not over 90% of the atmosphere by volume. Suitable conditions are readily determined by trial and I have found for example that in an electrically heated kiln having a capacity of 45 cubic feet, 8 ounces of flowers of sulfur is a satisfactory initial quantity but that subsequent heat treatments in the same kiln without permitting complete diffusion and dissipation of sulfur dioxide trapped in the refractories, require smaller amounts of sulfur, the quantity for the third consecutive heat treatment and all thereafter being 4 ounces.

While practically any compound of copper can be utilized in carrying out the invention, I have found that cupric oxide produces the best result. Although the addition of elemental sulfur to the staining composition might be expected to provide an atmosphere of sulfur dioxide effective for the present purpose, I have found that such is not the case. The presence of sulfur in the copper staining composition not only fails to produce the desired result but it causes non-uniformity of coloration due to variable local reaction caused by uneven combustion and/or evaporation of the sulfur.

Analysis shows that the amount of migrated copper per unit area in glass treated in accordance with the method of this invention is substantially larger than the amount produced by the same copper-staining composition in the same glass but heated in an atmosphere free of sulfur dioxide. Moreover such increase in the copper content of the glass may be brought about at a lower temperature. A borosilicate glass having a softening point of 780°C and an annealing point of 528°C, when treated according to the method of this invention and heated at 585°C, contains as much or more copper per unit area than when heated at 620°C in an atmosphere free of sulfur dioxide. With borosilicate glasses, generally good results are obtained by heating in accordance with this invention for about 30 minutes at a temperature about 50°C above the annealing point of the glass or for about 15 minutes at about 100°C above its annealing point. Soda-lime glasses and other glasses having similarly high alkali-metal oxide contents produce comparable results at temperatures relatively somewhat lower than those required for borosilicate glasses, on account of their higher alkali-metal oxide content and the resulting higher rate of exchange of the copper ion for alkali metal ions.

Following such heat treatment in the atmosphere containing sulfur dioxide, the treated glass has a yellow color which may be converted to a red color having the desired spectral characteristics by heating the glass in a reducing atmosphere such as an atmosphere of a reducing gas, such as hydrogen, carbon monoxide, a mixture of hydrogen and nitrogen or, preferably, natural gas which has been partially burned so as to contain substantial hydrogen and carbon monoxide, such dilute mixture being milder in action than the pure gases. For such reducing heat-treatment a temperature nearer the annealing-point of the glass may, if desired, be employed and at least 15 minutes is required with a strong reducing gas. While a relatively small amount of sulfur dioxide in the atmosphere is not objectionable at this stage, its presence in large amounts is not desirable because any substantial dilution of the more reactive reducing gases recited above by the sulfur dioxide which is relatively a mild reducing agent, objectionably increases the time required for proper reduction.

The residual staining composition is preferably removed from the glass following its heat-treatment in the sulfur dioxide atmosphere at which time it is easily scoured off. No harm results, however, if such residue is left on the glass until after the final or reducing heat-treatment.

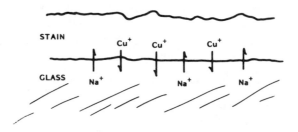

METHOD OF STAINING GLASS WITH COPPER HALIDE VAPORS

US Patent #2,428,600 (1947)

Helen S. Williams

This invention relates to improvements in glass manufacture and more particularly to the production of copper stains on glass or the introduction of copper into glass surfaces.

It is known that red glasses can be obtained by the use of copper in two fundamentally different ways. According to one method for producing a copper ruby, the copper compound is introduced as an ingredient of the glass batch; and under reducing conditions and in the presence of promoting oxides glasses are obtained which give a deep ruby color on annealing or reheating.

The other method called copper staining is based on a base exchange between solid or molten copper compounds and the alkali of the glass surface, this reaction being usually carried out by coating the surface of the glassware or a part of the surface with a mixture of a carrier substance and a copper compound, first firing in an oxidizing atmosphere to cause the copper to replace alkali in the glass and subsequently firing under reducing conditions to develop a red glass. This copper staining method is not well adapted for use with normal soda-lime glass such as window glass or bottle glass and requires special glass compositions, particularly the presence of substantial amounts of potash.

According to the present invention, the vapors of volatile copper salts are caused to react with hot glass surfaces. By using the vapors of volatile copper compounds it has been found that these react much more intensively than would be expected from the action of the solid or molten copper compounds in the so-called copper staining process. It has also been found that special glass compositions are not required and normal or ordinary soda lime glass can be readily and successfully colored.

It has been found that the vapors of both cupric and cuprous halides react with the hot glass surfaces. Different volatile copper compounds can be used which in vapor form react with the glass at high temperatures with replacement of alkali by copper, the copper ions migrating into the glass in replacing the alkali ions which in turn migrate out of the glass. Cuprous chloride is particularly advantageous as a volatile copper compound in the process.

The process of the present invention is applicable for the treatment of both soda and potash glasses. It is one advantage of the process that it does not require special glass compositions in that it may readily be applied to normal or ordinary soda lime glasses such a window glass, bottle glass, etc.

According to the present invention, the glass surfaces heated to a high temperature are exposed to the vapors of cuprous chloride and advantageously with subsequent reduction treatment. The temperature and time of treatment can be varied, and products of varying properties and characteristics obtained. Thus, for example, the glass may be heated to 500°C in a cuprous chloride atmosphere for varying lengths of time, e.g., from 15 minutes to 8 hours. The copper ions are thus introduced into the glass surface by the halide vapor treatment. The copper ions are thus introduced into the glass surface by a base exchange reaction with the sodium ions of the glass.

On subjecting the thus-treated glass to reduction, different results are obtained depending on the extent to which copper has entered the glass surface and the conditions of reduction. If the amount of cuprous ions entering the glass surface is sufficiently great, subsequent reduction will result in the production of a mirror. For this purpose, the treatment of cuprous ions entering the glass surface should be as great as possible and the depth of penetration is of secondary importance. In other words, the concentration gradient of the cuprous ions should be high.

By obtaining a low concentration gradient, the formation of a red copper stain is favored rather than the production of a mirror. For the production of a mirror, the reduction is advantageously carried out at a high temperature and for a short time, for example, at 700-800°C, by flash reduction with hydrogen of glass which has been exposed to cuprous chloride vapors for 6 hours at 550°C. **At this high temperature the copper mirror forms within the surface of the glass and does not dissolve in nitric acid.**

By introducing a regulated amount of copper into the glass surface and by reducing at low temperatures, e.g., around 400-500°C, a copper ruby or metallic luster can be produced with a sufficiently high concentration of cuprous ions.

If the amount of copper combined with the surface is not sufficiently high, the glass on reduction may not show a ruby color or metallic luster, but will nevertheless contain copper.

It is one advantage of the present invention that it enables products of different properties to be obtained with accurate control of the resulting color. If the reaction is allowed to take place at a low temperature, around 350-425°C, all color shades can be obtained, between a faint pink and a deep red, depending on the time of exposure to the cuprous chloride vapor. By using higher temperatures, around 500-550°C, a strong reaction takes place on the glass surface which leads to high concentration of cuprous ions in the glass. Upon reduction such a glass will not only develop a deep red color but it may also show a distinct metallic reflection. This metal luster can be used for decorative purposes and also as a basis for building up a layer of metallic copper by chemical deposition.

The invention is advantageously used for treating individual glass articles or objects for decorative purposes and for the formation of colored articles ranging in color from a faint pink to a deep red. Glass articles or surfaces can also be treated to adapt them for subsequent treatment to deposit copper or other metals thereon.

I have tried both of these staining techniques on glazed ware without outstanding success. Since I don't have a specific kiln (built just for the process of staining), I used my normal ceramic test kiln and adapted it to handle the processes described in the patents.

PASTE STAINING

Let us consider the first patent—staining by use of a paste. The technique I used was to make up a paste of clay and copper oxide and apply this to the areas of my ware that I wanted stained. The particular glaze that I used was a celadon, because I knew that celadons could be readily colored with copper red. The experiment was performed in the following manner: a kiln was heated to 800-1000°C so that it would act as a good heat sink; then when the temperature cooled to 6-800°C, the decorated ware was placed inside the kiln together with a cup full of sulfur; finally, the kiln was closed up tightly and was allowed to cool to ambient temperature. The objective was to allow the sulfur to burn to sulfur dioxide, meanwhile maintaining the heat as constant as possible during the cooling cycle. Whenever the sulfur was burned off, additional sulfur was added. However, the cooling process in this small kiln was such that the temperature did not remain at 600-800°C for more than one-half hour. After the ware had cooled, it was found to have a slight yellow stain on it. This cup was then replaced in the kiln and heavy reduction firing was started and maintained up to about 700°C. The reduction firing was kept as slow as possible, but again, because of the nature of my particular kiln, this was not simple. When the top temperature of 700°C was reached, the firing was stopped. When the ware had cooled, it was found that a red color had appeared in the areas where the paste had been fired. However, the color was rather poor. It was not a **bright** red, but was more of a **brick** color. If this were the best red that could be obtained by staining ceramic glazes, I would not recommend the procedure.

VAPOR STAINING

The copper chloride technique described by Mrs. Williams, was also attempted, although again, because of the lack of the proper firing facilities, the procedure was adapted for my particular kiln and ware. Since cuprous chloride is quite volatile, I decided to try and contain it near a sample. To do this, the sample glaze was placed in the kiln (with a small container of cuprous chloride next to it), and then the entire set-up was covered with a sagger. This was done with the kiln at a temperature of about 800°C so that the copper chloride immediately began volatilizing. The ware was then allowed to cool to room temperature, at which time it was found to have acquired some copper ions in the surface. When this treatment was followed by a reduction treatment (as before), some copper red coloration appeared. However, the stain was very irregular—some parts were stained well and others were not stained at all. The most interesting aspect of the coloration was the point mentioned previously: the stain showed up strongly in the crackle which was present on the glaze! Because of the crackle staining, it was reasoned that the as-formed surface of the test piece was deficient in alkali (due to volatilization) and that staining was only occurring where alkali-rich glaze was available. Red color showed in fracture areas, at craze surfaces, and at some ordinary surface locations where there happened to be more than an average amount of alkali. For the most part the glaze surface did not have enough alkali in it to exchange readily with cuprous chloride. Again, I wouldn't recommend this procedure for making copper red decorated ceramic ware.

I have included these techniques though, because they sound so tempting. The results **would** be beautiful if only we had glaze surfaces that had the same composition as the glaze interior. If you can find a glaze surface that is high in alkali, then I believe that these procedures would be practical. Of the two processes I think that the paste technique is the better one, and if this were worked on it might prove to be an acceptable procedure. For example, one might try staining a ceramic that had been fired in an electric kiln. Theoretically, there should be less alkali loss from a surface that has not been subjected to the washing of flames. Still another possibility is that a salt glazed piece might be readily stained, because one would expect that the surface of a salt glazed ware would be high in soda.

REDUCTION OF CUPRIC IONS

Since we have noted that in staining glass it is possible to reduce cuprous ions with hydrogen; and since we have noted that hydrogen will diffuse into a glass; we must ask ourselves whether hydrogen can also reduce **cupric** ions to copper metal and cause red colors to form in glass. An examination of the thermochemistry of the reaction:

$$CuO + H_2 = Cu + H_2O,$$

demonstrates that at $1300°K$ ($1027°C$) the free energy of the reaction is -31.1 Kcal. Thus we may rest assured that the reaction is **possible**. The question of whether it **will** occur in a glaze or glass can best be answered by an experiment that has already been done by George Wettlaufer, and, I am sure, others before him. Wettlaufer commented that it was possible to take a green copper glaze, reheat it to $800°C$ in heavy reduction and form a red color on the surface. After having read this, I immediately tried the reaction and found it to be successful. I had had some copper reds that had failed due to a lack of reduction in the kiln, so I took one of these green glazes and refired it at about $800°C$ in heavy reduction; then, sure enough, a copper red was formed. When the reduction was too heavy, a metallic looking copper finish was formed.

The only problem with such copper reds is that they are very thin. They are just a red skin on the surface of the glaze and it is possible to scratch the glaze lightly and make a mark in this copper red. Therefore, they are not entirely satisfactory as decorations. This is the sort of reaction that one would see if one reduced a copper containing glaze after a raku firing, when a hot pot is dumped into a barrel of straw or sawdust.

21 COLORS ASSOCIATED WITH COPPER

With copper materials, what you see is not necessarily what you get. If we consider something as simple as cupric oxide (CuO), we find that this material is described in the literature as being black. However, if we look at it under high magnification and with bright illumination we get the feeling that here is a brownish or greenish material. Certainly we know that if cupric oxide is dissolved in a silicate glass it gives a greenish color. Thus, it might be that the original material was a **very** deep green.

On the other hand, cuprous oxide is commonly described as red in color. And, in the case of this material we can actually see a transmitted color when we examine it with high magnification and a bright light source. In such an examination the appearance of cuprous oxide is that of garnet. It is a deep orange-red-brown color. It is definitely not a ruby red!

Some unusual colors in copper compounds are exemplified by the case of cuprous chloride, which is reported to be either yellow or brown in the anhydrous form, but which is a green color when hydrated. Cuprous chloride is also described as being white when precipitated from water or a brownish mass when prepared from copper and mercuric chloride.

Such differences are noticeable within one valence state, but as we go from the cupric (II) to the cuprous (I) state, we note even wider variations in color.

Our interest in the colors associated with copper may be connected with the colors which appear when copper compounds are dissolved in glass (or a glaze). The most common colors related to copper in glasses are blues and greens, which are due to the cupric ion. The variation between green and blue has been related to either the oxidation state, or the coordination state (i.e. the type of glass). On one hand, W. D. Bancroft believed that the color blue is the color to be expected from cupric ions dissolved in glasses, while the green color is due to the fact that some of the copper has been thermally reduced to a yellow, cuprous state, and that we are observing the combined blue plus yellow (or green) color. Since the color of a copper containing glass seems to be quite dependent on the base glass, subject to whether it is a borosilicate glass, a lead glass, or a soda-lime glass, there is the possibility that the color variation is due to the coordination number of copper in the glassy matrix, and that the color changes are caused by the substrate.

Traces of cupric oxide produce light blue colors in soda-lime glasses, but at the same concentrations green hues are found in borosilicate or high lead glasses.

Another authority, W. A. Weyl, felt that the green-blue color differences were due to polarization or coordination effects which were dependent on the number of ions surrounding the copper ion. In addition there is the thought that it is easiest to maintain an oxidized state in a highly alkaline medium, so the possibility exists that high alkali glasses, such as soda-lime types are producing blue colors because of their alkalinity and a propensity for forming oxidized melts.

In addition to the blues and greens, there is also a yellow color that can be formed in glass by the addition of cuprous oxide in the presence of a neutral atmosphere.

In fully reduced glasses, copper will, of course, give the color which is the subject of this book, red.

And finally, if one uses too high a concentration of **cupric** ion, a glass will become saturated with copper oxide, and a matte black surface will appear.

22 GLASSES VERSUS GLAZES

GLASSES

Since copper red glasses are easier to make than copper red glazes, they will be discussed first.

The classical work on copper ruby color in glass, done by Paul Ebell was reported in 1874 and can be found in part in a later chapter of this book. Ebell found that the best glass for making a copper ruby was one containing potash as the alkali, with high percentages (ca. 30%) of lead oxide in addition to silica. This potash-lead-silicate glass could then be used to form a copper ruby by the addition of small amounts of copper oxide and slightly larger quantities of tin oxide.

Glass, which is formed in a pot or tank, can be kept in a reduced state by the simple inclusion of a small amount of carbonaceous material in the batch. Hence, the firing atmosphere can be neutral or even oxidizing during the formation of the glass. The glass itself remains in a reduced state because of the difficulty that oxygen has in penetrating the surface and the bulk of the glass. This characteristic of glass melting is very convenient for high lead glasses, because the use of small amounts of a reducing agent will not be enough to reduce lead oxide to lead metal (which would give a grey or black appearance to the glass). The small amount of reducing agent needed to reduce the copper can be calculated so that only copper is formed. After the glass has been fined and conditioned to the correct temperature for blowing or pressing, pieces can be made by standard techniques. If the forming technique involves slow cooling from a high temperature, then the glass may strike-in to a ruby during the cooling process. If, however, the glass is cooled quickly, it may be relatively colorless after forming. The colorless state is actually the preferred condition, because this allows better control over the final purity of the red. If speed is the most important factor, then it is best to have the glass strike to a red color as it is formed. But, for exact control of color it is desirable to have a red formed during a reheating process, since this allows control of nuclei formation and crystallization around these nuclei.

As was discussed in the chapter on the mechanics of phase separation and nucleation, it is desirable to have a large number of small copper crystallites providing the color. Hence, it is preferable to take a colorless glass and reheat it to a nucleating temperature, and then finally treat it at the crystallizing temperature for appropriate periods as was discussed by Stookey (1949). In this way, an exact color can be produced time after time, as would be required in a commercial operation where the quality would be critical (as in glass filter applications).

One of the interesting aspects of copper red glasses is a comparison of them to copper stained glasses. While a lead based glass is preferred in the first case, both soda-lime and borosilicate glasses have been successfully stained. The patent by Grego and Howell (US# 3,429,724) shows us that a good red color can be obtained on borosilicate glass, while the patent by Williams (US# 2,428,600) illustrates red staining of a soda-lime glass.

In summary, we may state that the two advantages of making copper red glasses vis-a-vis copper red glazes are: first, the better homogeneity of a glass as compared to a typical glaze; and second, the ability, in many cases, to control the heat treatment and hence the copper red color quality in glasses. There is a drawback though, and that is that copper ruby glasses are deeply colored, and if a light red is desired, it becomes necessary to apply copper ruby to glass as a thin coating on the outside surface (flashing) rather than by using a solid glass color. A copper ruby glass is usually so deeply colored that extreme caution must be used to make it thin, otherwise the glass will not be transparent, and may even appear **black** to the eye.

Having considered copper red glasses, let us now compare them to copper red glazes. Glazes are quite a different situation for several reasons. In the first place, a glaze is a relatively thin layer of material compared to glass in a tank. Also, glazes are in intimate contact with two other phases: the solid body, and the gaseous atmosphere, while glass in a tank may be drawn from the center of the melt. Because of this, it is almost impossible to form a copper red glaze in an oxidizing or neutral atmosphere. It can be done (as has been demonstrated by Baggs and Littlefield in their work with silicon carbide as a glaze reducing material), but this procedure is very sensitive to over- and under-firing. For practical purposes, copper red glazes are formed in a reducing atmosphere, even though the atmosphere may not be continuously in a reduced state.

Naturally the converse situation has to be considered and the question arises of whether it is possible to overreduce a copper red glaze. It **is** possible. One can reduce to such an extent that carbon is left in the glaze; or, droplets of copper may form; or, the glaze may turn black due to lead reduction.

Temperature considerations are also crucial for the formation of copper red glazes. If one underfires, there are too many bubbles, and there may not be complete melting; then the glaze appears pinkish because of unmelted crystals and undissolved gas. On the other hand, if the glaze is overfired, there will be volatilization of copper and the color will be lost. Therefore, the firing operation requires fairly exact conditions.

The biggest problem with copper red glazes versus copper red glasses is concerned with the formation of copper crystallites. This is a delicate function of the cooling or the reheating process. In a glass, one can use quenching and reheating to control particle size. In glazes, this is not possible—because of the problem of quenching a body through crystal transformation temperatures. Hence, it is necessary to make a glaze which will strike on cooling and which will form the appropriate color in this process. The glaze has to have **exactly** the right concentration of copper in it. This is due to the fact that during the cooling process almost all of the copper will participate in the striking phenomenon and in the coloring of the glaze. In a glass, one can manipulate nuclei formation and the crystallization process so that only appropriate numbers of color sites and appropriate sizes of crystals are formed. In the case of glazes the cooling process will usually nucleate and crystallize all of the available copper. Thus, if there is too much copper in a glaze, a poor color will result due to too many crystals, or due to oversized crystals.

On the other hand, if not enough copper is present, then **no** coloration will result. It can be seen then that a very narrow copper concentration range is required for copper red glazes. An exact control of this copper concentration is one of the most delicate requirements for good copper red glazes.

While melting conditions are not much of a problem with glasses, they are critical here. If a glaze is overheated, it will react too strongly with the body, and this will change the composition of the glaze. Additionally, copper volatilization will occur if heating is excessive. Therefore, the heating procedure for good glaze formation must be exact and also at as low a temperature as possible.

As will be noted in the section on microscopy of glazes, the thickness of a glaze is critical to copper red formation. If we examine glazes in cross section, we see that the copper red color is in a layer in the center of the glaze. The red is not found in either the top (outer) surface or in the inner layer next to the body. Thus the problem of glaze thickness arises. It is possible to put a high concentration of copper in a glaze, but if it is too thin, no copper red will appear. The glaze has to be thick enough to furnish a central layer which can contain the red color. This is because of surface volatility, surface oxidation and glaze-body reactions. The extraction of materials from the body is a severe problem.

With regard to glaze compositions, the Ming potters undoubtedly used a simple feldspathic glaze fluxed with limestone (or ash). They also had severe problems, because such a glaze requires high temperature firing. As time went by, they may have turned to lead or boron-containing glazes in order to lower the glaze maturing temperature, so that the loss of copper could be minimized. For myself, I have found that lead-containing glazes do not give the brightest or purest red colors and I suspect that one of the reasons for this (which is in contradistinction to glasses), is that lead glazes react strongly with bodies. Also, in high tem-

COPPER RED VASE

The slender neck on this copper red vase (made in Ching-te Chen, China in 1981) has extensive bleaching at the top. This may be credited either to a high temperature, a thin glaze coating, or a combination of the two.

CHINESE COPPER RED VASES

These red vases were the successful products of firing ware in saggars in a wood-fired kiln in Ching-te Chen, China in 1981. Nearby were many white vases which were the unsuccessful products fired near the reds in a hotter portion of the kiln. The varying size of the white mouths on the red vases indicated the impact of slightly different temperatures in the kiln. The higher the temperature or the taller the vase, the whiter the mouth rim area became.

SAGGARS STACKED IN A WOOD-FIRED KILN

The 15-20 foot high stacks of saggars were tightly arranged in the wood-fired kiln (Ching-te Chen, China, 1981). However, the spacing between them allowed for easy passage of the flames and hot gasses. The saggars marked with white kiln wash were those containing the copper red pieces. Experience has shown that this is the optimum position for proper reduction and also results in an appropriate temperature for copper reds. All of the other wares fired in the kiln were less fussy as to their firing conditions. Even with all this care, many copper red pieces were either over- or under-fired.

FOOT GRINDING OF COPPER RED VASES IN CHING-TE CHEN, CHINA

Because of the fluidity of the copper red glaze used by the Chinese, it was necessary to hand grind the foot on most of the vases. They were also placed on soft clay supports before firing so that the glaze would not fuse the ware to the hard saggars and possibly crack it during removal.

FINAL INSPECTION

Here a worker inspects the ware for quality evaluation.

EXPERIMENTAL COPPER RED GLAZED BOWL

The pleasant red color on this experimental bowl was the result of over-firing an ox blood glaze. The foot had to be ground extensively to remove the glaze that ran down the sides. Note the variation in red color as the glaze collects in the throwing marks. This color variance is mainly due to a difference in glaze thickness in these areas. Since the copper red color is to be found only in the center of a glaze layer, too thin glaze will result in no color at all.

EXPERIMENTAL OX BLOOD GLAZES

Eight different ox blood glaze formulations were painted in panels on the sides and interior of this cup. The cup was then fired in light reduction to cone 8. Variations in the fluidity of the glazes can be recognized by the amount of white that appeared at the rim and in the amount of flow at the base.

OVER-FIRED
OX BLOOD GLAZES

Samples of ox blood glazes were painted in panels on the sides and interior of this cup and it was then fired to cone 12 in light reduction. The loss of red color in the glazes was due to at least two factors: the thinning of the glazes due to excessive flow; and the volatilization of copper salts from the glaze due to the high firing temperature.

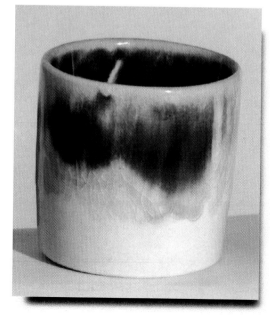

A Good Ox Blood Glaze

Occasionally a good ox blood results from a firing with no obvious variation from a firing that yields poor results. Here is such an example (though perhaps too dark to please all tastes). The glaze was indeed fluid, as can be seen by the drip on the right side, yet it did not run off the rim to any great extent. It was probably the result of a firing that was just a tad longer than usual and perhaps a few degrees lower than usual. Kiln conditions must be extremely uniform to produce consistent red glazes.

Good Peach Bloom Glazes

This cup was coated with eight panels of peach bloom glazes featuring different feldspars and different clays. The resulting, almost uniform, glazes indicate how easy it is to make good peach bloom glazes when compared to ox blood glazes. Ox bloods made with this much variation in their components would yield glazes with wildly different colors. Also note the lack of runniness at both the rim and base of the cup. This simplicity makes peach blooms the copper red glaze of choice for beginning potters. It is only necessary to make sure that the glazes are well homogenized.

An Oxidation Reduction Experiment

The cup in this picture was coated with panels of two different copper containing glazes. However, both glazes had the same percentage of copper and tin oxides. The glaze that became red had about 20% of a soft frit in it, while the green glaze did not. The firing technique consisted of firing in light reduction until the fritted glaze had sealed over. Then the fire was changed to light oxidation and was continued until the green glaze was fired to maturity. The result shows that once a red glaze is sealed over, it is unaffected by oxygen in the kiln. The green glaze, being unfused, was oxidized by the kiln atmosphere until it too was fused. The relative hardness of the two glazes can be deduced from the drip at the base of the red glaze and the lack of a drip on the green glaze.

Copper Color Variations in Reduction Firing

One eccentricity to be noted in peach bloom glazes is the appearance of both light and dark pink colors as well as green and black spots. In an effort to determine the cause of green spots on a glaze fired entirely in reduction, I performed an experiment with varying concentrations of copper on a color-less base glaze. The cup illustrated had varying quantities of copper batch placed in spots over the clear glaze. When the spot was especially thick or the copper concentrated, red areas would have bright green centers. Moreover, these central areas would be thinner than the rest of the spot. An indentation could be readily detected by running a finger over the spot. I am still trying to determine a reason for this anomalous result, but currently it baffles me. Since the glaze was fired in reduction from start to finish, how can any green (oxidized) copper exist in the glaze?

A SURFACE STAINED CUP

This cup was a green copper glazed piece before its final treatment. While still red hot, it was tossed in a can loosely filled with wet straw. In the reduction process which followed, the surface of the glaze became a deep red to copper metal color. The red or copper metal color was no more than skin deep, however, and could be erased by a very slight abrasion with emery paper. The point here is that while oxygen does not penetrate a glaze readily, this is not the case with hydrogen. It is unfortunate that the color made by this technique is difficult to control. It is more apt to progress completely to a metallic copper hue than a uniform good red. In addition, the thinness of the color limits its usefulness.

OUTSIDE VS. INSIDE VOLATILITY OF COPPER

This view of a high fired copper ox blood glazed cup is educational because of the difference in color between the outside and the inside of the cup. On the outside where flames and hot gasses have been impinging, most of the copper red color has been lost. However, on the inside of the cup where there is a more static atmosphere, the copper red color has survived to a greater extent. One is tempted to believe that a saggar coated on the inside with copper oxide would be an excellent way to preserve copper red colors from evaporation.

INCOMPLETELY FIRED OX BLOOD GLAZE

This ugly specimen was created by firing an ox blood glazed cup at 100 degrees Celsius lower than usual (1150 vs. 1250). There are interesting points to be observed on this specimen. For one thing, it has a peach bloom-like appearance, both in color and in speckles. It obviously isn't thoroughly fused since there is no running at the base. The glaze hasn't reacted with the body either, as very thin specks of glaze on the body are still pink colored. The extensive crawling of the glaze may account for some of the non-uniformities in many copper red glazes and is no doubt due to the low clay content of the glaze.

EXPERIMENTAL PEACH BLOOM GLAZE

In a peach bloom glaze, the copper does not seem to melt as freely and blend in as thoroughly as it does in an ox blood glaze. This is perfectly logical since the composition which I have used to replicate the Chinese color is loaded with clay (alumina) and thus is more viscous than an ox blood type which is required to be fluid. The Chinese peach blooms are frequently covered with red, green, or black specks or spots and my attempts at duplicates have some of the same problems. The Chinese peach bloom vase pictured on the frontispiece and the box pictured on page 28 are examples of non-uniformity and this cup shows some of the same variations.

VASE, "MILLENNIAL EGG"
PORCELAIN BY BROTHER THOMAS BEZANSON

Copper red glaze, 15¼″, TH1254.
Photo by Sean Kirby.
Courtesy of Pucker Gallery, Boston.

"SMALL VASE," PORCELAIN
BY BROTHER THOMAS BEZANSON

Copper red glaze 9¾″, TH1311.
Photo by Sean Kirby.
Courtesy of Pucker Gallery, Boston.

**PORCELAIN DISH
COPPER RED GLAZE
BY HARLAN HOUSE**

PORCELAIN VASE
COPPER RED GLAZE
BY HARLAN HOUSE

**PORCELAIN BOWL
8¼″ D
COPPER RED GLAZE,
PG51
BY FANCE FRANCK**

Photo by Andy Abrahamson.
Courtesy of Pucker Gallery, Boston.

**PORCELAIN BOWL
5½″D
COPPER RED GLAZE,
PG11
BY FANCE FRANCK**

Photo by Andy Abrahamson.
Courtesy of Pucker Gallery, Boston.

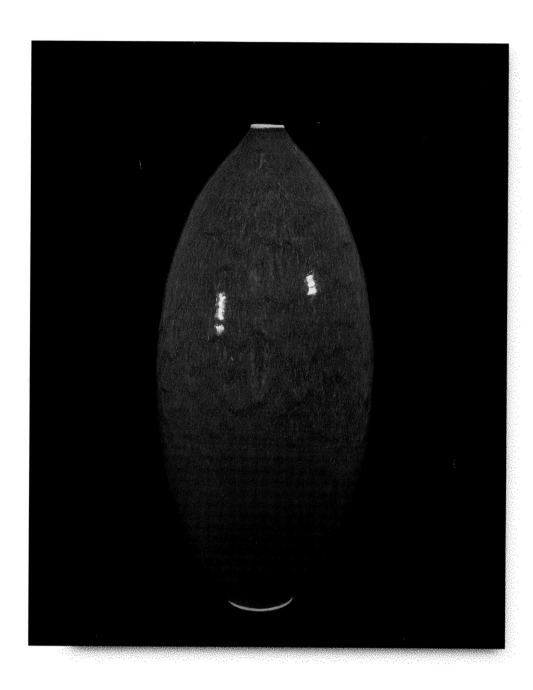

OVOID PORCELAIN VASE
BY BROTHER THOMAS BEZANSON

Rose red copper glaze, 19″, TH709.
Photo by Sean Kirby.
Courtesy of Pucker Gallery, Boston.

perature glazes lead is volatilized to a large extent and it may carry off copper with it or at least produce variable glaze compositions after high firing. Since lead is also susceptible to reduction, it is not a preferred component of copper red glazes. Lead can be used, but it is possible to get good-looking reds without it.

Boron, on the other hand, has been very useful to me for lowering the fusion temperature of glazes. Furthermore, it also lowers the coefficient of thermal expansion of glazes and can thus diminish the excessive crazing usually found in copper red glazes (due to their high alkali content). While boron does not attack ceramic bodies as actively as lead, it is volatile to a certain extent, and this is its major drawback. Ideally we would use glazes which are high in alkali to give us good colors and low melting points but practically this is not feasible because of the high expansion of alkali glazes as well as their poor durability. Boron additions improve both problems.

CONCLUSION

It can be seen that glasses and glazes of copper red type are quite dissimilar materials, and that they each have different problems. While there are some rules that apply to both glasses and glazes, and while they are both colored by the same copper chromophore the physical conditions in which glazes are formed contrast with those in which glasses are made. (In my vocabulary a glaze is usually a glass, but obviously most glasses are not glazes.)

Oh, my luve is like a red, red rose,
That's newly sprung in June;
Oh, my luve is like the melodie,
That's sweetly played in tune.

Robert Burns—A Red, Red Rose

23 SULFUR

This chapter is dedicated to Jim Cowan of the Corning Glass Works, who initiated these thoughts on the role of sulfur in copper red glazes.

The behavior of sulfur in copper red glazes could be two-fold. First, there is the possibility that it has a positive action as a stabilizer for the cuprous ion at high temperatures. Second, there is the certainty that sulfur has a strong negative action—either as a nucleating agent or as a secondary precipitate that destroys beautiful copper red colors.

Let us consider the possible positive action first.

STABILIZATION

In the formation of copper red **glazes** we commonly fire in reduction in the middle temperatures, before the glaze is sealed over. This technique unfortunately reduces all copper ions to copper metal. I say "unfortunately" because the glaze has yet to be melted and finished, and hence copper is appearing at the wrong time. If a finished glaze is quenched from 1250°C it is apparent that this reduction was too early, because no copper red shows up then.

It would be better if we could convert copper ions to the cuprous state so that the reaction with stannous oxide (or ferrous oxide) could occur when the glaze is cooled to the transformation range (600-800°C). Unfortunately, in the presence of hydrogen or carbon monoxide, copper ions will always be completely reduced to the metal. The dilemma is: how can cuprous ions be preserved; or be reformed in a cooling glaze?

In this situation we can examine a previous finding. In the Chinese underglaze sherd that was analyzed for Margaret Medley, Len Pruden noted that the droplets at the glaze-body interface consisted of a compound of copper and sulfur. Since this sample had been fired to high (ca. 1200°C) temperatures in reduction (as attested by the red color), I concluded that cuprous sulfide was the material of the droplets and that it is stable in a glaze, in reduction, at high temperatures. Weyl, in his book, also notes that cuprous sulfide is very stable in glasses.

So, although we might prefer to have cuprous **oxide**, we can have cuprous **sulfide** present in a finished glaze at high temperatures. The question of whether cuprous sulfide can be reduced to copper metal by stannous oxide, or whether it must first be converted to cuprous oxide via atmospheric oxidation, can be left as an exercise for some ceramist with a more sophisticated apparatus than mine.

Actually, there is some evidence from my experiments that a preliminary oxidation is necessary before reduction by stannous oxide can occur. When a sulfur-doped copper red glaze was cooled directly from a reduction firing, ugly colors resulted. However, if cooling was preceded by a high temperature oxidation step (1 hour at 1250°C), then a splendid red resulted.

DEGRADATION

While there may be some question about the role of sulfur in promoting good reds, there can be no doubt that sulfur, in almost any form, can sabotage our attempts at copper reds. In one test sequence that I ran, it was found that underglaze splashes, running the gamut from sulfur to sulfide to sulfate (in many varieties) always managed to produce ugly, off-colors when used in combination with my best ox blood glaze.

Since we usually do not add any sulfur-containing materials to glazes, the question is: where does sulfur come from to destroy our work?

A clue as to where some of the sulfur originates can be found by making a thin cross section of an average copper red glaze and then examining it with a microscope. When this is done, there is usually a bluish-grey layer to be found between the body and the central red layer.

This location of the blue color intimates that some contamination is originating from the body (although surface oxidation is also contributing to the localization of color).

An even more pronounced effect can be seen in a test where a sulfate is painted on the body before an ox blood glaze application. In this instance the red color becomes decidedly livery and in cross section the entire glaze coloration is blue-grey in transmitted light. Next, if this poor glaze is refired in oxidation, it will become a good red color and in cross section a fine red layer can be observed between the central region and the surface.

If this weren't indication enough that the average ceramic body contains sizable amounts of sulfur, then a test firing of an ox blood glaze over a pure silica body should certainly convince us. This test results in a fine copper red color and in cross section there is no evidence at all of a blue layer near the body.

It is thus obvious that sulfur can be detrimental and should be avoided. As to what the principal source of sulfur is, it will be variable. One commercial stoneware clay in the USA contains one fourth of a percent of sulfur, though obviously, high quality kaolins will have much less than that. One insidious source of sulfur in bodies is that found in slip cast or jiggered ware. This sulfur comes from the plaster (calcium sulfate) in which the body was formed. A third source of sulfur is the fuel used for firing. Natural gas, propane or butane should be low in sulfur, but not coal, wood, oil or manufactured gas. And lastly, the water supply may be contributing sulfur. A hard water source should always be suspect.

If I had my hundreds of experiments to do over again, I would use extremely pure raw materials and I would make all of my test pieces by hand on non-plaster bats. Then I would bisque fire the ware in oxidation and give all glost fires a long start in oxidation. But, who knows, perhaps the stabilizing influence of sulfur is worthwhile and an ultrapure operation might lead to other defects. In addition, it might be simpler to try to neutralize the sulfur effect. Perhaps it would be possible to tie sulfur up chemically with elements like zinc or barium and thus inactivate it. Maybe this is why Seger and Lauth and Dutailly used those elements in their glazes. I will leave it to you to try some of these experiments. Try making an ultrapure body and glaze, then try doping with sulfur to test its effect. And finally, add some barium carbonate and/or zinc oxide to see if the sulfur action can be neutralized.

Finally, to close this chapter, let me offer some reactions, comments and explanations from the literature and from experiments.

COMMENTS

One piece of information that can be deduced from the sulfur story is an explanation for poor colors in **low** temperature copper reds. Without an opportunity for high temperature oxidation of sulfides, low temperature glazes may always be plagued with cuprous sulfide discoloration. If this is true, then an extraordinary effort to remove sulfur might result in better low temperature glazes. Or, perhaps a very prolonged oxidation step at the top temperature might do the trick.

In quotes about ancient Chinese techniques it has been noted that they used a bisqued body in copper red production, whereas with other glazes they almost invariably used a raw body. We can imagine that in the bisquing operation any sulfur present in a clay (from organic matter) could be burned out by firing the bisqued ware in oxidation, so that sulfur could be converted to sulfur dioxide and pass out of the body. This might explain why the Chinese lost their ability to produce copper reds from time to time. A succeeding generation might not realize the importance of prefiring a body in oxidation.

This explanation also covers the use by Lauth and Dutailly (p. 247) of a **fired** body for copper red glazes. This would be even better as a base for copper reds, because all of the remaining sulfur would be fused in the body and there would be no tendency for sulfur to escape from the body. Thus by using a fully fired ware as the substrate, you might be able to get the best copper reds of all (other things being equal).

There is another possible reason why the Chinese may have lost the ability to make reds over the years, and that is that they may have had sources of clay or water that were either too high or too low in sulfur. I know that there are some American clays that are very high in sulfur. At one time an electric kiln firing almost drove us out of the house due to the evolution of sulfur dioxide from this clay during the bisquing operation. Thus a change from low to high sulfur clay might just be enough to ruin copper red production. Similarly a change from river water to well water might be enough to tip the scales against good copper reds.

Sulfur emanating from the body also explains the fact that we often have trouble with blue colors next to the body. Mellor and others have commented on this and I have found it to be invariably true in observations on thin sections. The place where the bluish color appears is always between the copper red layer and the body.

In addition to the above, we find that the sulfur explanation accounts for the fact that a silica body is an ideal substrate for copper red glazing and does not produce a bluish color between the body and the copper red layer of the glaze. One would expect that silica would have practically no sulfide or sulfate content.

We can also see why Seger used the technique of alternate oxidation and reduction firing during his formation of copper red glazes. We can imagine that he could form sulfur dioxide and sulfides as he alternately oxidized and reduced. This treatment would not have been necessary as far as the copper in the glaze was concerned, but it might have been extremely useful for the elimination of body sulfur.

Next, one can consider that the action of the final oxidation firing is not so much in its effect on copper, but in its influence on the sulfide. It may be oxidizing the glaze enough so that copper sulfide is oxidized to sulfate. In this case particulate matter might be converted to solubles with a resulting diminution of tinctorial power.

As mentioned before, the sulfur theory explains some of my troubles from using a slip cast body. Every once in a while a rogue glaze would show up which didn't seem to fit in at all with previous experiments. This may have been due to the use of a body that was either exceptionally high or low in sulfate, resulting in divergent effects.

Weyl, in his book COLOURED GLASSES, mentions that cuprous sulfide is very insoluble in glasses. This could explain the presence of bluish particles in a multilayered copper red glaze. It could also explain the location of this blue layer beneath the red layer. We can imagine, as Mellor has stated, that there is an oxidation gradient from the outside inward. The most oxidized layer is near the surface, and it gradually becomes more reduced as we go down into the glaze, so that as the body is approached a more reduced region is reached and this is where cuprous sulfide would be present.

Weyl also notes that sometimes one adds alkali or zinc to a glass to stabilize sulfur at high temperatures. If sulfur happens to be necessary for the reoxidation of copper metal (which may be the case), then this explains why a high alkali content is useful in copper red glazes. It could contribute to better reds if sulfur is a necessary element for converting copper metal to cuprous oxide which will later be reduced by stannous oxide to copper metal in the transformation temperature region.

Weyl, in referring to the insolubility of copper sulfide, remarks that in some instances cuprous sulfide would be an aid in providing nuclei for the precipitation of other materials. His comment is that in some glasses it is desirable to have fine particles of copper sulfide present so that cadmium sulfide can precipitate from solution around these nuclei. One could imagine a situation in a copper glaze where no nuclei at all would be present, with the result that either no precipitation would occur, or only a few large crystals might result. On the other hand, a **tiny** amount of copper sulfide in the form of many small nuclei might be just what is required for color development.

This leads us to the feeling that sulfur may be good as well as bad for copper glazes. It may be bad if there is too much of it, but it may be good if it takes part in the oxidation of copper metal (which has to be present at 1250°C after reduction). If it participates in a mild oxidation reaction for the formation of cuprous ion and thus causes cuprous ion to be present in order to react with stannous ion at temperatures in the annealing range, then that is useful.

So that this section doesn't end on a negative note, let us consider one other situation. If sulfur is a bad influence on our glazes, then this is another reason why it is easier to make copper red glasses than copper red glazes. Glass raw materials, being purer than glaze and body raw materials, could lead to better reds.

Actually there are many other possible comments that could be made—for instance with respect to Ebell's remarks on the haziness of copper red glasses—but these will be left for the reader to consider.

Since it is always wise to test a hypothesis, I would recommend that you try some sulfur tests to see what effect this element has on your glazes. I tried an underglaze wash test of several materials with sulfur in them. Using a paint brush, several stripes of different compounds were painted down the side of a test cup, until there were 6-12 stripes on the cup, then it was coated with a glaze which normally gave a good ox blood color. You might try a similar experiment, or you might try adding adding dabs of plaster, cuprous sulfide, etc. as test contaminants. You should find that sulfur is not beneficial. The question is: how little sulfur is necessary to cause some of our defects; and, is this within the range of the contaminant level in some of our raw materials?

Naturally I would like to be able to say that sulfur is the hidden culprit in all of the copper red problems, because it would be such a simple answer and would allow me to get out of a great number of tight corners. Whenever someone called me up and said: "Hey, I tried your glazes and they really didn't perform as specified." I could then say: "Well, you've probably got sulfur in your water supply." But, this is never 100% true. I think that you will find that sulfur is merely one of the numerous bad actors that we can suspect when we have difficulties in our copper red glazing; and it is just one more item to be aware of.

Sparkling and bright in liquid light
Does the wine our goblets gleam in;
With hue as red as the rosy bed
Which a bee would choose to dream in.

Charles F. Hoffman—*Sparkling and Bright*

24 PHASE SEPARATION

INTRODUCTION

It would be helpful if it weren't necessary to delve into the intricacies of phase separation in glasses (or glazes), but phase separation is a process that takes place during the formation of copper reds, so it must be considered for an understanding of these glazes. As a start, it must be emphasized that copper reds are not "solution" colors. The cause of color in a copper red glass is a dispersion of **very** fine copper particles in a glassy matrix. If the particles are too large, the color will be poor. If the particles are too small, there will be no color at all. Therefore, a procedure which gives the proper size copper grains is necessary for the production of good copper red glazes.

The delicacy that is required to make a copper red glaze is caused by the fact that the required particle size is extraordinarily fine. The preferred crystallite size is in the neighborhood of 20-200 Angstrom units (1 Angstrom = 1 hundred millionth of a centimeter). Since the wavelength of green light is 5500 Angstrom units, you can see that the copper red particles are far below the resolution limits of optical systems. Thus, there is always a certain amount of faith required to believe some of the facts about copper reds. The instruments which will detect the particles are not capable of expressing their results in color, and the instruments which recognize color are not capable of resolving the particles. Therefore, caution is needed when interpreting some of the experimental results. I personally believe that the following description of the copper red system is the correct one: first, that the coloring particles are made up of copper metal (and not an oxide or a silicate); next, that these particles should preferably have a size range of 20-200 Angstroms; and finally that a combination of these two factors is needed to form good copper red glasses and glazes.

THE CONCEPT OF PHASE SEPARATION

There are many phase separation phenomena which can be seen in everyday life, from mayonnaise, to fudge, to mists. Recognizing that there are three common phases of matter: gaseous, liquid and solid, it can be anticipated that there would be nine possibilities if we took these three items two at a time. However, since the gas-in-gas combination is always molecular, this eliminates the possibility of one type of dispersion, and therefore there are only eight types of phase separated systems. These are:

1. *Gas bubbles in a liquid.(foam)*
2. *Gas bubbles in a solid.(pumice)*
3. *Liquid droplets in a gas.(fog)*
4. *Liquid droplets in a solid.(water in butter)*
5. *Immiscible liquid droplets in another liquid.(mayonnaise)*
6. *Solid particles in a gas.(dust in air)*
7. *Solid particles in a liquid.(gold in water)*
8. *Solid particles in another solid.(some alloys)*

The easiest way for one phase to develop by precipitation in another is for it to form on some kind of nucleus. Without nuclei, a new phase is reluctant to form. Unfortunately, high temperature glass systems are nearly nuclei-free because of the tremendous fluxing capability of most glasses. When they are completely molten there are virtually no nuclei present (which is one of the reasons for the occurrence of the glassy state). Glasses are unstable at room temperature and should be crystalline, but because of their high viscosity and the lack of nuclei, the glassy state exists. Some basic problems in copper red glazes—and in most other phase separation situations—are: the formation of nuclei in the proper number; their formation in the proper size; and their formation in a proper distribution.

If the ideal case for the generation of phase separation in a glass were given, it might be stated in the following way:

1. *A glass would be formed by heating the raw materials to such a high temperature that they would be fluid and completely homogeneous.*
2. *The next preferred step would be to cool the glass quickly to room temperature, so that there would be no chance for either nucleation or crystallization.*
3. *Then the temperature of the rigid glass would be increased to a point in the annealing region where nucleation could occur.*
4. *After the desired number of nuclei had formed, the temperature would be raised slightly to move into a crystallization zone, where the temperature would be held until the preferred number of crystals appeared.*
5. *Finally, after the desired structure had been obtained, the article would be cooled to room temperature.*

In the field of glass-ceramics it is possible to use this sequence. Unfortunately these steps are not practical for ceramics. With glass articles the glass can be cooled through the annealing zone to a lower temperature before initiating nucleation and crystal growth. With ceramics and their glazes, this is a difficult task because the thermal conditions which are conducive to quenching, nucleation and crystal growth in the glaze are inappropriate for the ceramic body on which the glaze is formed. Normally, this type of thermal sequence cannot be followed with pottery. The usual procedure with a ceramic is to cool it slowly, so that at crystal inversion points no fractures will occur in the body. Thus, the glaze, instead of being taken through a nucleation zone and **then** through a crystallization zone, goes through the reverse order. On cooling, it passes through a crystallization zone and **then** through the nucleation zone. If these two regions overlap, it is possible for nuclei to form and for crystals to grow on these nuclei. But, it can be seen that this is not a preferred route for the glaze to take. The result is: that a glaze system must be picked very carefully so the overlap will be appropriate, and so that crystals will not grow too large. If copper crystals grow beyond a maximum of 200 Angstroms, then poor copper red colors will be the result. It is a very delicate situation.

THE CHEMISTRY

There are two ways to form fine copper metal particles in a glass. The first technique is to reduce copper oxide in the porous glaze and then bring the glaze up to the melting point. When this glaze is cooled at an appropriate rate, the copper can grow to the desired size. A second way of forming copper metal in glass is to have a chemical reaction which occurs during the cooling process. One such desirable reaction is the one which occurs between cuprous oxide and stannous oxide to give copper metal and stannic oxide.

$$(1) \qquad Cu_2O + SnO = 2 Cu^\circ + SnO_2.$$

That equation (1) represents a desirable reaction is brought out by the fact that nearly every modern worker in the copper red field recommends the use of tin oxide as an auxiliary agent in the formation of copper reds. And practice has also convinced me of the fact that tin is a desirable element to have present in the formation of these colors. It can be assumed that reaction (1) occurs at desirable temperatures for the formation of small copper particles and thus good copper red colors can be obtained.

GLASSES VERSUS GLAZES

As is mentioned in the chapter "Glasses versus Glazes," there is a vast difference between the average glaze and the ideal glass, since ideal glasses are uniform in composition. Although uniformity would be a desirable condition for glazes also, it is impossible in practice. In glazes we are faced with a very corrosive material in contact with a ceramic body of a different composition. Therefore, at the ceramic-glaze interface, there will be a great deal of reaction; also, there will be diffusion of body materials into the glaze and diffusion of glaze materials into the body. Thus, there will be a fairly large transition zone at most glaze-body interfaces. Whether we like this situation or not, it has to be true, for if there were not a good reaction between the glaze and the body, then the glaze would not adhere well.

Furthermore, since glaze-making occurs at a high temperature (ca. 1200°C), there is also the possibility of volatilization of material from the glaze surface. Although there are ways to avoid this problem (by providing elements in the atmosphere to compensate for the loss of these same elements from the glaze), nevertheless it is almost impossible to balance this loss exactly and there is usually a net loss from the glaze surface. For this reason, a composition will exist on the surface of the glaze which is different from that in the center.

We see then that every glaze is a sandwich, in which the original composition of the glaze will be found only in the "filling." This is why almost every copper ruby glaze is only red in the center of the glaze.

Obviously, if too thin a glaze is made, it will consist of only two zones—a glaze-body interface zone and an upper zone where volatilization has occurred. There will not be enough room for a red central zone. This one of the reasons why a glaze must be selected carefully and must be applied in the correct thickness. If too thin a glaze is made, it will be extremely difficult to get any red color to appear at all, no matter what the concentration of copper may be.

SUMMARY

In concluding comments on phase separation in copper reds, it may be stated that it is desirable to choose an appropriate base glaze. Primarily, it would be a glaze which is amenable to phase separation (i.e., the glaze would not have so much alumina present that the viscosity would be high enough to impede phase separation). Secondly, the correct concentration of copper should be selected so that the colloidal copper particles do not grow large enough to give poor coloration. And third, an auxiliary element (tin or iron) should be present to provide the reaction with cuprous oxide to give copper metal particles in the appropriate temperature range. And, in addition to all this, a practical firing schedule must be selected in order that copper will be reduced to the metal early in the firing, but that later the copper metal will be reoxidized to cuprous ions so that they can react with either stannous or ferrous ions to give copper metal in a finely dispersed form.

AFTERTHOUGHTS

One final cautionary note must be given here about something that is found in the literature on glass-ceramics. The discovery of these useful materials came about during work on a **metal** nucleated glass! It was discovered, by Dr. S. D. Stookey, that copper metal nuclei could form sites for further nucleation of the entire glass mass. To form one type of glass-ceramic, it was necessary to have copper or gold nuclei present; then further crystal growth could take place on these metal sites. The importance of this discovery is that we must be cautious about the kind of glazes that we select, so that an easily crystallizable glaze will not be used. Such a crystallizable glaze could precipitate once copper nuclei formed. Then a glaze could result which was completely white due to crystallization of the glassy material on the copper nuclei.

Oh green is the colour of faith and truth,
And rose the colour of love and youth,
And brown of the fruitful clay.

Charles Kingsley—Dartside

25 MECHANISMS FOR COPPER RED FORMATION

This chapter on the mechanisms of glaze formation will be concerned with many of the items which are taken up in greater detail in other chapters, but here the factors will be brought together in one place. In this way it is hoped that a better overall understanding of the process of copper red formation will be had.

As a starting point, the glaze materials should be well ground and mixed so that unnecessary problems can be avoided. Also, the well-blended glaze batch should be applied as uniformly as possible on a piece of bisqued ceramic. An exception to the uniform application rule will be found when one wishes to apply thicker layers near the top of a piece to compensate for the flow which occurs during glaze formation.

The body on which the glaze is applied should preferably be bisqued, so that there will be a minimum of blemishes. It is quite likely that a raw body could be used, but the extra defects which would be caused by this technique would merely add more problems to this already over-fussy glaze.

When firing commences, it should begin at a slow rate, in order to avert avoidable flaws. Whether the initial firing is in oxidation or reduction is not a matter of great importance, although I normally use a light reduction from the beginning, merely for convenience. As the temperature of firing gradually increases, we can observe a number of phenomena occurring. Some of these are physical, some chemical, some thermal, and some combination effects. One of the first things that occurs is the removal of water from the hydrated materials in the glaze and in the body. This is one of the reasons why a slow approach should be used, so that gas evolution from the body can be nearly complete by the time the glaze is sealed over. In this way, we can avoid some of the bubble formation that leads to nonuniformity in copper reds.

After water removal, the next chemical reaction will be the decomposition of calcium carbonate and copper carbonate into their oxide forms with the evolution of carbon dioxide. These reactions should occur over an extended temperature span, copper oxide being formed first, and later calcium oxide at temperatures of 800-900°C. These decompositions leave both copper oxide and calcium oxide in highly reactive states, at rather high temperatures, so they will be quite prone to react with other materials in the glaze batch and also in areas where they contact the body. Wherever glaze contacts the body, calcium oxide will react strongly with it. Fortunately calcium ions are not very mobile so there won't be much diffusion of calcium to the glaze-body interface, but there will be **some** reaction there. Another effect will be the release of alkali metal oxide by double decomposition reactions between calcium oxide and both the frit and feldspar in the glaze batch. This will produce sodium oxide and potassium oxide, which will be free to volatilize at the glaze surface and to react with the body at the glaze-body interface. It would be nice to be able to prevent this reaction, but I doubt if it could be done. Even if we used a completely fritted glaze, the high alkalinity of the glaze would result in the diffusion of sodium and potassium oxides.

With the liberation of calcium oxide and its reaction with the glaze materials, liquifaction of the glaze has begun. After this point we must be certain that the glaze atmosphere is definitely reducing. It need not be strongly reducing, because copper oxide is easily reduced to copper metal, but it does need to be completely reducing.

Because of the tenacity with which some of the gases are held in the body, it will be found that after the glaze has begun to liquify, there will continue to be bubble formation from the body as well as from the glaze itself. Hence, it will be difficult to avoid porosity in the glaze. There will always be some gas evolution, and this has to escape through the glaze. These bubbles will have a sort of mixing effect on the glaze, and if we had a more uniform system, this would be beneficial. Unfortunately, once the glaze has started to react with itself and with the body, it will become more and more nonuniform with the elapse of time. Any bubble which escapes and passes through the glaze will be forming striae as it goes through the various glaze layers.

The layering of the glaze is best understood through an examination of alkali migration. Alkali is lost from the outer surface of the glaze, evaporating into the atmosphere so the outer surface will be short of alkali. Meanwhile, the glaze laying next to the body will lose alkali though diffusion **into** the body, and this also will become an alkali deficient layer. Hence, even if no other events were occurring, our glaze would be a **three** layer sandwich. These layers are not uniform by any criterion, especially on a vertical surface, because the glaze will run off the uneven body surface and will become streaked due to these irregularities.

It is always depressing to see a nonuniform glaze after you have gone to great lengths to make a well-mixed batch. It is also hard to understand this until you realize what **unmixing** effects are taking place. The worst culprit in our system is the bubble movement through the glaze, carrying various layers into one another. This is the effect which produces hare's fur variations on the surface. It provides many irregularities, which, though sometimes pleasing to the eye, are more often distracting when one is trying to get a uniform glaze.

One experiment which is useful to try, and which you may sometimes do inadvertently, is that of pulling samples from the kiln after various degrees of firing. This allows you to understand what is happening to the glaze at various stages. One of the most interesting copper red glazes that I have is one that I fired to only 1150°C, using a glaze that should have matured at about 1250°C. The glaze was a real horror after being fired to 100°C less than the requisite temperature. Instead of being a deep red—which the composition should have given—it was, instead, a horrible matte pink color. And, rather than being a smooth glaze, it was exceedingly streaked. It had the typical "alligator skin" appearance that was so well described in Plumer's book on Temmokus. This is the kind of ware that he found on the sherd heaps of the Temmoku kilns in Fukien province, China. Plumer correctly assumed that these "alligator skin" glazes were underfired, but it is startling to see all of the large cracks in the glaze and all of the horrible colors that result when the glaze has not been completely fused.

Another experiment along these lines is the removal from the kiln of a copper red glaze at the **highest** point of the firing when the furnace is about to be turned off. In such a case, the glaze may be smooth and have good physical features, but the color will be missing from the copper red if it is quenched quickly from a high temperature. This is a startling thing to observe, but it should be tried at least once so that you can get an idea of the mechanics of copper red formation.

In this description of the mechanisms of glaze formation we really have two subject headings: one is the formation of the glaze as one would describe it for any normal glaze; the other is copper red formation as a distinct circumstance. Hence, we should emphasize this second part of the mechanism now.

COPPER RED FORMATION

At rather low temperatures, copper carbonate will decompose to copper oxide and carbon dioxide, presumably much below the temperature at which calcium carbonate decomposes. Also, in a reducing atmosphere, copper oxides will be readily reduced to copper metal, which will **not** be very finely dispersed. Copper metal will be scattered around in clumps corresponding to the clumps of copper oxide (that could be readily observed with an optical microscope). It will definitely not be found in the form of an atomic dispersion at these early stages, but it **will** be in the form of copper metal. The possibility of the reduction process being so delicately controlled that **cuprous** oxide would be formed is extremely unlikely.

With rising temperatures, copper metal will start to disperse slightly because of its vapor pressure but this will not occur to a marked degree. If we consider the copper-containing glaze at the final (maximum) temperature, just before the kiln is turned off, the copper should be disseminated in metallic form in the glaze. But, it will definitely **not** be uniformly dispersed, because it does not have a high vapor pressure at 1250°C. We can see problems arising even before the red color has begun to form, because at this stage (as you will find out if you pull a sample from the kiln) the glaze is transparent and has no red color.

As an aside, let us now think about the auxiliary agents that we add to a glaze to improve the copper red coloration. We could use either tin oxide or iron oxide to accomplish our result, but let's consider only tin oxide because it does give some of the best red colors.

Stannic oxide is a refractory material, and will not thermally decompose at the temperatures of glaze formation. However, in a reducing atmosphere there is the probability that stannous oxide will be formed. This is slightly questionable, but some of my experiments have indicated that the mechanism of copper red formation requires the presence of stannous oxide, so for this reason it can be assumed that at least some stannous oxide has been formed because of the reducing atmosphere in which it has been fired. Thus, when we look at the glaze at its highest temperature, we see that in addition to copper, there is stannous oxide dispersed in the glaze. This oxide, however, is not mobile, because stannous ion is divalent. Therefore, it behooves us to have it well dispersed at the start, because it will not move around like copper does.

At this moment, consider that we are at the maximum glaze temperature. Summarizing, we have a liquid glaze in contact with the atmosphere and a porous body. Because of this the glaze will be layered. The glaze also has bubbles passing through it, so it will be streaked to some extent too. At this maximum temperature there is copper metal (liquid) dispersed in the glaze; and there are also stannous ions in the glaze. We now need to do a bit of manipulation to improve the red color formation. What we need to do is: continue the firing at the maximum temperature, but in oxidation instead of reduction. This needs to be done because the desired reaction is not the coagulation of copper atoms that are floating around by themselves—because if this happens it will be found that the particles will be of large size and ugly colors will appear. Instead, a more subtle reaction is needed, such as the one between cuprous oxide and stannous oxide:

$$Cu_2O + SnO = 2 Cu° + SnO_2,$$

which will form copper metal in very finely dispersed form. Since copper metal is already present in the glaze, it needs to be converted to cuprous oxide so that it can react with stannous oxide and precipitate on an atomic scale. This is the reason for a final firing in oxygen.

The mechanism for this slight oxidation of copper metal to cuprous oxide can occur because of the fact that cuprous ions are mobile in glass. They are univalent and of the correct size, and hence can migrate easily in a glass. A mechanism that I am fond of, is the one in which copper metal diffuses to the surface, is oxidized there by air, and then diffuses back into the glaze in the form of cuprous ion. If the copper metal is oxidized too far (i.e. to cupric ion) at the surface, it can then react with copper metal to again form cuprous ion which can diffuse back in. Thus, rather than having oxygen moving in and out of the glaze, we have cuprous ion swimming around, carrying the charges and performing the necessary messenger boy operations. You may worry that stannous oxide will be reoxidized to stannic oxide at this time, but it will not, because of the divalency of the stannous oxide (which is not mobile). So, for the most part it will remain in place as stannous oxide. Therefore, after a final firing in oxygen, we are ready to turn off the kiln and observe what happens as cooling occurs.

Itemizing: a stratified liquid glaze is present and in this liquid there is some copper metal, some cuprous ions, some stannous ions, and no doubt some stannic ions. Then, as this glaze is cooled, reactions will occur and physical movement of ions will take place. The movable materials in the glaze as it cools down are: the alkali ions, the cuprous ions, the copper atoms (to a slight extent) and that is about all.

Finally, as cooling starts, a point will be reached where the viscosity of the glaze is appropriate, where thermal conditions are ripe for reactions, and where nucleation of copper metal can begin. In the first stage, copper atoms will agglomerate in very small clusters—perhaps in clumps of 2-5 atoms. If the temperature is too high, these clusters will break up. But, as the temperature slowly goes down, the clusters will tend to get bigger and will accumulate more and more copper atoms until a stable nucleus is formed. With further cooling, crystals will grow, until at a diameter of 50-200 Angstroms there will be absorption of light and a red color will be transmitted. Obviously, if the crystals grow too much, more light will be absorbed and ugly colors will be produced.

If the glaze were completely uniform, then operations could be adjusted so that a perfect red color would result. But, as you have already seen, a layered glaze is present in which the composition is nonuniform. Thus, a copper red with an optimum color will only be found in certain zones. These good copper red colors are usually found in the central zone of the glaze—especially on the side towards the surface. As the surface is approached a clear colorless area is found, while as the body is approached, distortions of the red color are to be noted. In a transmitted light view of a thin section, bluish colors may be noted near the body in association with visible particles. While, if a cross section is examined in reflected light a coppery metallic look can be observed in the lower layers of the glaze. The latter phenomenon is due to the growth of copper particles to sizes that are too big to transmit light. In this range of particle sizes, reflection is occurring to an increased extent. The particles that are detected with the light microscope are of relatively large size (on the order of thousands of Angstroms). When electron microscopy is used it will be found that good copper red glazes have particles in them with a size range of from 20-100 Angstroms.

These, then, are some of the reactions that occur physically, thermally and chemically during copper red glaze formation. And this is why some of the observed effects occur. If we could arrange affairs so that only a thin layer of fine copper red crystals would exist in the center of a glaze, then a very beautiful, transparent ruby red would result. But, because of irregularities from these several effects, it is rare that a uniform, transparent copper ruby color will be found.

The violet loves a sunny bank,
The cowslip loves the lea;
The scarlet creeper loves the elm,
But I love—thee.

Bayard Taylor—Proposal

26 RAW MATERIALS

Copper red glazes are basically reduction-fired high temperature glazes, therefore they are normally feldspathic in character. For a starting formula, one could use something as simple as Seger's cone 5 composition, but with a lower clay content. Or, a simple feldspar-lime-silica mixture with added copper and tin oxides would make a fine copper red glaze in reduction. The problem with such a basic glaze is that it must be fired to a high temperature and, since copper can be lost by volatilization, other additions should be made to this base glaze.

Seger, when speaking of copper red glazes, mentioned the technique of mixing one of his porcelain glazes with a frit, in the proportion of 3:1, as the base glaze for copper reds. I, too, have found this to be a practical glaze, although my frit is quite different from his. The frit addition lowers the final firing temperature and also minimizes glaze attack on the body.

The frit that I use is Pemco P-25 (a soda-potash-alumino-borosilicate), although a commercial product is not absolutely necessary. One could use an additive such as colemanite or any other combination which would lower the final firing temperature. The mere addition of several different components in low concentrations could have this same effect. It would be possible to add a percent or two of magnesia, zinc oxide, baria, lithium spar, or a fluoride and get an acceptable red glaze. The common glaze that I use for making an ox blood color is the following: 50 parts Custer feldspar; 30 parts Minusil-5 silica; 20 parts limestone; 27 parts P-25 frit; 1 part copper carbonate; and 2 parts tin oxide.

One characteristic of a glaze such as this one is that once you get good results from this formula, it is hard to avoid getting a good copper red glaze. The addition of minor amounts of other elements does not seem to affect the outcome.

Looking at the components of this suggested glaze, it is possible to comment on their roles and their desirable characteristics. Starting out with feldspar, I have become accustomed to using feldspars with about 10% potash in them. If one uses a soda spar instead of a potash spar, the copper red color tends to become orange and this is less pleasing to the eye than a ruby red. The addition of a lithium-containing feldspar, such as spodumene, has been suggested, and at one time I was convinced of its usefulness. But, after a number of experiments, I found that the above glaze gives just as good a color as one containing lithium. And, since lithium is both scarce and expensive, it is just as well to avoid spodumene.

Another base material for our glaze is silica. Due to the absence of clay in the batch, I have found it useful to employ a finely ground silica. One called "Minusil 5" is very satisfactory because it aids in the adhesion of the dried glaze to the body, and it is also good because it dissolves completely during the firing process. If a coarse silica is used, then a fair amount remains undissolved and the glaze composition is not quite what has been calculated. Probably an average silica could be improved for use in this glaze by ball milling it for an extended period of time. Although, if adhesion is no problem, then an ordinary silica can be used.

The next common component of our glaze is calcium carbonate, which should be used in the amount that I recommend. If the quantity of lime is increased to any extent, a bluish opal will appear instead of a good red color. Calcium carbonate also has one other drawback besides the blue tendency, and that is that it encourages attack of the body. For these two reasons, the amount of lime should be kept moderate.

For the same reason, the next ingredient—the frit—should be selected with its calcium content in mind. If the percentage of calcium carbonate plus calcium in the frit is too high, then you will be back into the problem of getting a blue opalescent appearance. Other than that, the frit should be low in alumina—to avoid a pink or orange color—and it should have only moderate amounts of boron, because this element can also lead to opal formation and blue tints.

The tin oxide that is put in the glaze should amount to about twice the concentration of the copper oxide. I would say that copper should be kept at as low a level as possible, because excess copper always gives ugly, dark red colors. On the other hand, too little copper will give no color, so this is a delicate balance, and once the copper concentration has been selected, then twice its weight of tin oxide can be added. As to how these two components should be placed in the glaze, one can smugly answer that they should be fritted. This is an extra (and difficult) step though, and is not absolutely essential. I have found that mixing a **color batch** containing copper carbonate, tin oxide and a portion of the frit will lead to good copper red colors. This mixture should be ground well and then be dispersed thoroughly in the batch. It is particularly important to have the tin oxide dispersed well. Copper is so mobile, both as an ion and as a vapor that there is not much difficulty in spreading it around, but tin oxide does not move at all in a glaze and it should be well mixed.

As mentioned before, clay should be omitted from this glaze if at all possible. If necessary, it can be added to the extent of 1-2% (perhaps as a bentonite addition). If the literature is examined for glaze recipes, one of the most striking things to be noted is that clay is either absent or is in low concentrations in almost every glaze listed by people who promise good copper red results.

Returning once more to copper, I have generally used copper carbonate as a copper source because of its fine, soft texture. It does have a variable copper content though (from 50-75%), and should be evaluated by testing. One also likes the carbonate because of the feeling that, during the thermal decomposition, it will form a reactive copper oxide which will contribute to good reactions with other glaze ingredients and will lead to good mixing in the finished glaze.

Minor elements are not as much of a problem as they are in some delicately colored glazes. Contaminants do not cause such wide variations in copper colors as they do in celadons for example, because copper gives such an intense red. Actually there is little need to worry about most of our raw materials because the ingredients used will be rather pure. The feldspars are relatively clean, as are the silicas, the limestones and the frits. Since we are avoiding the use of clay, we do not have to worry about the impurities that often appear in this material.

One interesting experiment that I ran was the addition of a percent of each of many different common contaminant oxides (one at a time) to a good ox blood glaze batch. In these tests it was found that no contaminant in the range of 1% will cause much of a color change in a standard ox blood copper red. When a frit is picked, there is not much of a problem if it has a percent or so of zinc, barium, lithium, fluoride or magnesium, because things like that will not upset the balance in the average copper red glaze.

Roses red and roses white
Plucked I for my love's delight.
She would none of all my posies—
Bade me gather her blue roses.

Rudyard Kipling—Blue Roses

27 GLAZE THICKNESS

Just as firing time and firing temperature are intimately related, so are glaze thickness and several other parameters. But, we have to consider items like this individually in order to have logical breaks in our descriptions. Obviously there will be times when repetition will occur, but it is hoped that this will help in imbedding facts rather than in leading to boredom.

The importance of glaze thickness may be realized by observations on both a gross and a microscopic scale. Whenever copper red glazes are too thin, there will be a tendency to lose the red color completely. In the reverse situation an overthick glaze would result in a dark—even black—color. Therefore, if one desires to make a transparent copper red glaze of just the right shade of color, it is found to be difficult because of the narrow thickness range that must be maintained.

A casual observation of almost any copper red vessel brings out one striking feature, and that is the great tendency for copper red glazes to be white (i.e., clear) in the top portions of ware. In fact, if one wants to obtain completely red ceramic objects, it would be advisable to spend much time contemplating the design of the object, because tall forms will almost inevitably have clear areas at the top unless extraordinary efforts are made to control glaze thickness and firing conditions. It must be noted that copper red glazes are definitely not like cobalt glazes or oxidized copper glazes. As the thickness of a red glaze diminishes, there comes a point where the color completely disappears. This is in contradistinction to cobalt blue glazes, for instance, where, with decreasing thickness, the blue color becomes paler and paler, yet is always in evidence.

Examination at high magnification will illustrate why this vanishing act occurs with copper reds. In copper red glazes, the color is a sandwich affair. The red is present in the central zone of the glaze, while on both the surface and next to the body it tends to be clear. This has even led some casual observers to hypothesize that the glaze must be applied in the form of three layers. A few experiments have convinced me that the layered structure is entirely normal and is not due to the application of separate layers. This layered effect can be observed on a fractured surface with a hand lens at 10X magnification, but it is very noticeable at 100X, using thin sections and observing with an optical microscope.

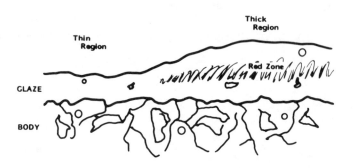

The clear glaze layer next to the body is evidently due to reaction of the glaze with the body and extraction of material (presumably alumina) which impedes the formation of copper reds. A clear zone at the surface seems to be best explained by the concept of volatilization of copper from the surface. Knowing these two facts, it should be possible to eliminate the effect. And, this can be done. But whether one wants to go to the extra effort, or whether one wants to merely control the thickness of the glaze is a personal decision. I have made copper red glazes on bodies that were 100% silica, and in such cases it was found that there was no clear glaze layer next to the body. Thus one might hope that by applying a slip to a clay body, that a clear layer between the glaze and the ware could be eliminated. The problem of course is the fact that a silica layer would have to be fairly thick, so that the body wouldn't be able to migrate through the silica. And, this thickness of silica would be rather hard to obtain because of the granularity of silica particles when compared to the fine, platy nature of the body particles (with the attendant difference in contraction during drying and firing processes). If you are able to make a silica slip and have it adhere to a body through all stages of fabrication and firing, then this would be a reasonable course to follow.

As for the clear zone at the surface of the copper red glaze, one might hope to eliminate this by means of copper washes on the inside of saggers. If one could provide the proper wash, so that the vaporization of copper from the inside of the sagger would exactly balance the loss of copper from the glaze, then one might be able to avoid the outer clear layer. It would seem logical that the application of some copper red glaze to the inside of the sagger would accomplish this, but I suspect that the actual use of this technique would not be straightforward. For instance, the loss of copper from a glaze is undoubtedly non-linear with respect to time and temperature. Therefore it is probable that while the loss of copper would be accelerated for a while during the firing process, that there would also be a contrary effect due to the fact that less and less copper would be available. Thus there would be a complex curve for the loss of copper from the glaze and maintaining a balanced copper gain and loss would be difficult.

It is unfortunate that an increase in copper concentration will not compensate for the clear inner and outer zones, but experiments which I have run show that thickness is not directly correlated with concentration in copper reds of a standard color. I have used increasing concentrations of copper in varying thicknesses and found that even at high concentrations of copper, there can be a dearth of copper red if the glaze is very thin. Thus there is a problem which can be met only by using a moderate glaze thickness and techniques that are available to maintain it uniformly over a body.

Obviously there are going to be variations in glaze thickness, but it behooves us to try and minimize them. When the usual techniques for applying glaze to a body are considered, it can be assumed that dipping would be one of the poorest, because it would not be easy to vary the thickness on a piece in relation to the tendency for the glaze to run off the body. In other words, by dipping it would be hard to provide a considerable thickness of copper red glaze at the top of a vessel and do it in a graded fashion so that there wouldn't be noticeable lines of demarcation. The next best technique would be to brush the glaze on so that one could blend the thickness of the glaze more carefully with the vertical features of the ware. Obviously the best way to control thickness and to vary it in relation to the shape and size of our ware would be to use spraying. I think that this would be the recommended technique for applying uniform copper red colors.

The relation of firing temperature to glaze thickness is of course extremely important. One must do everything possible to avoid the case of overfiring where there is a lot of running of the glaze. Such running would be caused either by too high a temperature, or by too long a firing time.

The glaze composition would also be important for control of the glaze viscosity. Primarily, one must avoid too high a flux content. Lime is an important flux in copper red glazes, but alkali is even more influential in making fluid glazes. Thus we must moderate the tendency to use excessive amounts of alkali—even though alkalies seem to improve the copper red color. Also, it would be desirable to have a relatively refractory and viscous glaze, so that it would maintain a uniformly thick layer on the ware. Unfortunately the best material for controlling refractoriness and viscosity is alumina, and this substance seems to be the number one plague as far as copper reds are concerned. Therefore, we must go to the next best material—silica—and use it in varying particle sizes and varying concentrations in order to provide the viscosity and refractoriness that are desirable for maintaining the appropriate thickness combined with good color.

Since it is advisable to have the firing proceed as rapidly and at as low a temperature as possible, it would be well to frit as much of the glaze as is reasonable, so that the glaze will already be melted and will be ready to be consolidated. It is appropriate that a fritted glaze needs to be sprayed on, when it is remembered that the spraying process is the preferred one to provide the correct glaze thickness on the ware. The only problem with fritting is that since a viscous, refractory glaze is desired, it will obviously be necessary to have a rather high-firing frit. But this is a criteria that has to be accepted.

As was mentioned previously, some workers have postulated that Chinese copper red glazes were applied in layers—thus giving a stratified appearance in the finished glaze. We have shown that the strata **could** be caused by natural glaze generation mechanisms, but we have not demonstrated (and probably could not demonstrate) that the Chinese copper red glazes **were not** made by use of layering techniques.

Therefore, the next step must be to ask ourselves: what happens when glazes are applied in layers? The experiments are easy enough to try, but unfortunately the combinations are manyfold. For example, one could try applying the following glazes in twos and threes:

1. Standard base glaze.
2. Base glaze plus copper.
3. Base glaze plus tin.
4. Base glaze plus copper and tin.
5. A softer base glaze.
6. Soft glaze plus copper.
7. Soft glaze plus tin.
8. Soft glaze plus copper and tin.
9. A harder base glaze.
10. Hard glaze plus copper.
11. Hard glaze plus tin.
12. Hard glaze plus copper and tin.
13. Et cetera.

Then if one considers the combinations of: tin glaze over copper glaze; copper glaze over tin; hard glaze over soft; soft over hard; and so forth; it becomes obvious that the problem of testing is a huge one.

I have tried the combinations of hard and soft glazes and the separated tin and copper contents in several over and under variations. From these experiments the major conclusion was: the ready diffusion of copper in molten glazes can nullify the significance of many of these tests. Some testing is definitely worthwhile, but one can look forward to being confused in at least half of the tests because of copper movement.

Of the numerous tests run, I had the best results in cases where a copper-containing glaze was applied **over** a tin-containing glaze. But, the effects vary, depending on whether the whole piece is covered with both glazes, or whether just a dappled decoration is used.

Other things noted were:

1. The alkali effect - with increasing alkali content, a better copper ruby developed

2. The body effect - copper glazes in contact with the body produced off-colors.

3. The concentration effect - below 0.2% copper content, reds began to disappear.

4. The thickness effect - better copper reds are found in thick glazes.

The thickness effect may be the major benefit of applying multi-layered glazes, because as noted before, when a copper red glaze is too thin the color can be completely lost.

Summarizing, a few multi-layer glaze tests seem warranted. Just be aware that the diffusion of copper will often cause the results to be puzzling.

Good morrow to thy sable beak
And glossy plumage dark and sleek,
Thy crimson moon and azure eye,
Cock of the heath, so wildly shy.

Joanna Baillie—The Heath-Cock

28 GLAZE-BODY INTERACTIONS

Since it is the nature of a glaze to liquify at high temperatures, it is to be expected that it will be the nature of a body to react with this corrosive glaze liquid. In light of such circumstances I feel that the glaze-body reaction could be responsible for as much as 50% of the problems in glaze firing. While that percentage may be slightly exaggerated, it certainly represents 25% of our glaze problems.

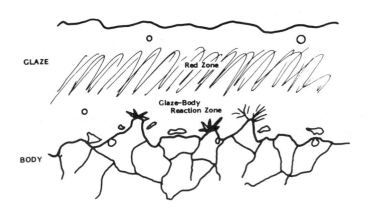

If a copper red glaze is examined—as illustrated in the figure—a number of observations can be made. In the simplest mode, one could take a fractured glaze-body section and look at it in a bright light using just the naked eye. Such a casual observation can show a number of facts about the glaze and the body. In the first place, it can give an indication of how glassy the glaze is and also how vitreous the body has become during firing. Furthermore, if a glaze chip is examined, an idea can be had of whether the glaze is red throughout, whether it has a clear layer on the outside, and whether it has a clear layer next to the body. The nature of a flake is such that it will show in its thin edges whether or not the redness is continuous.

It is so simple to use a hand lens to get a good fix on the character of the glaze and body, that I highly recommend this tool. A lens is really necessary for the serious potter, so that he can examine glazes in cross section and thus gain some insight on their character. With a 10X hand lens, you can observe bubbles and voids easily and can get a good notion of how uniform glaze coloration is. Also, you make an evaluation of the reaction zone between glaze and body with a hand lens.

Finally, if you are really serious about what is happening in glazes, a requirement is an optical microscope (with the capability of 100X magnification) and a means of preparing samples. Unfortunately sample preparation is the most difficult part of glaze examination, although you can go a long way just by examining glaze chips. Still, microscopy will require more equipment and time than the **average** glaze maker will want to invest, therefore my comments will emphasize my own microscope work in an effort to save time for the reader.

I don't think that I can make any claim to originality in the examination of copper red glazes, because almost every investigator in this field has taken a good look at cross sections. Typical of these is J. W. Mellor's thorough paper. Mellor's work is particularly valuable because of an optical micrograph he presents showing a cross section of a copper red glaze in contact with a body. In this micrograph, Mellor has identified a number of zones which are almost universally present in copper red glazes. His picture shows a clear layer near the surface, a yellowish layer next, then a central red layer, followed by a bluish layer, a clear layer, and finally the body. Since this chapter is just concerned with the reaction between the glaze and the body, it is only necessary to consider the lower half of the picture presented by Mellor, going from the central red layer through the blue layer, into the clear layer and finally to the body.

Two particular regions should be noted here: first the clear layer next to the body; and then the bluish layer between the clear layer and the red layer.

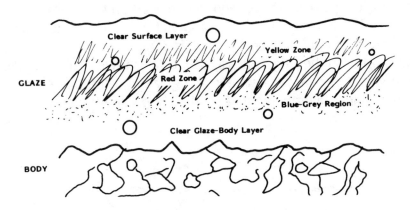

From experiments, I have found that the blue layer can be eliminated by varying the glaze composition or by making changes in the firing atmosphere. For instance, the blue layer is found to be absent if one uses a glaze which is quite glassy. At one time I made a glaze containing only lime, feldspar and a frit (in addition to copper and tin). With such a glaze, I found that no blue layer could be noted below the red zone. The glaze went from a central red layer directly to a clear layer, so there is some relationship between the glaze composition and this bluish zone.

On the other hand, I did not find that the clear layer next to the body was ever eliminated by merely changing the glaze composition. Almost every time I applied a glaze to a porcelain body, a clear layer would be evident between the glaze and the body, no matter what the glaze composition was. This is not strange, because one makes a glaze with the intent of having it melt freely—due to the fluxes in it. And, these fluxes can be expected to react with the body just as they react with the glaze components. Hence, we always find a clear (i.e. reaction) zone between the usual glaze and body.

However, I have found that the lower clear layer in copper red glazes can be eliminated by changing the **body** composition. Most ordinary ceramic bodies will form clear layers, but if you go to an extreme case and use a pure silica body (that has no clay and no feldspar), then you will find that the clear layer is not present. This was shown most strikingly by the following experiment. I took a flat piece of porcelain, applied a thick copper red glaze, and then placed on top of that a piece of pure silica body. Next I fired this sandwich in reduction to 1260°C and allowed it to cool slowly. When this sample was sectioned and examined in transmitted light, it was found (as shown in the diagram) that there was a clear layer between the glaze and the porcelain, but there was no clear layer between the silica body and the glaze.

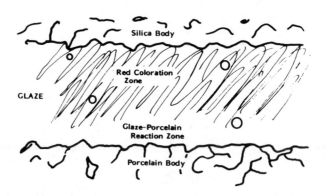

I therefore suspect that the clear zone is due either to a contaminant coming out of the body and entering the glaze or to some glaze ingredients moving out into the body.

To try to resolve these alternates, I ran some further experiments. In the first sequence I tried adding various materials to a good copper red glaze to see if any component would cause the glaze to become transparent. For example, I took some bisqued porcelain body (ground to a powder) and added it in varying proportions (5, 10, & 20%) to a glaze, and then melted these. While there was a change in color—tending towards pinks at high concentrations—there was no indication that the glaze was becoming clear because of additions of the body material. I had also suspected that clay was the culprit in the formation of clear zones, so I also tried adding various amounts of alumina and clay to the glaze. Again, this had no effect as far as changing the clarity, even though the color sometimes changed to pink. An alternative mechanism—that glaze components were diffusing into the body—now seemed more likely.

Another set of experiments was performed to test the importance of the time of firing. In this sequence I noted that a fast firing cycle resulted in a rather thin clear layer between the glaze and the body, whereas a slow melt would cause a thick clear layer to develop, so this indicated that the reaction rate was an important factor.

One further observation made on copper red glazes had to do with the appearance of gas bubbles. Often gas bubbles would be noted in a red portion of the glaze and it could be observed that the inner surfaces of some gas bubbles were transparent. This led me to believe that a volatile material inside the gas bubble was having an effect on the copper red glaze.

The next experimental observation was with peach bloom glazes—which are more refractory and less reactive than ox bloods. With them, one notes no clear zone at the glaze-body interface. This trait of peach blooms led me to believe that the loss of red color next to the body was not due to copper diffusion, because there would be no reason for copper **not** to diffuse into the body in the formation of a peach bloom glaze.

Since I have eliminated so many explanations for the cause of the clear layer of interaction at the glaze-body interface, I have become a bit desperate for a mechanism. My conclusion at the present time is that **lime**, in a roundabout way, is the cause of the clear zone between the glaze and the body. I postulate that calcium carbonate in the glaze (which decomposes at 800°C to calcium oxide) will react with either feldspar or frit to form a calcium feldspar and alkali oxide or a calcium frit and alkali oxide. The reasoning behind this is: calcium oxide is a very caustic material at high temperatures; it is very reactive; it is also refractory and has no tendency to volatilize. Therefore, in a high temperature glaze mix such as soda feldspar and reactive lime, it would be expected that a calcium feldspar and sodium oxide would be generated. The sodium oxide would be volatile, diffusible and very reactive (as would potassium oxide). However, one might ask: why not believe that calcium oxide is reacting with the body? This would be reasonable **if** there were some way for calcium oxide to move around inside the glaze. But, because it is divalent, and because it is so refractory, there would not be much tendency for calcium oxide to move. On the other hand, sodium oxide (or potassium oxide) is much more volatile, is just as reactive, and it can diffuse rapidly in a glass because of its monovalent nature. Thus, I can foresee sodium and potassium ions moving rapidly in all directions and even preferring to go to the body, because there the concentration of alkali was lowest originally. The high concentration gradient would encourage the movement of alkali into the body.

On looking at some x-ray work that was done on a Chun glaze, I think that I have seen enough evidence to confirm this explanation. When running analyses of: (1) the central body; (2) the body near the glaze; (3) the glaze near the body; and (4) the central glaze area on the Chun cross section, I found a definite concentration gradient of alkali from the glaze into the body when sodium was used as the marker.

Another interesting feature of this explanation of the clear zone is that it can also explain the blue zone. I have noted that whenever excessive amounts of calcium are added to a copper red glaze, that it tends to become a bluish color because of opal formation. This is a particle size effect and presumably is what the blue coloration is due to at the zone between the clear layer and the central red layer. Thus we can hypothesize that since the reaction of the lime with the feldspar results in the activation of alkalies and their removal by diffusion into the body, that this zone is actually higher in calcium than the average glaze composition. Therefore—for whatever reason—there is a tendency to form blue colloidal colors in the area just below the red layer and just above the clear layer next to the body.

My predilection for this mechanism of alkali movement from the glaze into the body is also due to an observation that I made on the movement of alkali from glass into a porous powder covering. If one heats a glass object to its softening point and cools it and rinses off the surface, a small amount of alkali will be found on the surface (perhaps 1-2 milligrams per 1000 square centimeters). If, however, a refractory powder is placed on the surface of the glass, and if the two are heated to the same temperature as before, then when the washings are analysed, the amount of alkali that will have moved from the glass into the powder will be 5-10 times as much as on the plain glass. Hence any porous material in close contact with a glass or glaze will act like a sponge and will absorb alkali when the system is heated. The higher the surface area of the porous material, the greater will be the amount of alkali that can be absorbed. This explains why less alkali moves into a silica body with a low surface area than into a clay-based body with a high surface area.

When the alkali migrates into the body, it leads to liquifaction of the body at the location where the alkali concentration is highest and behold, a clear zone is generated.

My only regret is that this mechanism is too complicated. Nature seems to have such simple explanations for our problems that I am suspicious whenever a complicated story is suggested.

Oh, bright as a berry,
They're red and they're rare,
The setters from Kerry,
And Cork and Kildare!

Patrick R. Chalmers—The Red Dogs

29 MICROSCOPY

Because microscopy is my trade, I tend to use it to a greater extent than the average person. And, since it is a useful tool, I will make certain recommendations for the microscopy of copper red glazes. Unfortunately, microscopy is very dependent on sample preparation, hence there is not much point for a ceramist to invest in an expensive microscope, because the difficult job of sample preparation would limit the usefulness of a good microscope.

My recommendation is that you spend a modest sum on a good 10X hand lens. This will be a high enough magnification for the average glaze examination, and together with a bright light source it will give at least twice as much information as the unaided eye could provide. Just remember when using a hand lens that the place for the eye is close to the lens, so that a large field of view can be seen.

LIGHTING

Lighting is as important as magnification for information gathering. As noted in a previous chapter, the color content of light can vary widely from the bluish tint of fluorescent lamps to the orange rendition afforded by low temperature incandescents. The brightness of a light source is important too. In general, a small, high intensity lamp (like a Tensor) will provide both high brightness and an acceptable color quality. If a lamp like this is available, it can be used to good advantage when examining a glaze at low magnification with a hand lens.

Another feature of lighting that is important is the different effect of reflected and transmitted light on samples. Examining ceramic glazes by both modes of illumination is vital to the evaluation of colors. A change in color when viewing samples by these two modes of illumination is a dead giveaway for phase separation in glazes. Frequently, copper red glazes will appear red in reflected light but blue in transmitted light, due to particle size effects.

SAMPLE PREPARATION

The obvious first step is to examine the outside surface of a sample glaze, first with the eye, and then with a hand lens. Going on from that, one should always examine the uppermost portion of the ware to observe what happens when the glaze runs thin on the body. Here one can see the body's effect on the color; and one can also note the amount of reaction that has occurred between the glaze and the body. At the upper edges, the glaze almost always runs very thin. At the opposite extreme is the drip which may be observed on a runny glaze at the base of a piece of ware. Dripping is especially noticeable when working with copper red glazes, because many of them have a tendency to run. Although many people have used drips for analyses—and have hoped to get an idea of glaze composition from these drips—I believe that most droplets are inappropriate sources of information because they are high in fluxes (after all, they have ended up at the bottom, where the glaze has run the most). Hence, glaze drips may have excessive amounts of alkalies, alkaline earths and borates present.

One way of observing a glaze that I favor, is taking a look at a fracture cross section. On a broken piece of ware, one can learn a great deal by looking at the glaze cross section with a hand lens. In this way one can find out about: the glaze-body reaction; the color dispersion; layering of the glaze; the glaze thickness; bubble evolution at the glaze-body interface; and finally, the number of bubbles to be found in the glaze.

Another way in which the glaze can be examined is by taking a look at a chip that has flaked off the piece. Naturally it would be preferable if one could cut a piece out of the sample with a diamond saw and then polish it as a thin section, but as this is not very practical, it is helpful to look at glaze chips. Again, you can get a good idea of the location of the color in the glaze and whether it is more highly concentrated at the top, middle or bottom of the glaze layer.

OBJECTIVES

There have to be some specific goals as we look at glazes. As mentioned above, we may be interested in the glaze thickness, the color variation, bubble formation and glaze-body reactions. Also we need to know if all of the batch has dissolved or whether there is a lot of silica and clay left in the glaze. Likewise we want to know if our glaze has crystallized—whether it is near devitrification and whether it has begun to form crystals. In the case of copper reds, devitrification would be detrimental to deep colors.

We can also get an idea about liquid-liquid phase separation from looking at a glaze at various angles in bright light. When opalization can be observed under optimum lighting conditions, it gives us a hint as to whether glass phases (or fine crystals) have separated out during the cooling process. This phase separation often has a strong effect on the color and it is good that we can observe this phenomenon without too much difficulty—even by using the naked eye.

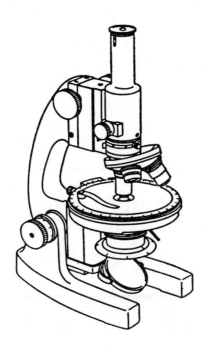

30 TORCH TESTING OF GLAZES

I do not recommend that the reader try torch testing of glazes because it is a hazardous operation. But, since I found it a useful technique I will describe my experiments and the results.

SAFETY

Before even thinking about torch testing, one should consider the safety aspects. **Always** wear safety glasses! **Always** work in the open air with plenty of ventilation! These points cannot be emphasized too strongly. Protect yourself effectively from: flying fragments, hot materials and noxious fumes before doing any torch testing.

TOOLS OF THE TRADE

If you are a sculptor in metal, or if you repair automobiles, or if you have friends who do things like this, you may want to try torch testing of glazes. I didn't have the appropriate equipment, so I found a friend who was willing to let me use his torch. Then, using this equipment, I saved myself a great deal of experimental work.

I don't think that an ordinary soldering-type propane torch would work, and I am afraid that the usual acetylene torch would be a little too powerful. An appropriate torch would be a gas-oxygen torch such as is used for brazing. This would definitely be better than a standard welding torch. The one I used was quite simple and was supplied with natural gas and oxygen at low pressure. It would have been just as effective to have used propane gas and oxygen, but natural gas happened to be

available to me. With a torch like this, one can attain temperatures that are comparable to those which are found in a cone 10 kiln. In addition, by appropriate adjustments of the controls, it is possible to fire in all degrees of oxidation and reduction. Unfortunately it is not possible to measure these degrees of oxidation and reduction, but the nature of the flame can tell you what state you are in and thus you can draw some general conclusions after such flame heating. When I did my firing, I took care that there were no inflammable materials around and that the work was done on an insulated, refractory surface in a hooded area. There was always a good current of air flowing past the work and away from me. Presumably it would be practical to run these experiments outdoors in good weather, especially when a gentle breeze was blowing in a direction away from the worker.

Torch testing, it must be remembered, is simply that, a testing operation. There will be no chance to make anything which will be permanent or useful. The idea behind this procedure is to test various operations, materials and temperatures, and then make estimates of how one should conduct a kiln firing. Also, if one has trouble in a kiln firing, a further torch test may give some insight as to the reason for the problem. The main benefit of torch testing is that it is very fast and allows you to make a lot of tests in a short period of time.

One of the problems of torch testing is that you will need to have a fair amount of experience before you can draw conclusions from the work. Obviously, it is quite different from running a kiln firing, but, because I have found it so useful, I would like to recommend it to those of you who have enough experience to benefit from the procedure.

Torching allows one to make test firings in place on a pot; on a section of a pot; on a sherd; or on a pile of unmelted glaze. I have even tried firing batches on a platinum strip, but this did not work out very well. Platinum, which is normally inert to glasses and glazes, unfortunately can alloy with copper metal, so reduction testing for copper red glazes on a platinum strip is not very practical. I had the feeling at the end of my experiments that much of my copper had alloyed with the strip.

I think that the best way to indicate how useful torch testing can be is to give examples of some of the tests that I have run, and some of the conclusions that I have drawn from these. While all of this work may not be profound, at least the experiments will illustrate some possibilities.

GLAZE TESTS

1. A useful experiment involved taking some of my copper red **glasses**—that showed no red coloration when quenched—and, by using a gentle oxidizing flame in the torch, heating them to see whether copper reds warmed in. This, when workable, was much faster than resorting to kiln testing.

2. If no red appeared during the above experiment, it was possible to take the same glass and try a gentle reduction flame treatment to see if copper showed up on the surface of the glass. Because of the short times involved, it wasn't possible to get penetration of the glass by hydrogen, but you could tell whether there was copper present, because reduction would occur on the very surface when it was bathed by a reducing flame.

3. The same type of experiment could be done with a quenched **glaze**. If you had a sample that had been yanked from the furnace at a high temperature, you could try warming-in or reducing-in to see if reds formed from a quenched glaze.

4. Another experiment involved working with the clear zone at the top of a fired copper red piece. It had been postulated that this clear zone might be due to oxidation of the copper; and yet there was also the option that it could be related to volatilization of the copper. By warming the top of a piece with a reducing flame, one can find out whether there is any copper present in the surface. If no copper red color appears, one may assume that there have been volatilization losses.

5. By taking a quenched glaze, and warming-in the color slowly, one can gain an insight as to what heat treatment will provide the best quality of copper red. One can see whether a short or a long firing is needed to produce a good red color.

6. Along these same lines, by using a torch it is possible to get a good idea of how fast copper reds form. From this it is possible to find that a very slow cooling is not needed to produce copper reds. My experience has been that copper reds will strike-in quite rapidly once the appropriate temperature is reached.

7. I have used torching to determine if there is an actual degradation of a copper red color by prolonged heating. Sometimes one gets a muddy glaze and it is useful to know if this glaze could have been saved by heating it at the striking temperature for a shorter length of time.

8. If torch testing is begun on an unconsolidated batch, it is possible to determine how the flame composition affects the color of the dissolved copper. One can note green, clear and red colors appearing under different flame conditions.

9. By using extremely hot flames, either in oxidation or reduction, and by looking at the color of the flame after it bounces off the glaze, you can come to conclusions about the volatility of copper and the extent of loss of copper in these different kinds of fires. The fact that only tiny amounts of copper will produce brilliant green flames allows this to be a very sensitive test. The loss of copper, besides being observed from the flame color, can also be noted by the color of the final glaze.

10. One can make up raw batches with varying components in them such as other redox agents (iron, tin, arsenic, antimony, etc.), and determine their effects on copper when subjected to reducing or oxidizing flames. Then one can see color changes and gas evolution, even though perfect glazes do not result from these tests.

11. One reaction that was of special interest was a test of the solubility of tin oxide in boric oxide. Fusion of a percent of tin oxide in a mix with powdered boric oxide, when fused into a glass, gave evidence that tin oxide was soluble to only a slight extent in boric oxide. This is probably one of the reasons why high alkali glazes are desirable. They may allow a material such as tin oxide to be dissolved in a glaze.

12. Another experiment that really surprised me was an attempt to reduce some tin oxide powder in a flame. I thought that surely a highly reducing flame at not too high a temperature would be able to reduce tin oxide to tin metal. This did not occur, and my conclusion was that the water from the combustion of gas in the flame prevented the reduction of tin oxide to tin metal. This probably is the same sort of thing that we encounter in glaze formation. Hydrogen and carbon monoxide in the presence of water are sufficient to reduce copper to the metal, but they are not adequate for reducing tin oxide to the metal.

13. The reaction of the glaze with the body is well demonstrated by a torch test. The amount of bubbling that occurs when a glaze is melted down in contact with a body is extraordinary. And, even when you have taken half-fired glazes out of the kiln, with lots of bubbles in them, there is nothing like running a torch test with the glaze-body combination for noting how great the evolution of bubbles is during this firing period.

14. Another test that I ran, involved the use of an extremely high firing temperature, which was done to determine just how feasible thermal reduction of copper and tin oxides could be in a glaze. I found that an extreme overfiring could result in both volatilization and thermal reduction of copper oxide. The result with tin was not too evident. I found that copper oxide could be entirely washed out of a glaze on high firing, even in strong oxidation. It also was evident that at very high temperatures and in strong oxidation, it was possible to get reduction of copper (which I presume was a thermal reduction). I could imagine that both cupric oxide and stannic oxide could be reduced to their lower valence states of cuprous oxide and stannous oxide by high temperatures, and that during the cooling operation these two materials could react together to give copper metal and stannic oxide, and therefore red colors.

15. I repeated the experiment that I had run in the kiln (of reducing the surface of a copper green glaze) only this time using the torch. There was no point in this experiment, because I knew what the results would be. It was just interesting to know that the same thing would happen with the hand torch as had happened in the kiln. At a moderate temperature (about 600°C) the surface of a copper green glaze could easily be reduced to copper metal to give a combined metallic and reddish looking surface.

16. A piece of ware that was incompletely fired in a kiln was placed on a ceramic block and was then fired by using a hand torch. This was a good way to note how glaze formation occurs, step by step, from the underfired condition, to the correctly fired condition and finally to an overfired state.

SUMMARY

Summarizing, I would like to emphasize that torch testing of glazes is not the complete answer to all of our problems, but it is another useful tool to have available when it is desired to find out what is happening during the glaze-forming process. It is not easy; it takes a lot of practice; and one learns about it only bit by bit; but it does help. And, we are always looking for techniques which will add one more dimension to our search and give us answers from another viewpoint.

Crimson glowed the furnace,
Bright red the clay;
Scarlet bloomed the ox bloods
The kiln disgorged today.

Old Potter's Chant

31 CLASSICAL LITERATURE

INTRODUCTION

Although the Chinese obviously knew how to make copper red glazes as early as the Sung dynasty, and although they wrote about their glazes, we have no descriptions from this era which would tell us **how** to make copper red glazes. The first pieces of literature which told about copper reds were two letters from the French missionary Pere d'Entrecolles to his superior Pere Orry. Since these are brief descriptions, the segments of d'Entrecolles' letters pertaining to copper red glazes will be included. Other pieces included as classics will be comments by Ebelemen and Salvetat, Paul Ebell, Lauth and Dutailly, Hermann Seger and Georges Vogt.

PERE D'ENTRECOLLES' REPORT ON COPPER RED GLAZES

Pere d'Entrecolles wrote two letters to France from China, concerning the manufacture of ceramics in the neighborhood of Ching-te-chen. The first letter was sent in 1712 and the second in 1722.

In the first letter, d'Entrecolles commented that the Chinese technique for making red colors for glazes used copperas (iron sulfate), which was treated in a furnace to form red ferric oxide. In his second letter, he noted that the iron red was merely an overglaze color, and that there was a better red (in glaze) which was due to copper. He then described, as well as he could, the technique and the materials involved in making copper reds.

LETTER I

Red is made from copperas (iron sulfate), *tsao-fan*. Perhaps the Chinese have something special in it, and because of that I am going to describe their method. One pound of copperas is put in a crucible that is luted well to a second crucible; at the top of this there is a small opening that one can easily cover if one desires; then the whole thing is surrounded with a circle of bricks. As long as the rising fumes from the hole are black, the material is not ready, but it is ready as soon as a kind of fine delicate cloud appears. Then one takes a little of this material, mixes it with water and makes a test on some fir wood. If it gives a beautiful red, one removes the surrounding fire and partly covers the crucible. One pound of copperas gives four ounces of red for painting porcelain.

LETTER II

I was mistaken when I said (in letter I) that the red glaze—*yeou-li-hum*—was made of a red derived from copperas, such as is used in the red for refired porcelain. This glaze-red is made from the shavings of red copper and a powder of a certain reddish stone. A Christian doctor told me that this stone was a sort of alum, used in medicine. Both ingredients are ground together in a mortar, adding the urine of a young man and some *pe-yeou* oil. I have not been able to get the exact quantities, as the secret is well-kept and not let out. This mixture is applied to the porcelain before it is fired, and no other glaze is applied. Only, care must be taken that the red color doesn't flow to the bottom of the vase. I have been assured that when this red is to be applied to porcelain, no *petun-tse* is used (in the porcelain), but in its place, some yellow earth, prepared in the same manner as the *petun-tse*, is used with *kao-lin*. It is probable that such earth is more likely to accept this sort of color.

Maybe it would be convenient to learn how these copper shavings are prepared. We know that, in China, there is no coined silver. Bulk silver is used in business, and there are many pieces of an alloy base. However, there are occasions where they have to be refined, as for example, when a tithe or similar contribution is to be paid. Then, we have recourse to workers whose trade is refining silver in furnaces specially-built for this purpose, at the same time separating the copper and lead. They form copper shavings, which, undoubtedly still contain some invisible bits of silver or lead. Before the liquid copper coagulates and hardens, a small broom is dipped lightly in water and, tapping on the handle, water is sprinkled onto the molten copper. A film forms on the surface, and is lifted off with small iron tweezers, and is plunged into cold water, where the the particles form piece by piece. I think that if nitric acid were used to dissolve the copper, this copper powder would be more suitable for making the red which I spoke about. But the Chinese don't know the secret of nitric acid and aqua regia, their inventions all being of extreme simplicity.

CONCERNING SOME GLAZES OF THE HIGH FIRE

J. J. Ebelmen and L. A. Salvetat

(Translated by Robert Tichane)

The research contained in this memoir was undertaken on a series of materials used in China for the fabrication and decoration of porcelain. Most of the material was collected by a Chinese Catholic priest, Father J. Ly, who sent it to the factory at Sevres in 1844 at the request of his Superior General and according to instructions from M. Brongniart, administrator of the Sevres factory.

COLORED GLAZES

In China, a great number of pieces are decorated with colored glazes. Using simple methods, one can obtain a variety of effects. For example, one can get (by means of relief) some very brilliant effects merely by using a thin coat of glaze and obtaining in this way an upper light coat detached from a background of a deeper color. One can see among these backgrounds: pale blues, deep blues and celadons.

Among the colors which one applies with a uniform thickness, we can mention: red in its variations; a greyish-green celadon—which is commonly applied over stoneware ceramics; an olive-brown green; a leaf brown; and a yellow golden brown. We shall give the results of the work that we have done on each of these colors.

RED GLAZES

This color, which the Chinese call *Tse-hong-yeou*, rarely presents a lively color; generally it is of a violet tint. Sometimes it is a brick red color; sometimes it is a bronze; and sometimes parts are decolorized or show a light bluish tint. This last effect is noted principally at the neck of vases. The most notable pieces of this kind of ware are those which are flambés and which present alternate reds and blues with a very gradual change from one shade to another. The symmetry of these streaks demonstrates that they are obtained by conventional mixtures made up of two different colored glazes, one, a blue made from cobalt oxide, and the other a red made from copper oxide. Contrary to previous beliefs, these flambés are not caused by variations of the furnace atmosphere acting on a single copper glaze.

In order to make an analysis, we have taken off some fragments of red glaze from some Chinese ware which we have sacrificed. One was a uniform color, and the other a flambé of red and blue. We have found the following numerical results for the composition of these glazes:

	Uniform Glaze	Flambé Glaze
Silica	73.9	69.0
Alumina	6.0	4.0
Iron Oxide	2.1	0.8
Lime	7.3	12.0
Cupric Oxide	4.6	0.2
Cobalt Oxide	0.0	1.5
Lead Oxide	0.1	0.7
Manganese Oxide	0.1	2.0
Potash	3.0	0.6
Soda	3.1	9.4
Total	100.0	100.3

The analysed glazes have also been submitted to some other examinations with the object of better understanding their nature. The blue glaze maintained its coloration in the blowpipe for both an oxidizing and a reducing flame. The red enamel, on the contrary, has given the following results in several tests; one fragment of the red glaze was submitted to the temperature of the porcelain furnace at Sevres. In these conditions the glaze has undergone different changes in accord with its composition; the glaze has run down sloping parts in thick droplets, and there it crackled; it has lost its red coloration totally at the surface, and there it has become light green and opalescent; the decoloration occurs only partially on the interior and it stays rose colored in those parts where it is thickly coated and is preserved from oxidation during the firing. The body, which was perfectly white at the start, became a brownish tint on all of the surfaces exposed to the influence of the furnace, because of the iron which it contained. The interior of the body, which was protected by the glaze, kept its original whiteness.

A fragment of this same vase was fired in a muffle and taken to a red heat; after removal from the muffle, it retained its coloration, the edges remained sharp, and there was no softening at the temperatures of this decoration firing. A repeat experiment was made on the same fragment, only firing to the temperature which gives a matte gold. The heat was then raised enough to soften a little of the glaze and to dull the edges of the fracture, but this was insufficient to cause adherence of the glaze to the sand in which the fragment had been placed during firing. The Sevres hard porcelain, under the same conditions, did not show any modification or any softening.

One can therefore confirm from the preceding experiments and analyses: that this glaze is fired to a high temperature (although somewhat lower than the temperature of the Sevres high fire, but perhaps equal to the high fire that is used in China); and that the fusibility of the feldspar in this glaze is increased by the use of limestone, of which the quantities can vary, and whose presence we have already noted in Chinese porcelain glazes.

In addition, the attempts that we have made up until now to obtain this color have confirmed the compositions that we have just given, and we can indicate the results here. However, it was necessary to determine the practical conditions for firing pieces covered with the cuprous oxide red glaze. We have adopted as the composition of this glaze:

Aumont Sand	38
Feldspar	50
Limestone (12); Lime	6
Cupric Oxide	6
Total	100

This corresponds to:

Silica	76.05
Alumina + Iron Oxide	7.75
Lime + Magnesia	6.08
Potash + Soda	3.72
Cupric Oxide	6.00
Total	99.60

One has to use a high percentage of copper oxide in this glaze because of its volatility in a reducing atmosphere. The composition that we have given is somewhat harder than that of the Chinese, but this condition seems necessary to us in order to avoid crazing. In order to avoid this defect one could also use a different body composition, possibly one that is more fusible, and which is closer in composition to the porcelain body used in China.

The following body has given us some good results:

Standard Sevres Body-80%
Glaze-type Feldspar-20%

The ordinary body is not desirable for use in making pieces covered with a copper red. The firing conditions necessary for the development of copper red glazes or which are amenable to the maintenance of copper in the cuprous state, are different from the furnace conditions for firing ordinary paste. If one tries to make the body translucent, one loses the red color, and because of the excessive firing temperature, the glaze runs off the piece.

By simply restricting the chimney on a small furnace, we have been able to obtain some red pieces using a standard body. Moreover, the glaze is not crazed (which is very unusual even on Chinese pieces). We have placed in the Sevres Ceramic Museum collection several samples to demonstrate this work. On one of these we have even used a gold flourished decoration, fired in the muffle kiln and burnished. We do not know of any Chinese piece which has received either gold or any other color on the red surface.

In addition, we have taken some samples of red glazed porcelain from the high fire—made at Sevres—and reglazed them with cobalt blue, and they have given violet tones and blues that are quite analogous to those presented by the flambé glazes of the Chinese.

We have also obtained in our first work some bizarre results, of which we have not been able to find any examples amid the porcelain of China. For example, when a piece is not sufficiently fired, it comes from the furnace covered with cracks. Or, if the atmosphere has not been reducing enough to keep copper in the cuprous state, the glaze is loaded with bubbles and blisters, which gives the surface a very rough aspect. In both of these cases, if one refires the pieces in a porcelain furnace, and if the heat is adjusted correctly, one obtains a very original coloration, namely an agate-like appearance, and this, in conjunction with the crackling, is a very remarkable effect. The crackles no longer exist, but their place is made apparent along their whole length by a decorating process, due no doubt to the action of air on the two lips of the crack. We have placed in the collection of the Sevres Museum some cups showing these very curious results, obtained simply by refiring some of these crazed or blistered and bubbled pieces. These are, no doubt, the kind of pieces which are analogous to those which the Chinese call *Yao-pien*, or transmutation pieces.

32 COPPER RUBY GLASSES

PAUL EBELL

(Translated by Thomas Elmer)

Ebell's article about copper red glasses is a fine example of what a scientist can do with some very simple experiments and a great deal of careful thought. His experiments with copper reds remind one of the work done by the early experimenters in the field of nuclear research; he made observations of reactions that were already known, performed peripheral tests, and then thought through the results to irrefutable conclusions. His paper is a gold mine and an inspiration to those working in the copper red field.

INTRODUCTION

On the basis of communications published in 1871 by Max Muller, regarding **gold** ruby glass, one can come to the logical conclusion that glass can dissolve metals in the elemental state, and that ruby glass can be looked upon as simply a solidified solution of metallic gold in glass. One cannot reach a definite conclusion regarding his works without also making basic studies of a related matter, namely glass that has been colored red with **copper**.

The present paper, in addition to dealing with gold-containing glass, includes results and studies made with copper ruby glasses, those prepared with silver, and some phenomena encountered with lead-containing glasses.

There are two main forms in which gold-containing glass occurs. The homogeneous, uniformly-transparent form has a practical importance; the other, in which the gold consists of a finely divided precipitate, has no application. With copper glasses, this is different. If one excludes the blue (cupric oxide colored) glass, which we shall not consider further, we know from experience that there are three types of copper red colored glasses: copper ruby (corresponding to the beautiful deep red gold ruby of church windows, et cetera), hematinone, and aventurine.

The most important work so far was that done by von Pettenkofer. It covers hematinone and aventurine, and deals briefly with ruby. He showed that hematinone, on melting is red-brown, but on subsequent processing (namely continued thermal treatment at temperatures near the softening point) the glass turns a deep opal—a true hematinone. Aventurine exists in two states: a melt without crystalline glitter, and a true aventurine in which the crystals are developed by a secondary process. According to von Pettenkofer, the formation of both glasses depends on the crystallization of siliceous cuprous oxide. The freshly molten glass, according to him, represents the amorphous state, and the thermally-produced hematinone and aventurine represent the crystalline state. However, there also exists a transparent copper ruby. It, too, exists in two states, colorless and red (strike-in type), but without any precipitate. Regarding this, von Pettenkofer says the following: the warming-in of color is related to the transition of siliceous cuprous oxide from the amorphous to the crystalline state; the red color is due to precipitation of crystallites of this compound, but the crystals are so small that they cannot be detected by means of a light microscope. This explanation is not readily acceptable. Crystals require, if they are to remain invisible in a matrix, not just minuteness; it is sufficient if their physical, namely optical properties are nearly the same as those of the matrix. The precipitates that we are dealing with here—hematinone and aventurine—are quite different from the matrix; one is transparent and green, the other opaque and red. They cannot be invisible even when diminished in dimension to the greatest degree, because they would have to remain undetected, not only by the naked eye, but also by the light beam.

According to von Pettenkofer's explanation, the nature of copper ruby remains doubtful, but that of hematinone and aventurine is related to very small microscopic and larger crystals composed of siliceous cuprous oxide. This compound, however, is considered completely problematic and its existence—as already indicated in Muller's publication—is to a high degree improbable because strong mineral acids cleave cuprous oxide into metallic copper and cupric oxide, and it is inconceivable that silica in the melt should behave itself differently. Furthermore, it is known that Wohler reached different opinions from those above, because he considers the crystals in such a type of glass to be simply metallic copper. Fremy and Clemandot support the views of Wohler as regards aventurine. We find however, that Hautefeuille attempts to demonstrate that the crystals in such glass are not metallic copper, because they do not turn white when treated with mercury salts (through a-malgamation). He assumes that the crystals are siliceous cuprous oxide as was also assumed by von Pettenkofer. It should be pointed out that mere melting together of glass batch with cuprous oxide produces no red colored glass. Von Pettenkofer, for example used copper scale that was so rich in cuprous oxide that it yielded a red powder on comminution. He also melted it with batch in an atmosphere containing only nitrogen, carbon dioxide and carbon monoxide. This melt was stirred with a copper rod. He, however, obtained only a green glass. Only when simultaneously using reducing agents, such as iron and carbon, was he able to form a red-brown melt, or a hematinone.

From the above, we see that the investigations published about red colored glasses produced with copper, contain gaps, contradictions, and obscurities; they have enriched our knowledge with numerous and important observations, but have not led us to a universally satisfying understanding of the nature of this artificial product.

REGARDING GLASSES COLORED RED WITH COPPER

1. Ruby Glass Stains

The art of glass making teaches us two ways of producing copper ruby, first by means of staining (as practiced in coloring glass with silver) and also by flashing (overlay).

The first involves a coloring of the formed glass article. One mills copper scale, iron scale, and ochre with turpentine oil to a fine slurry that can be applied by means of a sable brush to the areas to be colored, and then one fires the dried coating in a muffle. A portion of the copper-containing addition diffuses into the glass, causing it to turn dark green; the remainder, with ochre, is attached loosely on the surface and is removed with a brush. This completes the first step of the coloring cycle. The development of the ruby color is achieved by subjecting the glass article to a reducing atmosphere in a muffle in which charcoal has been uniformly distributed. Generally, the first firing results in a red that is somewhat dull. The full color is not achieved until a second and third firing. It is said that the color is achieved only in lead-free potassium glasses and not on lead crystal containing alkali. A coloration that is achieved in a similar manner is observed in chemical laboratories during burning of organic substances with copper oxide. Frequently the coloration is very pronounced and occurs in locations where the copper oxide is located. It may occasionally occur in places covered with copper chips, or it may be completely absent. This observation of incidental coloration of glass tubing was found to be a convenient way for studying the appearance of color on rigid glass by means of stains.

The experiments were carried out using so-called combustion tubes made of hard glass in the well-known gas furnaces used for the analysis of organic compounds. Some were made using a Bunsen burner as a heating source. In the tube furnace one can raise the temperature up to the softening point of the glass, but with the Bunsen burner this is hardly possible. The first experimental series involved a slurry comprised of a mixture of black copper oxide, charcoal and clay in oil of turpentine. This is similar to what is conventionally used. The clay helps to adhere the mixture to the glass. By introducing such a mixture inside tubing and then inverting the tube, it is readily possible to uniformly coat the inside wall. After drying, the coated glass tubes are fired in a gas-fired tube furnace for a period of time. No red coloration was obtained regardless of whether the glass tubes were fired in a dark, barely visible red glow, or at red heat which led to considerable sagging of the tubes. Elimination of the clay in the mix, or sweeping the inside of the tubes with illuminating gas or hydrogen did not result in red coloration either. The copper oxide was reduced to a metallic coating on the glass. Tubing, drawn from a more fluid glass, or from a section of plate glass, painted with the same mixture and then treated in the muffle, acted similarly to the above tubing and remained colorless. One sample of tubing which had been fired for 1-2 hours and which had been subsequently subjected to a stream of hydrogen, contained some sporadic traces of faint red spots. Following this hint, it was decided to treat tubing, that had been subjected to unsuccessful experiments, to the action of hydrogen gas. Such a tube of hard glass, that had been baked at a red heat after treatment with a mixture of copper oxide, carbon powder, clay and turpentine oil, was cut in half, the mixture was removed, and then the tube was subjected to the gas combustion furnace at maximum heat in a stream of hydrogen. Immediately a deep ruby color formed. The same also happened on repeating the experiment with the other half of the tube, and also with a tube which had been used for organic analysis with copper oxide. Another tube, which had been coated with copper oxide only (using some turpentine oil), and which was first heated for some time in a stream of oxygen and then in hydrogen, developed the same deep, full ruby color.

The identical observation was made when the copper oxide was replaced with metallic copper. Hard and soft tubing that had been filled with copper chips or coated with precipitated metallic copper (using clay and turpentine oil) and then had been heated in a stream of hydrogen, showed no coloration except for a few faint isolated spots. However, if the tubing containing copper was first heated for 3/4 hour in air and then in hydrogen, a deep red color formed in the previously colorless or yellowish glass. Upon subjecting a tube that had been colored red (by using copper chips and then removing them) for two hours in a stream of air, it was found that it completely lost its color. After having become colorless, the red color reappeared upon exposing it to hydrogen at red heat. However, the color was not quite as intense a red as before.

A small piece of plate glass that had been heated just to the point where it begins to soften (while in the presence of copper oxide, charcoal and clay), was found to have a red color after removal of the coating. The weight gain after removal of the loosely attached layer, was 60 milligrams.

The facts speak for themselves. The development of color on a glass article occurs only when the surface has first been impregnated with a copper compound which is then reduced in the glass by hydrogen (or carbon monoxide). In the muffle, where immediate coloration took place, there occurred: first, the impregnation upon gradual raising of the temperature; and then, the reduction by the carbon monoxide atmosphere at full heat.

There is little doubt that copper enters the glass as the oxide. The oxide imparts a blue or blue-green color of very low intensity. The diffusion zone is generally so thin that it is not readily perceptible to the eye. Upon reduction firing of the stain, such color imparted by copper oxide becomes clearly visible. The ruby color which results is intense and confronts the eye even when the layer is extremely thin. The reducing agents that were added to the mixture initially are not required, they have no significance. Turpentine oil vaporizes, and the carbon powder does not remain in the mix, because it is present in too small an amount to prevent regeneration of copper oxide. Hydrogen (or illuminating gas) if passed over the glass at the beginning does not color it red, because premature reduction prevents impregnation (copper oxide diffusion). It is not surprising that impregnation of the glass occurs prior to softening of the glass, because this phenomenon is observed frequently, e.g., the color of glass with silver preparations occurs at even lower temperatures.

Cuprous oxide generally forms only on oxidation when there is a large excess of metal; in the above experiments only small amounts are active. The formation of cuprous oxide during initial heating, for this reason, is improbable or can be considered only with experiments involving copper chips. We may then ask, what form of solid is responsible for the ruby color in the glass?

Generally one believes it to be due to formation of cuprous oxide, but this assumption is subject to important reconsideration. On heating of copper chips in air in a hard glass tube, one finds that it becomes coated with a thick layer of black cupric oxide. Upon subsequently subjecting it, without altering anything, to a stream of hydrogen, the tube turns a nice ruby red, while the cupric oxide is reduced to metal (not cuprous oxide). The copper oxide thus must be simultaneously (and at the same temperature) reduced to copper in the glass and outside the glass. Direct experiments with cuprous oxide are not easily carried out because it is too easily reduced or oxidized.

Ruby glass produced from batch by melting processes differs from ruby glass produced by the staining process. It exists in two states, colorless or deep red. Glass that has been rapidly cooled after melting and fining appears colorless or weakly greenish, depending on the accidental secondary constituents such as iron, et cetera. If properly molten glass is subsequently heated to temperatures which cause it to soften, there suddenly appears a deep red color throughout the body. This well-known phenomenon is known as striking-in and is similar to the warming-in of a gold ruby glass. On the cooling of a glass melt in a crucible (laboratory-size) the copper ruby is generally not uniform throughout the glass. Occasionally one encounters colorless regions, while parts are livery in color, dark red brown (transparent) or opaque deep red. All of these states may appear as streaks or bands and spots next to one another.

When coloring glass by the staining process, one finds that small amounts of copper suffice to achieve a full red coloration. Such small quantities are not able to produce a ruby by the melting process, perhaps because it is difficult to avoid oxidation. Large quantities also fail to produce the desired color because other phenomena, such as hematinone formation take place. The following experiments are intended to help determine the amount of copper that needs to be incorporated in the glass, and also the choice of a suitable copper preparation. Unless indicated otherwise, the glass batch preferably consists of:

GLASS BATCH "A"

Silica	48
Litharge	60
Potash	12
Saltpeter	8
Total	128

This batch was preferred for laboratory experiments because it melts readily and also because lead glasses are well suited for coloring. Among the substances used as additives were: copper oxide, iron oxide, metallic tin, zinc and carbon powder; but some of these materials are of little practical value. Carbon leads to gas evolution, and because of its high reactivity, produces copper deposits in the bottom of the crucible. Zinc oxidizes too rapidly. Iron scale reacts properly, but colors the glass too intensely. Tin foil looked promising when immersed in the glass melt while stirring. It, however, can cause the lead glass to turn black under certain conditions, which is a secondary phenomenon that has nothing to do with the coloration by copper.

The above glass batch "A" with 0.04% copper oxide produced no ruby glass regardless of whether the copper oxide was added as such or in the form of a dilute copper sulfate solution prior to melting. Tin foil and iron oxide were also not effective in reducing this glass. A melt of glass containing copper poured into a melted glass containing iron oxide, while stirring, also did not produce a ruby. The same batch "A" with 0.2% copper oxide and tin as above, or with an excess of iron oxide, results in a completely colorless glass (with 1% tin) when fritted in water, and a beautiful and rapidly-striking ruby glass when reheated. All other experiments with the same addition of copper were failures.

One sees that the addition of 0.2% copper is sufficient, but the treatment is too difficult. No successful melts were achieved when adding 0.5% copper oxide plus iron oxide, but with tin (1.5%) the glass was dark red; it was colorless when quenched in water, but the color struck-in nicely when reheated. Only upon adding 1% copper oxide did the melts consistently yield a ruby, not only with iron oxide (1.5%), but also with tinfoil (2%) when using a melting time of 1.5 hours. The heat generated by a portable blower furnace fired with coke worked satisfactorily. Among 12 melts there was only one melt that was not quite completely ruby, and none were failures. During one of these experiments with 1% copper oxide it was decided to pull glass samples after introducing tin and achieving a complete melt. The first pull was made after 2 hours of melting, all subsequent pulls were made at one hour intervals until a total of 5 pulls had been made. It was striking to see that the ruby color was at first insufficient, but that it eventually developed to its full extent as the melting time increased. The glass that had cooled in the crucible was livery in color with opaque red stripes and occasionally the color was that of red sealing wax. On pouring in water, one finds thicker clumps of red and thin, thread-like colorless glass. Pouring onto a dry refractory plate gave results which were similar, but in which only the thinnest parts were colorless. In order to judge the melted product it was indispensable to use overlays (besides the microscope, about which we shall report later). On a small scale one proceeds as follows: one closes one end of a glass tube, drops a lentil-sized piece of the melt into the tube, and upon remelting in a flame, blows the end into a ball. The dark, livery-brown grain of melt yields a yellowish spot that is shaded brownish and is about the size of a cherry, which strikes-in immediately over a gas flame, giving a beautiful blood red color.

It was of interest to compare the copper content of the finished glass, after it had been converted to copper ruby, with the quantity of copper initially added. This was done by melting lead glass batch "A" with 1% copper oxide, adding 2% tin foil after achieving a complete melt (pressing it under the glass), stirring and continuing the melting cycle for 1.5 hours (in a portable coke-fired blower furnace), pouring aliquots into water, until one achieves a colorless, somewhat yellowish tinged glass, that on warming-in results in a deep and beautiful ruby glass.

A sample of 2.0435 grams of the glass gave 0.0165 grams of cuprous sulfide and 0.023 grams of stannic oxide, corresponding to 0.66% copper and 1.38% tin in the ruby glass, or nearly an atomic ratio of 1 part copper to 1.1 part tin.

In another experiment, glass batch "A" was divided into two equal parts and each was melted down separately, one with 1% copper oxide, the other with 1.5% iron oxide. After both flowed equally, they were combined and stirred. After this, the mixture was allowed to remain in the fire of the blower furnace as above, for another 1.5 hours; then test specimens were poured into water where they solidified as colorless, yellowish glass that could be warmed-in nicely to produce a ruby. From this water-quenched glass, it was found that: 2.064 grams contained 0.011 grams of cuprous sulfide and 0.0205 grams of ferric oxide, corresponding to 0.42% copper and 0.959% ferrous oxide in the final ruby glass. Calculations show:

	Copper	Ferric Oxide
Glass	0.42%	0.96%
Batch	0.44%	0.75%

Similarly for the previous glass:

	Copper	Tin
Glass	0.66%	1.38%
Batch	0.88%	2.00%

Since the batch undergoes a considerable loss in weight on melting, it would have been expected that the copper content in the final ruby glass will be proportionately higher than in the batch, but on the contrary, we find that the copper content in one case is about the same, and in the other case markedly smaller. From this it can be concluded that some metallic copper segregated on melting or that the ruby glass was not homogeneous. The latter, in practice, is rather difficult to verify, especially when carrying out melting studies on a small scale. In another trial, which was mentioned earlier, a ruby glass with a completely saturated color was obtained using an addition of 0.2% copper oxide in the glass batch. According to the above analyses, it was found that 1% copper oxide in the batch resulted in 0.7-0.9% copper in the glass, or, in other words, considerably more. Using a larger batch with copper oxide, therefore, assures that the glass will retain a greater amount of the copper which is needed for coloring; and more importantly, that it does so with reliability.

It was previously supposed that to achieve red color with copper it is not possible to replace lead glass. However, melts of cullet composed of commercial hollow glass plus 1% copper oxide also gives a ruby color. A glass melt composed of 20 parts by weight sand and 46 parts by weight calcined soda, without lime or lead oxide, also produced a red color when mixed with 0.2% copper oxide and iron filings.

The following experiments were carried out to determine whether, and to what extent, copper oxide can be replaced by metallic copper when making ruby glass. A melt of pulverized plate glass and 1% metallic copper with the addition of iron oxide, when remelted for one hour in the blower furnace, gave a negative result. The resulting glass was green and did not change color on warming-in. Apparently the temperature was too low for this difficult-to-fuse glass. One should select for the following melts, an easily fusible glass and a higher temperature in a brick-lined blower furnace with a 40 foot flue. The lead batch "A" with a 1% reduced copper was placed in a Hessian crucible (with a tightly sealed cover) and was subjected to the maximum temperature for 2 hours. The glass that was cooled slowly in the crucible consisted of a red and a black-brown layer, none of which developed a warm-in color in the lab-worker's burner. Only a few colorless areas on the surface gave any red color. However, a repeat experiment involving rapid cooling in the crucible or quenching in water resulted in warmed-in ruby glass with the former being livery and the latter a good ruby. The formation of a copper ruby by direct melting with metallic copper is possible; however, it is more difficult, produces a less fiery color, and is less suited for use as an overlay. The difficulty is undoubtedly associated with the fact that the desired amount of coloring material is incorporated only slowly in the glass and only at higher temperatures.

The usual viewpoint regarding the assignment of the red color of the ruby glass to cuprous oxide or its silicate gives rise to experiments with this body, and the last series of melts will be dedicated to it. There are no hints available based on experience. Cuprous oxide or cupric oxide in combination with reducing agents is frequently considered necessary to achieve the objective. In the experiments to be undertaken, it was decided to avoid reduction as well as oxidation. Therefore, the melt was prepared with very finely divided cuprous oxide. In the first experiment, the cuprous oxide was added as uniformly as possible to the batch (lead-containing batch "A"). Attempts were made to avoid harmful influences during the 2.5 hour melting cycle by introducing carbon dioxide into the crucible. A dark green glass with some red stripes resulted; the glass was colored in spots, but a color-free glass as an overlay remained, and it did not produce color on warming-in. This disappointing result is apparently related to the incompleteness of the chemical equilibrium. The action of carbon dioxide is stopped by the strong currents of the highly radiating surroundings; the long period required to form the melt gives the cuprous oxide too much time to undergo chemical changes; and, the long time in the open crucible leads to disturbing secondary phenomena. In subsequent melts, the batch was first allowed to melt into a clear glass, and then cuprous oxide was added with vigorous stirring. Then the well-covered crucible was allowed to remain in the fire for from one to at most two hours. In this manner the lead batch "A" with 1% cuprous oxide melted for two hours at a high temperature, resulting in a blue-green glass with small spheres of copper in the bottom; the same thing happened with 4% cuprous oxide after a one hour melting at a moderate red heat. Plate glass (as well as a melt prepared from sand, potash and barium nitrate), both with 1% cuprous oxide also acted in the same way. The former was a stiff glass, and the latter was a fluid, lead-free glass. Stirring was done with copper and glass rods to avoid contamination with iron. Directly-added cuprous oxide does not compare in its action to cupric oxide plus a reducing agent. Also, von Pettenkofer obtained only a glass with a black-green color when working with a melt containing lime and soda to which he added 10% cuprous oxide in an oxygen-free atmosphere of the melting furnace. There was no trace of red or of a mixed color that might contain red. Thus it can be said that cuprous oxide, when incorporated in the glass, does not lead to a red color. It is simply dissociated into metallic copper and cupric oxide. The latter is not reduced by the combustion gases over the glass, but is responsible for the blue-green color. The red coloration results from the continuous action of the fluid glass with the deposited metal. The red color is often observed around metallic spheres. The bulk of the copper settles to the bottom of the crucible as a mass at temperatures above that of the melting point of the metal (1083°C). If one adds cuprous oxde to the batch, the metal remains dispersed for longer times, thereby increasing conditions for red coloration of the glass. This was the case with the first experiment involving cuprous oxide.

If one heats transparent red ruby glass, that was produced by the staining method (and was not colored too deeply) in a tube furnace, for about three hours while passing hydrogen through the furnace tube, one finds that the red color disappears completely and that the glass does not color on reheating (warming-in). Apparently, the ruby color which was initially achieved by a hydrogen treatment is destroyed by subsequent treatment in the same hydrogen atmosphere. The destruction of color is probably not due to the action of hydrogen, but to the continuous action of heating.

It was found that the phenomenon was the same when heating was continued in carbon dioxide or in nitrogen; even though the air in the tube was expelled by flushing with carbon dioxide for some time prior to the heating. It is sufficient that the ruby glass (obtained by staining) is subjected to indifferent atmospheres. In no case can the phenomenon be based on oxidation, or conversion of copper to oxide. Apparently the phenomenon is related to the fact that the red color exists only in an immeasurably thin layer on the outside surface and that the amount of copper that has entered the glass is exceedingly small. On continuous heating, this small amount of copper moves into the interior of the tubing wall away from the hot surface. The color can then no longer be brought forth, perhaps because the dilution of colorant has proceeded too far, or because the small amount of copper has found an opportunity in the interior to oxidize and can no longer be reached by the reducing agents—which is the essential condition for ruby coloration. In connection with this, the following facts are worth mentioning: copper-rich ruby produced by melting does not lose its color under similar conditions; furthermore, there is the behaviour of blue-green copper oxide glass, which upon heating in a stream of hydrogen turns red and does this only at the external surface.

3. Optical Behavior of Ruby Glass

There are differences in appearances among ruby glasses prepared by various methods, or even by the same recipes. Copper rubies produced by the staining method, using light impregnation of the glass are under all conditions equally red. When using moderate impregnation, they are clear, transparent and blood red, but when impregnated beyond what is required to develop a saturated red, the glass turns turbid or carnelian-like, and is more copper red in color. Copper rubies made in glass houses by overlay and warming-in methods, appear similar to moderately impregnated, stained glasses when viewed against the light (namely clear blood-red). They appear to be an opaque red when viewed against a dark background or when they are stacked in layers. Copper ruby produced by quenching a melt in water is colorless; but when cooled in the crucible or poured onto a plate, it is generally livery, and is almost never homogeneous. Lighter opaque stripes alternate with dark clear regions. The opaque stripes range from brown-red to the color of sealing wax. The more or less strong degree of variation in appearance depends on the method and the success of the melt, the distribution of the coloring material, the procedure of cooling (pouring, left in the crucible, et cetera), and the dimensions of the cooling body— whether thick or thin. To reach a clearer understanding of the reasons for the above-described phenomena, calls for the use of microscopic examination. Two types of lighting conditions are needed for such an approach. In transmitted light, one obtains views of a one-sided nature which can lead to important conclusions. On the other hand, views obtained with incident light are more useful and instructive. Only by a combination of the two types of views is it possible to obtain a complete knowledge of the phenomena.

Overlay ruby glasses prepared commercially, and ruby glasses made by the staining process appear cloudy or turbid when viewed with the naked eye in reflected light. They also appear this way when viewed under the microscope using transmitted light. At 80-150X magnification, the microscope reveals a delicate fog-like haze which does not impair the transparency. Small objects viewed through the glass have a completely sharp definition. In reflected light, the microscope reveals a similar appearance only less clear. The light haze appears turbid against the lighter illuminating color, but the turbidity cannot be resolved even at the highest magnification. However, the non-transparent, opal-like stains are coarsely turbid when viewed with the naked eye. The turbidity, when viewed in reflected light under the microscope, begins to be resolved as ultrafine shiny particles in the form of a cloud comprised of illuminated points. Both types of ruby glass, overlay and stain, appear red in various degrees when viewed under the microscope. They are hardly ever completely free of turbidity, but the overlays are sometimes clear on a fine scale.

If one melts a particle of copper glass in a glass tube, one obtains a sphere, on blowing, that is coated with a colorless or colophany-colored copper glass. Upon holding the sphere over the flame of a Bunsen burner and moving it carefully towards the hottest zone, one can achieve a gradual striking-in of the ruby. If one now pulls the sphere back at the moment when the red has just started to appear, one obtains a blood red ruby without any turbidity—an absolute ruby. The turbidity is a sign that the glass has already passed the condition of ruby and has entered the stage where opaque precipitates begin to form. These show up as a light, microscopic insoluble haze in commercial overlay glass and in non carnelian-type stains. This can be seen by the naked eye in reflected light, but remains undetected in transmitted light. It is not normally seen—just as one does not see the dust on eyeglasses when reading—because the objects on the other side of the glass are recognized clearly and in full outline when the incident light is bright. The immeasurably small particles responsible for the turbidity simply cannot be focused, because of their immediate nearness.

Under the microscope, with transmitted light, there are no images of other distant objects that could disturb the eye when the highly magnified particles comprising the fog are in focus. Thus the eye is forced to look at them, and the fog becomes visible. On examining the same glasses against a dark background, the naked eye receives only little light from the clear portion of the glass because the dominant portion of the beam passes on through and becomes absorbed in the dark surface of the background, where it becomes lost. On the other hand, the light from the turbid region is reflected back, becoming one object, which the eye can grasp and consequently detect. In opal-like stains the turbidity is not equally intense; the particles are more fully developed, and are present in higher concentrations although not uniformly. The eye, on looking through such glass, does not see the outline of objects on the other side. It can only see the turbidity as illuminated points that are visible in incident light under the microscope. The relation of turbidity to the clearest parts of the glass—in other words the amount and the nature of the precipitate—depends mostly on the type of cooling and can vary significantly for a given glass, as will be seen in the instructive experiment below.

A piece of commercial overlay ruby, which revealed a light haze only in reflected light, was held for several hours in a muffle at a temperature where the glass barely starts to soften (such that neither deformation nor rounding of the edges takes place). Its appearance was completely altered. The regions that had been a transparent, deep red became opaque brown (a coarse turbidity resulted). Under the microscope, in transmitted light, the opaque brown-red glass appeared as a light green transparent ground mass with dark, deep black-brown clouds intermixed. The latter under high magnification were clearly recognized as granulation. In incident light, the glass offered a completely different picture. It appeared as a beautiful, bright-colored, red glowing mass, which could be resolved at medium magnification as a milky way of shiny red-yellow points imbedded in a groundmass of dark indefinite color. This behaviour—black points in a green glass, or red-yellow shiny points in a dark mass—proves that the precipitates must be opaque and of yellow-red color. The same is the case with most of the ruby glasses produced by melting.

It is difficult to obtain ruby glass by melting (if it is not quenched in water), because an absolute ruby, without precipitates, is rarely achieved by fusion alone. A product of a previously described melt, with 0.2% copper oxide plus tin as a reducing agent, represents such a ruby in the strictest sense of the word. Glass melted in a crucible and poured onto a plate contains no opaque streaks and zones, but consists of a uniform, deep red, non-livery mass. Splinters and thin fragments appear transparent ruby red in transmitted light when viewed with the naked eye and under the microscope. The same holds for incident light, because the glass contains no reflecting particles—i.e. precipitates. Due to absorbtion of light, the glass appears dark to the naked eye. The occurrence of such a glass requires special lucky conditions; the glass must not be cooled too rapidly nor too slowly; furthermore, the coloring constituents must not be present in excess. Results obtained with melts containing 0.5% copper oxide with tin were almost as good.

Reds produced by melting with more copper oxide—one percent and more—are not rubies, no matter how homogeneous they may appear. They invariably contain precipitates in the heterogeneous groundmass—which is indicated by their livery nature. In transmitted light, under the microscope, the livery color is completely gone and, instead, one sees a green glass seeded with dark points. In incident light this color also disappears and the glass splinters appear surprisingly and delusively like a strikingly red body in a bright red color, which upon sufficient enlargement can be resolved into numerous extremely fine points of the same color. The glass thus consists (just like overlay ruby that has been heated in a muffle) of a transparent green groundmass with precipitated bright red particles. With the unaided eye, the two colors mix into a brown color, as was shown by von Pettenkofer. In transmitted light, one observes the groundmass with its real color and the precipitate appears as a projection of opaque, non-illuminated particles (i.e. as dark points). In incident light, the groundmass disappears in the reverse manner, and only the brightly illuminated particles of precipitate with their characteristic color are discerned by the eye; then, they alone reflect light, since they are opaque. Occasionally one finds regions with a red groundmass in the melt—namely in thin bodies, threads, fibers, et cetera. Overlays of the livery glass yield a weakly-hued brown color, which as already mentioned above, warms-in nicely.

If one increases the copper still more, e.g. from one percent to four and five and even to nine percent, always with an appropriate addition of reducing agent, then these larger additions remain incorporated in the glass. To determine how much copper oxide can be assimilated by the glass under the action of reducing agents, we prepared a melt at a high red heat and this melt was composed of the following batch:

Lead Glass Batch "A"	60
Cupric Oxide	20
Metallic Tin	40

Upon cooling of the crucible in air, the glass was found to be an opaque red-brown color, striated and with a dull luster; in some ways it was slag-like in appearance with many coarse and fine round copper particles in the body. A portion of the glass was poured into water during removal of the crucible from the fire, and selected pieces that did not contain any copper particles (as examined by the eye), were used for analysis. Upon pulverizing in an agate mortar, it was possible to remove the remaining tiny copper particles that had been missed by visual examination (since they became perceptible under the pestle and were evident upon flattening of the powder). The determination of silica was made by fusion with sodium carbonate and tin was determined as tin sulfide; another portion that was decomposed with barium hydroxide was used for the determination of copper as sulfide; and a third portion that was dissolved in hydrofluoric acid was used to determine potassium as sulfate. We obtained:

Silica	38.55%
Stannic oxide	13.79
Litharge	36.34
Potash	3.86
Copper Metal	6.75
Oxygen	0.71
Total	100.00%

If one starts with 100 parts by weight silica in order to make a ready comparison, one finds that the batch contained 88.9 cupric oxide or 70.4 copper metal, and the final glass contained only 17.5 (also based on a hundred parts silica), thus, only one fourth of the copper added (as oxide) is incorporated in the glass. Nevertheless, the assimilation (solubility) for copper is dramatic and without equal—it is at least 30 times greater than with gold under the most favorable conditions.

This copper-rich glass, when taken from the crucible after melting, behaved not at all differently from glass melts containing only small amounts of copper. It yielded a livery, occasionally grey and black colored melt with deep red veins; the glass was dull in appearance and completely opaque. Under the microscope, where only the thinnest splinters appeared transparent (viewed in incident light), one observed a ruby color and a precipitate; the latter consisting of innumerable sparkles in a shiny, bright red matrix. When quenched in cold water, the glass contains deep brown-black shiny particles, neither opaque nor dull, but instead glassy in appearance; under magnification, the glass appeared to be colorless on the surface, ruby red in the interior, and transparent with a sparse precipitate. The glass, which had not been quenched, but which was poured onto a plate (and also that which had remained stuck to the wall of the crucible), upon comminution was red-brown like a wood extract. Under high magnification, one observed individual, widely separated, angular particles in a dark, colorless groundmass. They were considerably larger and more distinct than the above precipitates in the red matrix, and appeared to be crystalline; in projection, as far as one could discern, they were square. It was not possible to make overlays because the glass was too viscous due to the high tin concentration.

Two other samples of glass (lead containing batch) melted with 9% cupric oxide had properties which were between the previous and the glasses with 1% or less cuprous oxide. When cooled in the crucible they appeared livery, shiny, reflective and dark brown, with red-brown opaque stripes. In the water-quenched state, the opaque stripes were absent, and the glass was a deep black-brown. Thin splinters under the microscope were nearly completely colorless, with a few areas a transparent ruby red. The latter were black in appearance in incident light, and had some indications of precipitation. An overlay was red and contained yellow-red precipitates when viewed under magnification with top lighting. Drawn threads of glass were similar, except that the precipitate was more clearly defined as points. A pea-sized piece that had been heated for some time in a blast flame and had been cooled in air, showed stripes that were twisted, marble-like and a mixed sealing wax red and dark brown. The powder—which had a brownish appearance to the naked eye—showed up under the microscope (in transmitted light) as a transparent ruby red, and in incident light as a red-green iron color.

A phenomenon that is observed rarely and at isolated regions in both of the above melts , was a canary yellow and a grass green color. In the case of the previously described glass with 6.7% copper content, this condition can be achieved by fusing it in a glass tube and pulling the ball into a thick thread. The color of the melt was molasses-brown, quite transparent, and upon subsequent light heating did not turn red; but instead it became a siskin yellow to light loam color (which was opaque). Under the microscope, using incident light, the loam colored glass appeared to contain precipitates of shiny, very fine, tightly heaped yellow glitter imbedded in a groundmass of a weak, indeterminate color.

The mentioning of these details is only meant to serve as proof that the exterior appearance and nature of copper-containing glasses that are melted with reducing agents, depends to a great extent on the conditions existing during treatment, especially on cooling. The color can change appreciably for the same melt—depending on how the threads are pulled or how the glass is poured from the melt—i.e. in thicker or thinner mass, on plates or in water, solidifying in the crucible, et cetera. All glasses from 0.1% copper oxide to the highest copper oxide content, exhibited chiefly the same appearance which the opaque melts produced on cooling—namely being livery with a high or low degree of opaqueness. The batch with 9% cupric oxide corresponds to hematinone, one with 4-5% corresponds to aventurine, but even these glasses, when prepared by simple melting were no exception from the rule as regards appearance. One can only say that glasses with an increasing content of cupric oxide have an increasing tendency to form precipitates and turn opaque. A glass does not form hematinones because it forms a glass with 4-5% cupric oxide, nor an aventurine because it has been melted with 9% cupric oxide; but only becomes these glasses after melting and cooling develops certain precipitates. Such precipitates are best formed when these glasses contain those amounts of copper oxide.

From the Chemical-Technical Laboratory of the Collegium Carolinum in Braunschweig, Germany.

33 RESEARCH ON COPPER REDS

C. LAUTH AND G. DUTAILLY

(Translated by Robert Tichane)

> This piece by Lauth and Dutailly, in my opinion, is the best article ever written about copper red glazes. True, they did have the advantage of having Ebell's article available and undoubtedly they benefited from their associates at Sevres, but nevertheless, they put it all together and they did it in writing, which is what really matters.

The names flambé and high-fired red are used to describe the colors of some glazes which are obtained on porcelain by means of copper and its derivatives. These descriptions separate these red products from those made with iron oxide, which can only stand lower firing temperatures.

The porcelains coming from China and decorated by means of copper have a variety of aspects; sometimes they are covered uniformly by an opaque red glaze, while on the other hand the glaze is sometimes of a transparent red color, which is very brilliant and in an artificial light has a beautiful clear quality. In addition to the red vases that have a more or less uniform tint, we also find some which are given the general name of flambé. Such a glaze, instead of being a uniform color, is veined in streaks going from red to all kinds of violet, blue and even green colors. All of the colors are intimately melted together and are mixed in all kinds of bizarre manners, and yet they have an unexpected charm and an inexpressible quality. Such glazes are nearly always crackled. Also, on certain rather rare objects, one finds some copper red used as an ordinary color—like those which one uses to paint ornamentals like flowers, animals, and so forth. In this case, the copper red generally appears in the form of strokes or hatchings of an opaque red; although sometimes the color, instead of being a beautiful red, is only an ugly brownish black, and the lines, instead of being clean and neat, are surrounded by a halo of red. These underglaze red decorations are often accompanied by underglaze blue color.

HISTORICAL

For many hundreds of years now, the Chinese have known how to make copper reds, but it is probable that they have done this purely from an empirical standpoint. It is known that they have lost the process at different times, sometimes for long periods, and particularly after they have changed their primary materials. At the end of the last century, the imperial factory at Ching-te-chen was still in the possesion of this "secret;" but then they lost it again, and it seems that it is still lost at the present time, at least insofar as the beautiful transparent glaze of long ago is concerned.

We can read in the report addressed to the minister of Public Instruction, from M. Scherzer, the following comment: "The copper red called *Tsi-houng* or sang de boeuf, so appreciated by collectors, has been lost since the death of the last possessor of the secret of its fabrication; for the last twenty years, the administration at the imperial factory has been making excuses in its reports to the throne about not being able to execute a command to make vases covered in *Tsi-houng*, which was requested by her majesty."

And further along, M. Scherzer says, "One lone family claims to possess the secret of the manufacture of the red called *Kun-houng*; but this glaze, with regard to its vitreous aspects, is usually too thick, and rarely offers a beautiful color."

The composition of red glaze for the high fire has always been a secret; the formulas which have been received—as for example those which we find in the letters of Pere d'Entrecolles—are rather obscure, and only merit a limited confidence. It is about the same for that information sent from China by M. Scherzer. According to him, the red glaze was lead-containing, and, in addition to copper, it also contained several complex products, samples of which he sent to us.

It is necessary to add at this point, that all of this information can have value only if it is complemented by data concerning the complete method for making copper red glazes. We do know that the red colors are obtained by the use of copper, but of what use can this knowledge be put—even if one knew the exact composition of the glaze—if one did not possess at the same time the details and circumstances on: the nature of the paste on which it is to be placed; the base glaze; the temperature of firing; and the method of firing, et cetera. In ceramics everything is tied together and related; one isolated detail does not help to solve the whole problem.

The first French attempt to make a reproduction of copper red for the high fire, was made by Ebelmen and Salvetat, who described this in detail in their memoir on the composition of the materials used in the fabrication and in the decoration of Chinese porcelains (in 1852). These scientists, having analysed some fragments of red glaze broken off a Chinese vase, attributed to it the following composition: Silica-73.9%; Alumina-6.0%; Iron Oxide-2.1%; Lime-7.3%; Potash-3.0%; Soda-3.1%; and Copper Oxide-4.6%.

They formulated a glaze from this percentage composition, which was made up of: d'Aumont Sand-38.0%; Feldspar-50%; Lime-6.0%; and Copper Oxide-6.0%.

This corresponded to a composition of: Silica-76.05%; Alumina plus Iron Oxide-7.75%; Lime plus Magnesia-6.08%; Potash plus Soda-3.72%; and Copper Oxide-6.00%.

They applied this to a body that was more fusible than the usual Sevres porcelain, and which was similar to the porcelain of China; they made up this body by using: 80% ordinary paste and 20% pegmatite.

With this paste and this glaze, and by firing in a small furnace in which the chimney was adjusted to afford a reducing atmosphere, they obtained, "Some red pieces on which the glaze was not crackled, which is rarely the case in pieces of Chinese manufacture."

The examples of this work were deposited in the collection of the Sevres Ceramic Museum; another of the vases obtained in this manner was decorated with a frieze of gold, which cannot be done with Chinese porcelain, since it breaks up when it is refired for gold application.

We have expanded on these preliminary experiments because we wanted to establish that it was to these two illustrious scientists of the Sevres factory that the honor belongs for having been the first Europeans to have found and made known these manufacturing techniques.

It is astonishing that there were no further sequels to these experiments, all the more so because other work was done at the Sevres factory in a way that was completely different and imperfect. This consisted of taking some previously biscuit-fired pieces to a red heat and then plunging them in this state into melted glass, which was colored red by cuprous oxide.

Some years later, Reynaud repeated these experiments of high fired reds, by firing some hard porcelain pieces coated with a copper glaze, either in charcoal-lined saggers, or in the presence of reducing gases in ordinary unlined saggers. The account rendered of these experiences indicated that they did not give satisfactory results.

Recently the question of Chinese red glazes has been raised again and has been elucidated by different ceramic scientists. At the top of the list we find H. Boulenger & Co., which in 1877 produced, in collaboration with the late C. Feil, a splendid red on faience. In 1879, M. Deck obtained a whole series of flambés on porcelain which he showed in a remarkable collection at the Exposition of 1880. M. Optat Milet at the Sevres factory also obtained some interesting results. And finally, in the last three years, M. Chaplet and M. Haviland, have succeeded brilliantly in their work.

In foreign countries, the problem has been tackled and resolved by M. Seger at the Berlin factory and by M. Bunzli at Krummnusbaum (Austria).

As one can see, the fabrication of flambés and of copper reds has been realized in several places in the last ten years, so that it is less experimental today, even though the procedures used have remained secret. To our knowledge, nothing has been published on this subject since the observations of Ebelmen and Salvetat. In 1879, one of us was charged, at the direction of the Sevres factory, to undertake the research to establish the scientific facts and to make known the rules of copper red fabrication, the question of which had begun to be clarified in 1852.

EXPERIMENTAL

Our first high-fired copper red firing was made at Sevres in 1882, following a long series of preliminary laboratory studies. The account of the results obtained will be made the object of this memoir.

The uncertainty which we had as to the composition of the red as well as to the nature of the glaze and the paste on which it was placed, led us to repeat from the very beginning the experiments of Ebelmen and Salvetat.

Several fragments of red Chinese porcelain were put in a sagger of a Sevres furnace and were fired to the temperature usually taken for ordinary hard porcelain. On opening the furnace we found that these samples were nearly totally deprived of their glaze, which had run down to the lowest parts and was there to be found in round droplets of a pale, greenish colored glass.

Some identical fragments were then submitted to the temperature required for firing the "new" Sevres porcelain, which one of us, in collaboration with M. Vogt introduced to the Sevres factory. This glaze maintained its glassiness and didn't present any evidence of being overfired, and one did not observe any coloring. On firing in oxidation, it became greenish on account of the copper oxide that it contained, but on firing in a neutral atmosphere, the glaze was decolorized. More curiously, it regained some of its red color, going to a pale red when it was reheated later to a low temperature in a neutral or slightly reducing atmosphere.

These experiments prove that the Chinese glaze on which we were working cannot be maintained at the temperature of the usual Sevres firing, and that the red color disappears in the normal conditions of our firing. On the other hand, it shows that these glazes are resistant to the firing temperature of the "new porcelain," and that then the color (and all of its modifications) is not destroyed when submitted to such a firing. It is only partially volatilized and only after three or four firings is it completely evaporated.

It was therefore possible to suppose that one could obtain this red color in a furnace used for firing "new porcelain." the problem consisted of resolving two things: one, determining the condition of firing which the red would develop; and two, determining the nature of the glaze to use. As to the nature of the coloring, there was no doubt after what we have learned on this question and after several of our experiments, that it is copper that produces the red color.

The description of these researches will be divided into three parts: one, the laboratory experiments; two, the application of these results in an experimental furnace; and three, an extension of the results to the normal Sevres furnace.

LABORATORY EXPERIMENTS

It may appear strange on first sight that even though we had many furnaces of large size available to us, that we would think of doing the experiments in the laboratory. However, it would be impractical to proceed otherwise. When it is only a question of making a small modification in the work which goes into a ceramic furnace, it is advantageous to make a test run immediately in an industrial furnace, so that one can see what happens to this idea. But, when it is a question of varying the nature of the firing (such as neutral, oxidizing or reducing) or in changing the degree of temperature to which the firing is taken, the experiment ought to be made in the laboratory, because it is impossible to modify the course of firing of an ordinary furnace either as to its conduct or to the degree of firing it attains without compromising a whole furnace full of ware. This kind of reasoning explains the difficulty that one has in introducing new ideas into industrial ceramics, no matter how attractive or how carefully one changes the type of firing. The manufacturer cannot easily decide on a new furnace or risk a whole furnace full of ware and hence he cannot put into his current production some experiments which require special circumstances.

Let us also add that even if there were no other considerations, the infrequency of firing at Sevres would prolong obtaining results to an exaggerated extent and would be a serious obstacle to research of long duration.

Up until now, no one has ever indicated the procedure which allows one to make experiments on firing porcelain in the laboratory, so we will describe this subject in some detail.

M. Lauth, who was preoccupied by this question from the beginning of his researches at Sevres, had the idea of making use of a Perrot gas furnace for these experiments, and the result has been very advantageous on all sides. This apparatus allows firing of porcelain in the laboratory in a very short length of time (2 or 3 hours), with a relatively low cost and under variable conditions, at the whim of the experimenter. Nothing is more practical than this piece of apparatus, which occupies so little space. It seems to us to be an ideal piece of equipment for all ceramic laboratories, so that instead of waiting weeks for the results of experiments as would be the case in an industrial furnace, a Perrot furnace gives experimental results three or four times a day.

Here is the process that we adopted; in the interior of the furnace, one places a crucible provided with a false bottom, on which one places (on some clay pieces) the specimens destined to be fired; for special experiments, the crucible can be perforated in the lower part and can be supplied with a hollow ceramic tube which allows one to inject into the interior a current of air or other gas. When it is used just to modify the atmosphere of the furnace and to make it more or less oxidizing or reducing, one can use an ordinary crucible, and by simply regulating the supply of air or gas, one can vary the nature of the firing. To make more intimate contact between the furnace atmosphere and the object being fired, one can also pierce a series of holes in the walls of the crucible so that the flame can then penetrate freely over the sample.

In the first series of experiments, we determined, by means of test pieces, the maximum temperature which could be used without altering the Chinese red glazes. Since this temperature is in the neighborhood of that used to fire the "new" Sevres porcelain, we have adopted it for the fabrication of the reds. More recently, however, our research temperatures have been reduced to about 1300°C.

Next, we have determined in the same way (by means of different fragments of Chinese red porcelain), the conditions under which it is necessary to treat them without destroying their color, and have assumed that these same conditions would allow us to obtain the development of reds in our porcelain. We have therefore fired these fragments at the desired temperature, sometimes in a reducing atmosphere and sometimes in an oxidizing atmosphere, and it has been demonstrated that every time that the fire is oxidizing, the red disappears and in its place there is a greenish glaze. While on the contrary, when the firing is done in the presence of reducing gases, the red is not altered at all. The ease with which one can vary (using the Perrot furnace) the nature of the firing, has allowed us to determine quickly the most favorable conditions for obtaining a beautiful red. We have evaluated the importance of: the duration and the time of strong reduction; the rapidity of the firing; and finally the technique required at the end of the operation. The final technique may need to be reducing, neutral or even slightly oxidizing, according to whether the first period was more or less reducing itself.

We shall return to these different phases again in indicating the path adopted and then they will be described in detail.

We have considered as probable that one would obtain the copper red color at the temperature and in the conditions that we are going to determine and it is on that basis that the final experience has been based. The porcelain that we are going to use for our experiments, by its point of fusion and from its composition, resembles oriental porcelain. That is to say, it is more siliceous and less aluminous than the usual hard porcelain of Sevres.

The work on glazes has given rise to numerous experiments which, as we shall see later, have had to be repeated again and again. The goal that we have searched for, consisted not in obtaining just **any kind** of red, but in determining the rules that are necessary in order to obtain: first, a red glaze of an intense transparent kind that is not crackled; and secondly, different glazes called flambés, which appear to us to be varieties of copper red.

We first tried to make only simple additions to an ordinary glaze used on the "new" Sevres porcelain by adding oxides and other compounds of copper. We have fired in the fixed conditions described above and in the presence of samples of Chinese red (so as to evaluate the results of the operation). The results have been bad. One obtains in this manner only traces of red and it is a brownish-red without any clarity and is poorly fused. In each case, without fail, one has observed the formation of this poor color modification instead of the beautiful and interesting red Chinese color.

Basing our experiments on the fact that copper gives a beautiful red color in the blowpipe (using a borax or phosphate bead in a reducing flame), we thought that the addition of these fluxes to the ordinary glaze would be favorable. It has such a special effect in the case of borax, but we have not been able to obtain any good glazes when using phosphates. Although the many glazes prepared with varying proportions of borax gives superior results to those of the preceding glazes, they still are not comparable to the Chinese copper reds.

It was thus necessary to look for a glaze of a different type, so first a mixture was made up according to the ancient one given by Ebelmen and Salvetat according to the following formulation: Pegmatite-40; Sand-44; Limestone-12; Chalcothar-2; Potash-7.5; Copper Oxide-4.6. Which corresponds to: Silica-70.7%; Alumina-7.0%; Alkalies-9.3%; Lime-6.5%; Iron Oxide-2.0%; and Copper Oxide-4.5%/ This glaze differs from a normal one by its lower content of alumina and lime and by its higher content of silica and alkalies.

This mixture, having given a satisfactory result, has served as a point of departure for a series of methodical tests in which we have determined the importance and the advantage of silica, alumina, and alkalies; and on which we have examined the action of other chemical agents.

Here are the conclusions:

1. The glaze ought to have very little alumina;
2. It ought to have very little lime and quite a bit of alkali;
3. The presence of borax is useful as it tends to repress crackle formation (which may be due to excessive alkalies and low quantities of alumina); borax also favors the development of red, not only because of the alkali which it contains, but also because of the boric acid, which helps to dissolve everything;
4. It is good to add tin oxide to the glaze, for it protects the copper against oxidation during fusion and during cooling (the percentage of tin ought to be less than the percentage of copper);
5. The use of lead has only given bad results.

These first experiments having been completed, we considered that the period of preliminary trials had ended and we now decided to try an industrial firing.

APPLICATION OF THE RESULTS FROM THE TEST FURNACE

The small furnace which we used had a reversed flame (down draft), and it had a capacity of about 1.5 cubic meters (53 cubic feet).

From all the glazes which had been tested in the laboratory, we chose the six which had given the most interesting results. They were made up of compositions covering the following ranges:

Alumina	5.4 - 10.5%
Silica	46.5 - 66.0%
Alkalies	6.2 - 28.0%

These glazes were applied to the porcelain in many ways: sometimes on the biscuit by dipping; sometimes over covered and sometimes over uncovered ordinary white glazes; and sometimes they were placed on the porcelain biscuit in stripes as one often does with the underglaze blue of the Sevres high fire.

In order to be certain of the course of the firing we took a series of each of the different kinds of glazes (according to their different mode of application), and put them in all of the different stacks of saggers and at three different levels; and finally, for those placed in saggers, some of them were luted and some were left open—to facilitate the access of reducing gases to the samples.

The firing was maintained in a manner so that the atmosphere was constantly reducing. This result was obtained by continually keeping the firebox full of fuel and enclosing the draft vents in such a manner that the entrance of air was difficult. This produced a sort of distillation from the wood. The composition of the gaseous products produced in this manner was determined approximately by means of an **Orsat Apparatus** and the indications were controlled by means of draw trials from the furnace.

Here are the results obtained in this first firing:

1. The two following glazes have given a transparent
   red which was quite satisfactory in certain places
   in the furnace.

	I	II
Pegmatite	40	40
Sand	40	44
Lime	18	12
Fused Borax	12	0
Soda Ash	0	25
Copper Oxide	6	6
Tin Oxide	6	3

The percentage compositions of these two frits are:

	I	II
Silica	67.0	70.0
Alumina	7.1	6.8
Alkali	7.8	17.8
Lime	9.9	6.4
Boric Oxide	8.2	0.0

2. Our best results were obtained with glazes that were
   put on **already glazed porcelain.**
3. The red developed best in the stacks of saggers that
   were incompletely luted.
4. The proportion of copper oxide ought to be around
   6%. The glazes which contained less copper oxide
   had more decoloration in the conditions of firing
   that we used.
5. The amount of oxide of tin ought to be less than that
   of the oxide of copper.

After this first experience, which demonstrated that the results of a big furnace were exactly the same as those of the laboratory, the industrial fabrication of copper reds and the flambés was then organized and we rapidly began to produce some rather important pieces—that is to say, pieces of from 30-40 cm, in height.

The firings took place in the experimental furnace over a period of two years. The glaze which was adopted as the best in this period was that which we listed above as #I. Glaze #II was too alkaline to fit on our body without frequently breaking it into pieces.

Up until now, nothing has been said about the nature of copper red, and although the question has not been absolutely elucidated, it would be appropriate for us to comment briefly on our ideas on this subject. It is certain that the red is obtained by the reduction of oxygenated compounds of copper. But, what is the exact nature of the red? Is the opaque red different from the transparent red and from the flambé glaze?

Most of the scientists who have spoken about copper red have considered it to be either cuprous oxide or a silicate of cuprous oxide. But nothing appears to have been demonstrated. How could cuprous oxide manage to preserve itself at the high temperatures of which we are speaking? Especially, how could it be preserved in the presence of reduction, which should take it to the metallic state. And, shouldn't it on oxidation turn green? How can such an unstable combination of silica and cuprous oxide be able to maintain itself?

It appears to us more rational to admit that the copper coloration is due to the metal itself. Under the influence of a reducing atmosphere, and further favored by the presence of tin, the copper mixture in the glaze is amenable to conversion to copper metal at high temperatures. If the composition of the glaze permits it, the metal dissolves in the glaze, and when the amount of copper is not too high, the solution stays clear, even down to the solidification point. This is a phenomenon which is analogous to that which occurs for metallic gold in the colors called gold rose and gold red. Next there occurs the matter that we have talked about before on two occasions. When the chilling of dissolved copper occurs under certain conditions—most notably when it is cooled rapidly—the glaze is transformed into a colorless glass. Nevertheless, it is capable of turning to red if one rewarms it at a low temperature.

However, when the chilling process takes place slowly, the red develops in all its splendor and it retains a transparency similar to that of precious stones. It is a veritable dyeing of the glaze. If, on the contrary, the composition of the glaze contains more metal than it is possible to dissolve, or if the concentration of copper is too high, then at the moment of recrystallization, there is precipitation; and then, the finely divided metallic copper appears as an opaque color, a dark red, and the glaze in which it is mixed is neither clear nor transparent.

These phenomena are of the same kind that one finds for gold in glass, and this analogy appears forceful enough to us so that our hypotheses seems reasonable.

M. Paul Ebell, in 1874, made this question the object of a long memoir in his studies on the red colorations in **glass**; His conclusions appear to us to be applicable in all their points as regards porcelain.

The irregularities and the difficulties of making copper red glazes are due to the chemical properties of copper and its compounds. Let us suppose that the period of strong reduction be prolonged to a great extent, or that the temperature be raised much higher than we wished; in this case, the metallic copper volatilizes, and the enamel, which is more or less stripped of it, becomes colorless in the furnace. If, on the contrary, the firing is made too quickly, the partial volatilization of copper, on which one depended, would not have time to take place; in this case, the amount of metal would be too high to be able to be dissolved, and the glaze, instead of being transparent, would be opaque and saturated.

Other phenomena can also take place. For example, during the completion of the firing or during the period of cooling, air can penetrate into certain parts of the furnace. It doesn't matter whether it is from the firebox or from some of the many fissures which exist all over the surface of the masonry, because at that moment when the air comes into contact with the melted copper glaze, it will oxidize it. The spots struck by the air, turn more or less bluish or greenish, and, since the glaze continues to flow—as it is extremely hot—it traps in its mass those oxidized parts which then melt into the rest and thus give birth to flambés. Without having recourse to this explanation, based on the entrance of air, it is also possible that the flame—which is variable in composition along all of its length—could itself be the cause of these innumerable fantasies, which indicates that the surface of the glaze has been touched by the flame and has been instantly transformed. In addition, there is another cause to which we can attribute certain flambés. That is the ease with which some glazes decompose by themselves, setting free opaque bodies, which form in the body of the glaze. These form some zones, as well as some white streaks of the most beautiful aspect

These different phenomena can also all happen at the same time, and their effects can then combine and give results which sometimes have a very great charm. In summary, we consider that the transparent copper red and the opaque copper red are the product of copper dissolution, followed by precipitation of metallic copper in a glaze.

The rules to be followed in order to obtain copper reds vary almost infinitely. They obviously depend on a number of causes, none of which seem to depend on the other. Some of the factors are: the form and dimension of the furnace in which the work is done; the nature of the porcelain selected; and the composition and fusibility of the base glaze adopted.

One can even conceive of methods of fabrication which are absolutely different from one another. We personally have applied copper red as a product of the high fire, because we know that the ancient Chinese worked at a very high temperature. However, it would be possible to arrive at similar results under completely different conditions. Nothing is opposed to the fact that one could apply copper reds on porcelain biscuit or enameled porcelain using some copper glaze melting at 1000-1200°C. Such a glaze could then be transformed to a red in an appropriate muffle furnace. In such an apparatus and at a relatively low temperature, the difficulties would be greatly lessened. Furthermore, it should be possible for one to apply a copper red glaze on raw porcelain or on biscuited porcelain, which could be fired in a high fire, and then be transformed later into red in a muffle furnace. In the course of our research we have been able to perform some of these experiments on occasion and some of the results have been very interesting. We will speak about them in the third part of this memoir.

Let us now concern ourselves with the red and flambé obtained from the porcelain furnace. We believe that one ought to consider these technical details relative to the fabrication of copper reds in order to outline precisely the method of operation which has been followed.

The materials which compose the glaze should be intimately mixed before fusion; it is especially beneficial to grind the oxides of copper and tin together before introducing them into the mixture. The total batch can then be melted at a high temperature until it is transformed into a completely transparent glass; after several hours of fusion (which is necessary in order to ensure that the glaze has been freed from bubbles), one pours it into water; there, because it is cooled so quickly it is present in the form of a beautifully tinted green glass (if the fusion has taken place in an oxidizing atmosphere). On the other hand, if the fusion has been made in a reducing atmosphere the glaze comes out absolutely colorless; it is this reduced glass, which, if reheated in a gentle reducing flame, transforms itself into a beautiful transparent red glass. There is no advantage to firing the glass in a reducing flame. In fact, we prefer to use it in the form of a green glass, because the successive changes in color which it undergoes during firing, and which one can observe in the middle of the furnace, allows one to follow more easily the process of the operation and to control the composition of the combustion gas.

The finely pulverized glaze, mixed with an essential oil, is then applied to the **fired** porcelain and then is enameled, as is the practice for the underglaze blue of high fired hard porcelain; it ought to be completely dry before it is fused; one trace of humidity makes it ball up and this can cause the displacement of the color during firing. The thickness which ought to be used for application is given by the term "three supported layers."

Drying of the pieces in a muffle is more dangerous than useful; in effect, during this drying , the cover for the glaze begins to melt and it reacts with the body before the white glaze begins to soften; it therefore begins to combine with this and forms a kind of nonadherent envelope which tears itself up during the resolidification; and sometimes it falls off in flakes.

Then again, if one pushes the temperature of drying too high, so that fixation takes place, the red glaze may completely seal over without submitting itself to the action of the reducing gas in the furnace (or at least this action is less profound than when the glaze is porous at the surface).

SAGGERING AND FIRING

In the process of saggering the pieces, it is necessary that there should be interposed between the ware and the sagger which supports them, a little block of porcelain, thoroughly dusted with clay, in order to prevent the glaze on cooling from gluing the piece to the sagger. With a little experience the placement of the bottoms can be made well enough to give the glaze on the bottom part of the object some convenient space for the enamel with too much flow, so it can equalize itself; in general, one ought to keep a zone at the foot of a vase of about one centimeter in width on which one doesn't apply any glaze.

The saggers are only luted partially in order to permit the reducing gas to penetrate more easily into the pile. Still, it is not advisable to favor the access of the gas too much, because it has happened that when we fired one vase in the full force of the flames, without saggering it at all, then we found on opening the furnace that the glaze was completely devoid of copper (which had volatilized).

At the start of a firing and before the furnace becomes red hot, the gas is not able to act on the glaze; therefore, it is not absolutely necessary at this time to have a reducing atmosphere. Nevertheless, it is preferable, because it is often difficult to modify the kind of gas in a furnace once it has been established in a certain mode. Hence, if one begins with an oxidizing fire it is more difficult to change the type of firing to reducing, as needs to be done later.

At the moment when the furnace gets up to red heat, one should produce a maximum of reducing gas, and maintain this program until all indications show that the glaze has turned completely black, without any trace of green. If, at the moment when the glaze begins to flow, it doesn't present this character, it is necessary to increase the smoking and to keep the temperature steady until this result is obtained.

This reducing atmosphere can be obtained in two ways, either by the use of an excess of fuel, or by diminution of the draft. The first procedure, we believe has the most to recommend it, because a diminution of the draft causes shortening of the flame, which, at its extremity, can then become oxidizing, and on licking the piles of saggers, could oxidize the pieces.

During this reduction period the glaze is frequently bubbly. However, a slow progression of the firing prevents this problem (which is really not too worrisome), for one would still obtain a beautiful glaze even if the end of the firing is carried out in a conventional way.

When one judges that the period of reduction has been carried out for a sufficient length of time (and only experience allows one to appreciate exactly when this point arrives), one changes little by little the course of the firing; one slows down the reduction, one raises the temperature, and one takes all the dispositions necessary in order that the end of the firing be made in an atmosphere that is either lightly reducing or neutral. Sometimes it is even useful to use an oxidizing atmosphere in order to complete the formation of the red and to obtain a very vivid and very pure color.

We have tried different procedures in order to determine the state of the interior of the furnace during the firing of the reds, seeking to avoid the use of test pieces which require the opening of the apparatus and occasionally cause serious trouble in the progress of the operation. However, we have not been able to find a procedure that is absolutely satisfactory and we have continued to look for something which would show the state of the firing. The glazes pass successively from a matte black to a brownish black at the onset of glazing, then to a brownish red, next to an opaque red, and finally when the point of fusion is attained, they become a beautiful transparent red. In order to observe this last tint, one must avoid cooling the samples quickly when one withdraws them from the furnace, otherwise they would appear colorless or that modification that we have already described several times. The whole furnace is without doubt in this state at this moment and the development of the red only happens under the influence of a gradual cooling.

However, it is not necessary to try to slow down the cooling process (here again one finds oneself in the presence of one of these numerous questions, the appreciation of which makes the fabrication so delicate and so interesting at this time); actually, it is necessary to remove the red glaze as quickly as possible from air oxidation, which unfortunately—despite all precautions that we can take—will penetrate into the interior of the furnace. Another reason for a relatively rapid cooling is that we have observed that when the sample stays in the furnace for a **long** time at a high temperature, it produces a kind of liquid-liquid separation in the glaze. It becomes covered by opaque spots and streaks of a greenish-white which entirely masks the red. In such a firing, a vase will be found to be covered uniformly with a greenish-opaque enamel, very icy looking, under which one can find a red if one removes the upper surface by abrasion. This is not, as one might first believe, a simple phenomenon of oxidation; there is a veritable separation of products. But, we shall return to this later.

Our firings have always been made with a low fire for the period of strong reduction and in a high fire for the period of final ascension. In a firing of 16-18 hours, one usually fires 11 hours at low fire and seven hours at high fire.

The rise in the temperature has been observed with the help of a water circulation pyrometer, which has always given comparable results among the samples, as long as the rate of the temperature rise has been normal, and as long as one has not made use of the damper in the chimney to modify the firing in the furnace. In such a case, the velocity of the gas itself is modified and these observations are not comparable. The most favorable firing conditions have been realized by setting the high fire at a temperature corresponding to a thermometric rise of 9.5°C (the total rise being 14.5°C) according to the thermometer of the apparatus. One must not neglect, during the reduction firing, to frequently withdraw the pyrometer from the furnace in order to scrape off the coating of black soot which has deposited on it and which would place the readings in error and make the apparatus more susceptible to giving a false reading from the heat of the gaseous environment.

Such are the general rules which we have followed in the firings made at the factory from 1882-1885. These rules have allowed us to obtain a large number of pieces with very beautiful results and with a variety of interesting aspects. We have presented some of the principal types at the Paris Exposition of 1884 and also at d'Anvers in 1885. The yield of choice pieces in this fabrication has been, according to the registrar of the factory, about 82%.

EXTENSION OF THE RESULTS TO ORDINARY FURNACES

The use of a furnace of small dimensions is indispensable in a period of experimentation; it allows one to make experiments frequently and rapidly and it does not entail much expense. However, the production that one is able to obtain in this manner is obviously very limited and the pieces are naturally of small dimension. In addition, it is sometimes difficult to regulate the furnace so that it has reproducible temperatures, and gas compositions. This again restricts the amount of usable space. Also, it is necessary to decide at what point the rules for fabricating copper reds have been established and assured by a sufficient number of firings, so that one can try some experiments in a large furnace. During the first months of 1885, two firings were made in this fashion. They allowed us to make the following observations; reds and flambés have been obtained of a very beautiful nature, well glazed, without crackle and in an extended area of the furnace; in other parts of the furnace, it has not been possible to get reds. This furnace was constructed with an objective that was precisely the opposite to that which we were aiming at—it was meant to be used for oxidation firings. The resources which the factory placed at our disposal did not permit making a specially constructed apparatus for the use of this new manufacturing technique of ours. It was necessary to use the materials that we had at hand. In several zones of this furnace it was impossible to maintain the gas in the necessary reduction state; likewise, by reason of the mass of the furnace, the cooling was much slower than in the test furnace, therefore the glaze was fluid for a relatively long time while in contact with an oxidizing atmosphere; as a result, the copper was frequently reoxidized. Then, instead of obtaining a red, one obtained a green sort of copper celadon. On the other hand, as we have already verified and as we have indicated above, with the glaze adopted, one gets flambés more frequently than pure reds. By firing very high one could hope to remedy this inconvenience, but the elevation of the temperature then causes a very exaggerated slowing of the cooling process and a much greater chance to obtain flambé in place of red. With the existing glaze, which ordinarily gives reds with a fast firing of the kiln, we found that in this kiln this is a difficult condition to realize.

These inconveniences had already been noted in part, but they were more marked in the large furnace than in the experimental furnace. It is probable, moreover, that all manufacturers have run into these problems, since beautiful pieces of sizable dimensions in red and flambé are rare.

It would have been easy to get around this problem, since the places in the furnace favorable to the development of copper red have been clearly determined and they could be reserved for this purpose, meanwhile using the less favorable zones to fire white porcelain or porcelain decorated by other techniques.

But our program was not fulfilled in this manner; we desired to make a complete furnace full of red glazes. In these circumstances it was judged useful to look for perfection in our glazes and to remedy the defects that were presented at different times. These new researches had as their aim the discovery of a flux that was more apt than the old one to dissolve copper and maintain the desired degree of reduction without a predisposition to giving dulled, opaque reds and flambés.

All of the elements capable of entering into a colorless glaze were successively put together, and when the empirical research (whose tediousness would be devoid of interest here) finally ended, one could then try to accumulate the optimum results. After having established the chemical composition of the best glazes, their degree of acidity, the ratio between the alumina and alkali content, between the alkalies and the bases used, et cetera, one arrived at the following conclusions: in the same series of glazes, made up of the same bases, the most beautiful red was obtained in those glazes which had the highest degree of acidity.

In a series of glazes of the same acidity, the most beautiful red was obtained when the ratio of alkalies to alumina was the highest.

In the glazes containing alkalies and alkaline earths associated with a constant quantity of alumina, the most beautiful red was obtained when the ratio of alkalies to alkaline earths is the highest; but in the two cases, one cannot go beyond certain limits, because of the tendency for the alkalies to cause crackle; boric acid is used in this combination in order to neutralize the crackling tendency.

Lime and magnesia give rise to opaque streaks and flambés.

The oxide of zinc associated with barium gives the most beautiful reds.

Fluorides, lead oxide and iron oxide lead to defects of several different kinds.

Copper can be introduced in the glaze in several different forms; copper oxalate simply mixed and not fritted gives useful results; but the oxide, mixed in the glaze and melted with it, is more useful; the amount to use varies according to the duration of the firing and the maximum temperature of the furnace; five percent is the quantity that we have adopted; it is useful to add tin oxide in lower amounts than copper oxide.

The glaze (fritted), composed using the above factors, with which we have found the best results, has been prepared with the following components:

Pegmatite	31.2%
Sand	36.4·
Fused Borax	12.9
Anhydrous	
Sodium Carbonate	4.8
Barium Carbonate	10.4
Zinc Oxide	4.3

This corresponds to an oxide composition of:

Silica	61.0%
Alumina	5.8
Alkali	10.7
Barium Oxide	8.4
Zinc Oxide	4.5
Boric Oxide	9.5

The ratio of bases in this recipe is expressed in the following formula:

$$Al_2O_3 \; , \; 3NaKO \; , \; BaO \; , \; ZnO.$$

Its degree of acidity is 5.39, that of glaze number I was 5.14.

This glaze, when fired to a lower temperature than that used for number I gives a beautiful red which is transparent.

This glaze is reduced more easily than all the other glazes tried and presents in the most accentuated manner the properties of maintaining dissolved copper in a decolorized modification. It even appeared possible on several occasions to maintain dissolved copper in some samples which had been fired without any special precautions in an ordinary fire. On reheating these glazes in a muffle in a reducing atmosphere, the red then developed. It was less vivid and less profound than that which was obtained directly in the furnace, but this observation nevertheless appeared to us to indicate that the nature of the glaze is more important in the fabrication of copper reds than the type of firing that occurs.

This same glaze, which we gave to M. Vogt, has allowed him to obtain, by a special technique, an underglaze copper red.

The following glaze was composed in order to give a flambé which had opaque white streaks in it; it is the lime that appears to have the attribute of causing this kind of glaze.

Pegmatite	26.5%
Sand	42.6
Soda Ash	6.0
Limestone	19.3
Copper Oxide	3.8
Tin Oxide	1.9

The juxtaposition of these two glazes allows one to obtain a clear red alongside a flambé red at places determined in advance, and thus one can realize some beautiful effects, which can be varied even more by the addition of blue, green, brown and black glazes, and in general in any glaze which develops in a reducing fire.

Such are the principal facts that our researches on copper red have allowed us to observe. And, even though we have obtained some interesting results, and even though the factory has actually had at its disposal a process and some practical formulas which allowed it to produce a number of beautiful pieces, we still do not consider that the subject has been completely investigated.

Other experiments remain to be made which circumstances did not allow us the time for. Undoubtedly it would be of great interest to apply the method that we have indicated to obtain a red on an extremely siliceous porcelain. One would thus be able to use as glazes very alkaline mixtures, which we, for several reasons, have found to be too dangerous to use on ordinary porcelain.

It would be good to find a way to replace the necessity of coating a fired porcelain, by either soaking or spraying the glaze on raw or biscuited pieces.

It would be equally interesting, in our opinion, to construct a special furnace. This furnace would be moderately tall, and of the downdraft variety; the ratio of the height to the diameter would be much less than that which is generally used in Europe; the fire boxes should be larger and more numerous than usual, and would be placed at a level that is lower than the hearth of the furnace, in which case the flame would penetrate by channels dispersed regularly around the outside of the wall; the furnace would be arched at the highest part, so that the entrance of air would be more difficult; the furnace would also be longer and narrower instead of being rectangular; the air which penetrates into the furnace would be required to pass over a thick bed of carbon, so that it would enter the furnace completely depleted of oxygen, and would be highly charged with oxides of carbon; lastly, an energetic draft would be required so that the elongated flame would have the same composition throughout its length.

These modifications would certainly improve the process of manufacture which in actual conditions is subject to an unforeseen number of problems and requires taking special precautions.

CELADONS

We would like to finish off this memoir by describing our research work on the area of making glazes that are called celadons. It is one of the most delicate glazes of the Chinese palette. It has a bluish-green tone of very fine character, and takes, in artificial light, some very harmonious and soft nuances. It is used principally on carved pieces where it plays the role of a shading agent. Stanislaus Julien, in his translation, says that it is obtained from a mixture of feldspar, lime and a ferruginous earth. Ebelmen and Salvetat confirmed that the coloration is due to silicates of lime and iron and that one develops the iron at a low point of oxidation. When this composition is submitted to an oxidizing atmosphere, it loses its color and takes on all the varieties of tone which exist because of the coloration of the higher oxides of iron.

These comments are correct. The conditions under which celadons are obtained are identical to those which allow development of copper reds. The requirement for reduction of ferric oxide is more energetic still than that demanded by copper reds.

The nature of the base glaze exerts a large influence on the results, and it is on this point that we have principally carried out our researches, which unfortunately remain incomplete. We have been able to discern the following facts: alkaline glazes are less advantageous than magnesia or calcareous glazes as they are more subject to oxidation; phosphates and borates do not give good results; and the use of tin oxide is not necessary.

The best results that we have obtained were arrived at through the use of an exclusively calcareous glaze in which the iron was introduced in the form of an iron containing clay.

Here is the composition used:

Calcined Red Earth	35
Sand of Aumont	50
Calcium Fluoride	22

It is good to use an earth that is very ferruginous. One can also increase the intensity of the celadon by the addition of a couple of tenths of a percent of chrome oxide, which in these proportions dissolves and does not cause the glaze to lose its transparency.

We have found, that if one fires in the same sagger some celadons along with vases colored with copper, that the celadons will sometimes be colored red by the copper which is volatilized and which has a great tendency to fix itself on the ferruginous glaze. One could use this observation in a procedure to obtain a red decoration on celadons.

The roseate hues of early dawn,
The brightness of the day,
The crimson of the sunset sky,
How fast they fade away!

Cecil F. Alexander—The Roseate Hues of Early Dawn

34 RED AND FLAMBÉ CUPROUS OXIDE GLAZES

HERMANN A. SEGER

(Translated by A. Bleininger)

Seger's article is included because it is a classic in the copper red glaze field. However there are a couple of problems that I have in evaluating his comments. For example I find it hard to believe that he would try to promote cuprous oxide as the red coloring agent when he must have read Ebell's paper. Furthermore his comment that copper is volatilized in an oxidizing flame but not in a reducing flame seems to be the opposite of common experience. On this last point I would prefer to believe that there was either a translation slip-up or a typographical error involved.

Of special interest is the peculiar red glaze which is found on old Chinese porcelain and which for this reason is called Chinese red, also *sang de boeuf* or ox blood. On the character of the color of this glaze, Messrs. Lauth and Dutailly published an extensive treatise in which they describe the method used by them in its production. In this treatise these gentlemen, formerly active in the factory at Sevres, proved that this color can be imparted only to a body which requires a lower finishing temperature than that which is necessary for European porcelain. The porcelain used by them is, like the Chinese, one containing very much silica, and which hence vitrifies easily, a body which is now made quite extensively at Sevres as "*pate nouvelle de Sevres,*" and whose glost temperature is stated as being 1300°C. They give the mixtures of two glazes of this kind and say that the red color of the glaze is produced in the presence of tin oxide by a violent process of reduction, to which the ware is exposed on burning. The copper oxide is reduced to metallic copper, this being dissolved in the glaze and imparting to it on slow cooling a copper red color, while on more rapid cooling a colorless glaze is produced, which, however becomes red on slow gradual heating. The mixtures stated above as being the best glazes are, according to the writers mentioned above:

	I	II
Pegmatite	40	40
Sand	40	44
Chalk	18	12
Calcined Borax	12	—
Soda	—	24
Oxide of Copper	6	6
Oxide of Tin	6	3

Whether a part of the ingredients is previously melted to a frit they do not say, but this is very probable. The ingredients of a glaze, soluble in water, here soda and borax, are as a rule fritted with other compounds in order to render them insoluble. Since I have also worked a great deal on the production of such a red glaze and have made such glazed porcelain bodies on a larger and commercial scale at a time before Messrs. Lauth and Dutailly appeared with their invention, I believe that I am likewise in a position to express some opinion concerning this extremely difficult process. I shall not give in detail the many experiments that I made in this direction, which comprise 300-400 glazes of different composition. This would involve too much and would not benefit the manufacturer; but I will give my theoretical objections to the reasoning of Messrs. Lauth and Dutailly, and shall support these by proofs.

I cannot agree at all with the opinion of these investigators regarding the production of the red color by a segregation of metallic copper from the glaze, that is, by a simple and strongly reducing firing condition. On the contrary, alternately reducing and oxidizing conditions of the fire-gases are required in order to produce it, and the difficulties of the manufacture lie less in the composition of the glaze itself (although this is also of importance) than in the proper constitution of the fire-gases. It was shown in the production of the red color that in using one and the same glaze, not only the shade of color in the same burn is subjected to extraordinary fluctuations, so that it runs through all shades from black through brown to sealing-wax red and light bluish green, but also that some pieces are colored differently on one side than on the other, according to the intensity of the draft through the piles of saggers; some burns may produce in the same glaze a more or less beautiful color than others, and again some burns may be totally spoiled and not produce any red color at all, everything appearing gray or black.

Now let us see, how cuprous glazes behave in a reducing fire or fusing in a reducing gas, and let us first take such lead-free whiteware glazes, which besides copper oxide contain no other metallic oxide that could be reduced. For example, a glaze having the stoichiometric composition:

$$0.5 \ Na_2O, \ 0.5 \ CaO, \ 2.5 \ SiO_2, \ 0.5 \ B_2O_3,$$

a glaze which melts smooth at about the melting point of silver (960°C), and which is made by fritting together:

Sodium Carbonate	26.5
Marble	25.0
Ground Quartz	75.0
Hydrous Boric Acid	31.0

and which, after melting, is ground together with one percent of copper oxide. This mixture is put into a small porcelain crucible, which is placed in a platinum crucible; the crucible is provided with a perforated porcelain lid, and through the opening a thin porcelain tube is introduced, as in the Rose reduction crucible of the laboratories. The mixture is not put into the platinum crucible directly in order to prevent the platinum from alloying with the copper of the mixture.

If we heat the glaze mixture in a stream of hydrogen or carbon monoxide introduced through the porcelain tube, to dark red heat, that is, to 400°C or at most 500°C, the copper oxide is reduced and the glaze does not melt but is only fritted together. It has a red color caused by the copper segregated out.

If we now apply a higher heat, maintaining a current of hydrogen or carbon monoxide, about to silver melting heat (960°C)—the highest temperature obtained by the Bunsen burner—the metallic copper disappears, the copper flakes dissolve in the melting glaze, the red color vanishes and the completely molten glaze now has received a greenish gray color. If we coarsely powder this gray mass and again melt it together with the same white glaze, to which a trifle of some oxidizing agent is added, say one percent of ferric oxide, stannic oxide, or a sulfate like gypsum (but this time in a stream of air, in the crucible of the test kiln mentioned below), there is obtained a glass of a beautiful red color.

We must attribute this reaction to the fact that, by the oxidizing agents which are contained in the copper-free glaze, the black metallic copper enclosed in the copper glaze is changed to cuprous silicate and this imparts to the glass a red color, for the ingredients react as follows:

$$2\ Cu + Fe_2O_3 = Cu_2O + 2\ FeO$$
$$2\ Cu + SnO_2 = Cu_2O + SnO_2$$
$$2\ Cu + SO_3 = Cu_2O + SO_2.$$

The last reaction is remarkable, owing to the fact that a lively evolution of gas takes place in the fusion. If the glass is allowed to cool before it has become entirely clear, thus still retaining some bubbles, the presence of sulfur dioxide can be proved by the smell on opening the bubbles.

If we now produce a glaze of a higher melting point, mixing the whiteware glaze used before, with the white porcelain glaze mentioned below,

$$0.3\ K_2O,\ 0.7\ CaO,\ 0.5\ Al_2O_3,\ 4\ SiO_2,$$

we obtain a glaze, which, at silver-melting heat only vitrifies but doesn't fuse. This glaze consists of 25 parts of the above copper whiteware glaze and 75 parts of the porcelain glaze. If we heat this likewise in a crucible, as was done before, at a silver-melting heat, introducing hydrogen gas or carbon monoxide, we again obtain a gray vitrified mass. On heating this in air, that is, in the open crucible, we observe that it assumes after a short time a reddish brown or red color, which, however, fades quickly, and whose place is taken by a light green color. We also observe in this connection that the strongest reducing action of the gases produces a black color, since it causes the reduction to metallic copper; that the copper is first changed to cuprous silicate; and that finally the green color of the cupric silicate appears.

If we heat the mixture more strongly over the blast lamp, admitting a reducing gas, so that the glaze is fused, the mass thus formed remains gray in color and on heating in the air, turns to a reddish color only on the surface, but in the interior it retains its gray color. On the vitrification of the glaze, further oxidation (and with it the red color) is excluded. A striking phenomenon is at the same time caused by the carbon deposited in the glaze. If the reduction is accomplished with illuminating gas instead of with hydrogen or carbon monoxide, a part of its carbon is deposited owing to the decomposition of the gas, which surrounds the glaze particles and thus prevents fusion. The glaze thus becomes apparently less fusible and retains its porous character even at the temperatures which lie above its melting point. If glazes, reduced in this manner, are heated in air, the carbon is burned out, but at the same time the copper segregated out is also oxidized to cuprous oxide and the glaze is now enabled to fuse. In this manner red glazes are always produced.

These experiments, performed in the crucible with pure reducing gases, were supplemented by others carried on in the test kiln, using a small test kiln fired with gas. This little furnace not only increases the rapidity of the experiments, but also enables the experimenter to effect alternate reducing and oxidizing kiln conditions quickly and to control them by gas analysis. As trial pieces there are used small cups of biscuit-burned porcelain body, coated with a glaze composed of 25 parts of whiteware glaze, compounded with one percent of copper oxide and 75 parts of porcelain glaze.

On heating these in the kiln, first in an oxidizing flame, until a glow is just visible, then in a strongly reducing flame, so that about ten percent of carbon monoxide is contained in the fire gases, up to a temperature not exceeding gold-melting heat (1060°C), we observe on pulling small glazed trials from the kiln with a pair of tongs, that the glaze as well as the body possesses a dark color due to the deposition of carbon.

If we now allow the kiln to cool and do not close the damper, so that the air passes through the kiln for some time, we observe that the vitrified glaze coating has become beautifully red. When we fire under the same conditions, but higher—up to the temperature of cone 1 (1100°C), we obtain a fused glaze, gray in color, which, on properly melting the glaze in the oxidizing flame at about cone 1, changes more or less to reddish or brownish, but never assumes a fine red color. Repeating the same operation with another small porcelain cup, but with a lower content of carbon monoxide in the fire gases (2-3 percent), the gray color appears still more intensely.

On firing a trial cup so that we first burn with a strongly reducing flame about up to the silver melting heat, and then burn alternately with a strongly reducing and oxidizing fire up to incipient fusion, about five minutes reducing and two minutes oxidizing, and after the fusion of the glaze finish the burning of the porcelain in the oxidizing flame, we obtain a fine red glaze. This red glaze is retained quite satisfactorily in the oxidizing fire after it is once fused, and it can remain in the latter fire five to six hours without changing in color, though on the surface it may assume a pale green color due to oxidation. This nearly colorless, extremely thin surface coating produced by oxidation gives the pottery a special charm. Only when the glaze is very thin is it possible that the change in color might extend through the entire thickness of the glaze on remaining in the oxidizing atmosphere for a longer time; and such thinly glazed places, as well as the edges, and the relief decoration under the glaze, assume a green color.

It is of special importance in the burning of red glazed porcelain that the fire be very sooty. Between the sagger rings which form the stack of saggers, I have always inserted on top and at the bottom of the ring, at the height of the ware, three small pieces of fire-clay tile of 1.5-2 cm. in thickness, so that the flame was freely admitted to the ware, and could always draw freely though the saggers. The deposition of carbon from the fire gases has by no means the purpose of bringing about a very strong reducing effect, for the copper oxide is changed to copper even under weakly reducing conditions, but it should be the function of the carbon to retard the fusion of the glaze by depositing the soot in it. If now, oxidizing conditions are suddenly brought about, avoiding neutral firing conditions as much as possible, the copper, during the burning out of the carbon from the glaze, again changes to cuprous oxide and is retained as such by the glaze which is fused soon after this change in firing. When the burning is accomplished without the deposition of soot on the surface of the ware, the red color will never develop, and the copper glaze always assumes a grey color, since then the closing of the pores of the glaze is not retarded and the metallic copper segregated out is deprived of the possibility of reoxidizing to cuprous oxide.

An experiment which I carried out, endeavoring to burn a glaze (burning to a beautiful red with wood as fuel), using coke as a fuel, failed entirely; gray colored ware was always obtained.

Although on following the rules outlined above, a red color can be produced from every cuprous glaze in the crucible or in the small experimental furnace, the conditions in the large kiln are essentially different. It will not always be possible to produce a uniformly reducing atmosphere with a deposition of soot and it is especially difficult to produce strongly oxidizing conditions during a short time interval (one to two minutes); the red color in using any cuprous glaze will be obtained only rarely and in exceptional cases. But the production of the red color may be facilitated by imparting to the glaze a certain chemical and physical constitution.

The means of accomplishing this purpose consist first of a small addition of ferric or stannic oxide, in order to be independent of the oxygen of the atmospheric air alone for the translation of the copper to cuprous oxide. These metallic oxides are likewise changed to ferrous oxide and stannous oxide, but their reformation to the higher oxides takes place quickly and thus they are enabled to oxidize the copper. Although an addition of these oxides by no means prevents the formation of the gray color, yet in their presence the red color appears much more readily. The tin or iron oxide is best melted in quantities of not more than 2 percent, together with the copper oxide and the very fusible whiteware glaze which serves as a frit.

The quantity of copper oxide which is used is also of great importance for the beauty of the color. In my many experiments, I have always used a content of copper of from 0.5-1 percent and always obtained very good results. The more copper there is in the glaze, the greater is the liability of some of the gray coloring metallic copper to remain in it and to change the sealing wax red color, which is produced by the pure cuprous oxide into a brownish color. With a content of 0.5 percent of copper oxide to 100 parts of the finished porcelain glaze, the glaze where it is colored red is perfectly opaque. For transparent red glazes, which on account of their transparency produce a deeper red color similar to gold ruby, I have always used 0.10-0.15 percent of copper oxide. With this content of copper oxide, the glaze tends to produce green colors more readily, but at the same time, the portions which have retained the red color are so much more beautiful. In regard to the quantity of the very fusible whiteware glaze (serving as a frit) necessary, this will always depend upon the temperature to which the body must be subjected in order to burn it to a good porcelain. It may vary from 12-50 percent of the finished glaze. The more fusible the glaze is to be, the lower in silica it must be kept, the smaller may be its quantity, and the more beautiful will be the red color developed; the less fusible it is, the more difficult is the production of the red and the more readily will the gray color of the ware be shown. As to the composition of the porcelain glaze which is a component of the glaze, I have discussed it in the introduction; other porcelain glazes may very well be used, but care must be taken that the mixture remains as porous as possible; fused porcelain glazes cannot be used for this purpose, as they are too dense.

Fluctuations in the composition of the white porcelain glaze are permissible according to the composition of the body and the temperature it requires; care must be taken, however, that it does not vitrify at too high a temperature, which is controlled by the addition of a very fusible whiteware glaze (i.e., a frit). Whatever the composition of the glaze for the Chinese red or ox blood color may be, a satisfactory result will never be obtained if the firing is not directed in a suitable manner.

After the ware is glazed, either by dipping or spraying, and has been set so that the smoke can reach it freely, at first, a fire as oxidizing as possible is maintained. As soon as a dark red heat shows in the kiln, as much smoke as possible is to be produced and continued up to a temperature at which the glaze commences to vitrify. This is followed by short periods of oxidizing fire, kept up at short intervals, about one to two minutes for each quarter of an hour; between these, however, a strongly reducing kiln atmosphere must prevail. This mode of firing must be continued until the glaze has become dense and somewhat glossy. Thereupon, the burning may proceed with oxidizing or reducing kiln conditions up to the close of the burn. This method of burning, however, will not be easy to carry out in ordinary coal furnaces, especially will it not be possible, as a rule, to produce the oxidizing fire gases for so short a time without maintaining between time a longer or shorter period of neutral conditions. But, in furnaces with inclined grates, fired with wood, one is enabled to produce such a change almost instantaneously by opening the air passages beneath the charge of wood, and for this reason, firing with wood will always remain the most satisfactory way of firing for the production of red copper glazes, if for no other reason than that it, more than any other, permits of a uniform and intense evolution of smoke.

For the porcelain compounded according to the composition of the Japanese, the following mixtures are suitable; that is, they have the proper fusibility and adhere without crazing. There is to be considered: **that the ones containing less cuprous oxide are always darker in color because transparent**, and the ones higher in copper appear lighter in color because they are opaque.

Dark Red Chinese Glaze:

White porcelain glaze	75.00
Copper oxide	0.15
Tin oxide	1.00
Ferric oxide	0.50
Barium frit	23.35

Light Chinese Red Glaze

White porcelain glaze	70.0
Zettlitz kaolin	5.0
Copper oxide	0.8
Tin oxide	2.0
Barium frit	22.0

Blue Iridescent Chinese Glaze

White porcelain glaze	70
Zettlitz kaolin	5
Copper oxide	1
Tin oxide	2
Ferric oxide	1
Barium frit	21

In each formulation the barium frit and the coloring oxides are fritted together in a reducing fire.

The blue iridescence of the glaze appears especially when the latter is again covered with a thin barium glaze and again burnt in the glost burn.

There is yet to be stated, that fine red colors are obtained only when the difference between the melting points of the two glazes used for this purpose is very great, and that they will be the finer and appear the more readily when the whiteware glaze (frit) is very fusible. It is produced the more difficultly the less fusible the glazes are, and it is impossible to obtain a pure red, when the red glaze is first fused completely and, when again ground, is applied as a glaze. In this case it is always a grayish black, with a brownish or reddish cast at best. This glaze differs considerably from the original Chinese glaze in that **the latter is always very low in alumina**. For this reason it devitrifies very easily, and the surface becomes dull owing to the crystalline compounds segregating out at a low temperature. Consequently the Chinese red ware can be decorated only with difficult with gold and enamels or overglaze colors. But with the glaze given here, this can very easily be done; care must, however, be taken, especially with the glazes low in copper oxide, that the vessels are cooled very slowly after the burning; it might happen that they lose their red color on quick cooling and come from the muffle burn perfectly colorless.

Some interesting results have also been produced in the experiments which I have carried on in the direction of using the red glaze as a ground, and to inlay in it different colored glaze designs as I have described in previous work. It sounds somewhat odd that it should be possible to burn a red ground-glaze on the same piece in the reducing fire, while the other colors, as I have previously stated, are produced satisfactorily only under oxidizing conditions. But it will be clear that it is possible to produce such work, if one remembers that the Chinese red is produced at a comparitively low temperature and that a reducing kiln atmosphere does not injure the colors to be burned under oxidizing conditions, provided reduction prevails at a temperature at which they have not yet been rendered dense by incipient fusion. But the Chinese red glazes given above and the previously mentioned colored glazes have different melting points, so that this can be accomplished without any trouble. For this reason ware thus decorated is first burned in a strongly reducing fire up to silver melting heat (960°C), then in the oxidizing fire one to two minutes at intervals of fifteen minutes up to the melting point of gold (1060°C) or not far above it. At gold melting heat, the red of the ground must be dense, and in this condition is capable of withstanding the oxidizing fire gases without material injury of the color for several hours. The oxidizing burning is carried on very carefully in order to remove the effects of the preceding reduction, that is, to transform, in the glazes containing manganese, copper, iron and uranium, the lower oxides again to the higher forms.

When the temperature has risen to the melting point of the colored glazes, it will not be necessary to watch the oxidizing conditions of the kiln so carefully; on the contrary, it is advisable to reduce again during the last stage of the burn, because by this means the red glaze loses its egg-shell-like appearance, which it often shows, and becomes perfectly smooth. It is possible in this manner to burn even the very sensitive yellow glazes containing uranium (as well as the pink glazes) simultaneously with the Chinese red.

This is always successful if the fire gases are kept as strongly oxidizing as possible throughout, up to its melting point, and care is taken that a reducing effect of the gases never occurs. Of course, this process can be considered only from the standpoint of an art ware manufacturer, and for ordinary cheap ware this method, requiring such a difficult handling of the fire, cannot be considered. It can be put into practical operation only under certain conditions, which not every manufacturer is enabled to meet. In this connection it is especially necessary to know one's kiln accurately, so as to be able to handle it perfectly. Pottery of this character of Chinese or Japanese origin is not known to me.

RED UNDERGLAZE COLORS

On older Chinese vases there are sometimes noticed, beside the blue decoration, red underglaze colors apparently produced like the red glaze of the Chinese porcelain, with copper oxide. Now the copper oxide is by no means a suitable underglaze color, for it possesses the undesirable property of volatilizing strongly, and of spreading its coloring effect far around the decorated portions. This undesirable effect is noticeable only when the copper oxide is burned under oxidizing conditions; volatilization is not observed when reducing conditions prevail in the kiln. [I have always found the reverse to be true—RMT] I have always noticed the spreading of the copper when it imparted a green color to the glaze, but never when the color was red.

It is suitable as an underglaze color when the porcelain glaze has a low fusing point; if the glaze is less fusible, the composition of the fire gases must approach close to the neutral condition in order to produce a higher temperature at all, and then the color is, as I have shown before in the burning of the red porcelain glaze with copper oxide, generally not red, but grey or black. The copper oxide dissolved in a low fusing glaze also proved better suited for underglaze decoration than the pure copper oxide, and the colors in this way always appeared finer and surer. I have always obtained good results with the following mixture:

Copper oxide	7.5
Tin oxide	10.0
Barium frit	82.5

which should be fritted together in a reducing fire.

The production of the red decoration requires the same precautions as the production of the red glaze on porcelain. It is necessary here too, that the cuprous silicate remain as such in the burning by excluding the atmospheric air by means of the covering of glaze. The reducing action of the fire gases must not be stopped before the glaze covering the color has fused, thus protecting the copper compound from a reoxidation. If the white porcelain glaze is melted to a glass in the glost burn, and the ware, after being decorated, is glazed with this fused glaze, the latter will fuse somewhat earlier than if it is applied to the surface in the raw condition, and thus there is more assurance of obtaining the red. Furthermore, it is not absolutely necessary, although it is desirable, that the red color be applied to a body which has been well burnt. The body is often colored gray by the carbon deposited by the fire gases, which is always taken up into the pores of the porcelain during the strongly reducing fire, and hence the ware does not show the pure white color peculiar to porcelain. This is prevented if the body has been previously burned dense in an oxidizing burn. A simultaneous application of other colors is only permissible in a limited measure, as the fire gases must always be kept strongly reducing in the burning of the red glaze; only the black, blue and green colors resist reducing conditions. Other colors cannot be burned simultaneously with the red.

Now in the sea's red vintage melts the sun,
As Egypt's pearl dissolved in rosy wine,
And Cleopatra night drinks all.

Sidney Lanier—Evening Song.

35 STUDIES ON CHINESE PORCELAIN

> Although on the surface Vogt's work may not appear to be as useful as some of the others, his extraordinary analytical results are a prized accomplishment. In conjunction with Scherzer's excellent sample collection effort, Vogt not only tells us what materials were present in Chinese glazes, but also tells us what things were not present.

In 1882, M. Scherzer, who was then French consul at Hankow, traveled to Ching-te-chen for the express purpose of obtaining samples and learning techniques that the Chinese used to make all of their glazes, bodies and enamels. M. Brongniart, then director of the Sevres Porcelain Works, requested this information and provided M. Scherzer with exact details as to what was desired. In the process of obtaining all of this information, Scherzer was able to get numerous samples and much information on the techniques then used by the Chinese to make copper red glazes and underglaze copper reds. M. Scherzer did a splendid piece of work in the area of what we would now call "industrial espionage."

When the samples were returned to France, they came under the charge of M. Georges Vogt, head of the Sevres laboratories. Vogt then proceeded to analyse all of the samples with meticulous care and splendid techniques. In 1899 M. Vogt published the results of these analyses (as found in CHING-TE-CHEN by R. Tichane). From that book we have excerpted the work that was done on copper red glazes and underglaze colors. This includes some comments by M. Scherzer and the comments and analyses performed by M. Vogt. While this may not be a practical way of making copper reds today, it does give us the historical background to much recent work.

COMMENTS BY F. SCHERZER (1882)

(Translated by Robert Tichane)

Copper red, *chi-houng,* or sang de boeuf, so appreciated by private collectors has not been made since the death of the last possessor of the secret of manufacture. And for 20 years the factory administration has been making excuses to the throne for not being able to execute the command by her majesty to make *chi-houng* glazes.

...I also visited the lone, unique factory from which came the actual masterpieces, the vases with copper red glazes called *kun-houng.*

The head of this establishment refused categorically to tell me the formula which serves to make this high-fired glaze; however, unknown to him I succeeded in obtaining it anyway, and in a second visit I was able to make sure of the ingredients which had been indicated to me by the employees in the red vase factory. I will note that the paste for this glaze is very hard, which is necessary in order to resist several successive high firings.

The *kun-houng* glaze is applied to the biscuit at first by immersion, and then by sprinkling. I have in my possession some vases with glazes just as they are about to go into the kiln; and I have besides, received some samples of the paste used, and some materials which enter into its composition.

As for the *yeou-li-houng* (underglaze red), it is applied to the raw porcelain and receives an ordinary glaze; one does not use it alone on many occasions; it is generally associated with cobalt in the decoration of certain vases. The dark, wine red shade that it gives is rarely successful and again only on small pieces; I have brought back a sample of this high fired color, and the formula that is used to make it.

Finally, I made them apply, in my presence, different glazes on different vases (raw) under the foot of which I engraved my mark!! I also had my people bring bottles which were filled before my eyes with the different glazes that I had seen used; I also took samples of the pastes which were made into the vases used.

CHINESE COPPER REDS—ANALYSES

GEORGES VOGT

(Translated by Robert Tichane)

COPPER RED

Scherzer has been able to furnish us numerous details on this interesting subject, in spite of the difficulties that he had to overcome in order to get the information and the products relative to this beautiful glaze which stayed a mystery to European ceramists for so long.

We read in his memoire:

"Copper red, *kun-houng*, or imitation of sang de boeuf glaze, *ki-houng*:

"The imperial factory no longer makes vases with sang de boeuf glaze. One lone family, the Ho's, claims to possess the secret of making *kun-houng* red, but in the vitreous aspect of this glaze it is often too thick and it rarely has an even color.

"I experienced great difficulty in getting either material or information relative to red glazes, but I succeeded for the most part in checking its correctness.

"*Kun-houng* glaze is made with the help of a flux called *ting-leao* analogous to one of our fluxes (rocaille). They prepare this in the following manner:

"One melts in a pot a mixture of:

Lead filings *(Yuan)*	50
Silex powder *(Ma long ting)*	50

"This mixture is stirred up then to form a homogeneous mixture. After cooling, the material is broken up in a porcelain mortar with salt-peter in the following proportions:

Lead-silex powder	10 livres
Saltpeter	3 livres, 4 ounces

"The mixing completed, the whole thing is placed in the bottom of a well luted sagger that is sunk 3 inches deep in the gravel at the bottom of a porcelain furnace. The result of this fritting is a water-green colored glass. It is *ting-leao*.

"One pulverizes with care these materials that one mixes in the following proportions:

COPPER RED GLAZE COMPOSITION

Potash-lead Silicate	39.0
Artificial Jade	39.0
Ground Copper Filings	7.3
Beads of Colored Glass	7.3
Bottle Glass	7.3

"This last mixture is ground for a month in a porcelain mortar, then it is mixed in a white glaze made of milk of *yeou-ko* and milk of lime.

"If the liquid is too clear, one adds a small quantity of common salt which curdles it, and helps in the suspension of the different pulverized materials. This glaze, when it is well prepared ought to look like a muddy liquid.

"The first coat is applied by immersion of the biscuited vase.

"The paste of the vase contains some ferruginous clay which gives the biscuit a yellowish tint on the surface, although a fracture edge is relatively white.

"The biscuited vase is inserted, neck down, for 5 minutes into the liquid glaze. One allows it to dry in the sun, then with a brush one carefully applies three more layers which one dries successively in the sun and in plain air.

"One adds an extra layer of glaze on the rim and the upper part of the vase so that the top is not left with too little glaze because of glaze flow.

"The glazed vase is, on placement in its sagger, put on two round patties isolated by a layer of carbonized rice hulls. The vase is also isolated from the top patty by a layer of the same material. The top patty is smaller than the one below it and doesn't rest directly on the bottom of the sagger, but on a bed about 8 mm thick formed of fine gravel obtained by crushing old bricks and sagger debris. This disposition facilitates the flowing of excess melted glaze and prevents all adherence of the vase to the sides of the sagger.

"The firing takes place in the back part of the *laboratory* porcelain kiln, where the temperature is highest.

"If, after the first firing, the glaze does not attain the desired color, one applies a new coat of *kun-houng* glaze and refires it. This operation can be repeated without inconvenience up to three times."

We see from this that the Chinese put a red glaze on previously fired porcelain; Scherzer's shipment includes a fragment of porcelain destined for this use. It was interesting to see what the composition of this fired paste was and in what state of oxidation its iron was; analysis shows that a large portion of iron is in the form of iron monoxide, proving positively that this porcelain was fired in a reducing atmosphere.

The biscuit for copper red contained:

COPPER RED BODY COMPOSITION

Silica	67.66%
Alumina	23.57
Iron Oxide	2.98
Lime	0.67
Magnesia	0.32
Potash	3.61
Soda	1.38

The paste of this vase for red glazing is an ordinary composition, as Scherzer writes, except that it is markedly more ferruginous than those used for white glazes. The high percentage of iron in this porcelain causes it to lose its transparency and be closer to grey.

The Chinese have, by using a red over a nontransparent body, made a very judicious use of their porcelain. They use the white body under the beautiful and transparent blanc de chine and use the strongly colored glaze over the grey body, which would look terrible under a white glaze.

TING-LEAO

The first material that is used in the red composition, the *ting-leao*, ought to be, according to the information of Scherzer, a glass quite analogous to our crystal, which we obtain by quite a different method than the Chinese (who use metallic lead to make the melt!).

The qualitative analysis shows that *ting-leao* contains silica, lead oxide, potash, and soda as well as small amounts of iron oxide, alumina, manganese, lime and magnesia; which results are in accord with what ought to be found according to the indicated preparation.

One finds:

LEAD GLASS COMPOSITIONS

	Ting-leao	English Crystal
Silica	57.74%	57.5%
Lead Oxide	31.97	32.5
Alumina	1.43	—
Lime	0.65	—
Magnesia	0.29	—
Potash	7.62	9.0
Soda	0.52	1.0

This composition is that of crystal in general and especially of English crystal analysed by Salvetat, which composition I give alongside the other.

The Chinese have been sincere in giving their recipe for the preparation of *ting-leao*. In mixing silica and the lead melted in air, this metal oxidizes for the most part, and if some granules escape oxidation, they will be completely oxidized during the second fusion of lead silicate with saltpeter. Next, the temperature rises, lead oxide and potash combine with the silica and form the alkali-lead glass for which we have given the analysis.

ARTIFICIAL JADE

The second material which enters into the composition of red and in the same proportion as *ting-leao*, is artificial jade, on which Scherzer doesn't give us any information.

This substance melts in the blowpipe, and gives a greenish bead, which becomes red in a reducing flame; this characterizes copper; wet quantitative analysis indicates the presence of silica, fluorine, traces of lead and copper, lime magnesia, alumina, iron oxide, traces of manganese and some soda and potash. These elements are found in artificial jade in the following proportions:

ARTIFICIAL JADE COMPOSITION

Silica	57.81%
Fluorine	4.60
Alumina	2.56
Iron Oxide	0.49
Lead Oxide	0.86
Copper Oxide	0.06
Manganese Oxide	0.02
Lime	18.16
Magnesia	4.50
Potash	9.31
Soda	2.55
Volatiles	0.45

Artificial jade, according to this analysis is an alkali-lime glass, more basic than ordinary glass, greenish colored because of small amounts of iron and copper, and made opalescent by the presence of calcium fluoride.

COPPER FILINGS

The copper filings which are part of the red preparation, *kun-houng*, are far from being pure metal. One finds by qualitative analysis, cupric oxide, cuprous oxide, traces of lead, oxides of iron, aluminum, manganese, calcium and silicon, plus a sizable amount of carbonaceous material.

Nitric acid divides this material into a soluble part, composed mainly of copper and an insoluble part composed of a grey ferruginous clay (which should become red after firing), and carbonaceous material.

Analysis of the two parts gives:

COPPER FILINGS COMPOSITION

Silica	22.71%
Copper Oxide	52.71
Alumina	5.49
Iron Oxide	4.12
Manganese Oxide	0.19
Lime	2.12
Magnesia	0.77
Lead Oxide	0.83
Volatile	11.63

It was necessary to subtract from these results a certain amount of oxygen because all of the copper was not present as cupric oxide.

This aspect, the action of nitric acid and the analysis of the material called ground copper powder, leaves no doubt as to its nature. it is a mixture of more or less oxidized copper and a clay rich in iron and silica, no doubt introduced with the carbonaceous material to aid in grinding the material.

The fourth material which forms *kun-houng* is called beads of colored glass; this material was sent to us in the form of a white powder; its Chinese name is *tchou-tze*. Just as it is, this material melts into a greenish glass; melted in a blowpipe flame with borax, it gives in oxidation a yellowish bead because iron masks the copper; and in a reducing flame it gives a red bead; with phosphate one confirms the presence of silica.

Quantitative analysis gives:

GLASS BEAD ANALYSIS

Silica	54.74%
Fluoride	1.05
Cupric Oxide	0.08
Lead Oxide	20.97
Alumina	1.44
Iron Oxide	0.58
Lime	5.40
Magnesia	1.03
Potash	7.87
Soda	5.53
Volatiles	1.63

This analysis shows that the glass beads closely approach the composition of a hard crystal glass, which is lightly colored (green) by copper and made opalescent by the presence of fluorine as was the artificial jade just studied.

PA-LI

According to the Scherzer memoire, there is one more ingredient in the red glaze, it is bottle glass, called in the Chinese *pa-li*. This product, which came to us pulverized, melts with difficulty in the blowpipe, giving a yellowish green color; with microcosmic salt, it gives a skeleton of silica and the characteristic iron color.

Quantitative analysis of this bottle glass gives:

BOTTLE GLASS COMPOSITION

Silica	60.55%
Tin Oxide	0.07
Lead Oxide	0.29
Iron Oxide	1.75
Alumina	4.45
Manganese Oxide	0.45
Lime	20.42
Magnesia	4.21
Potash	1.09
Soda	5.41
Volatile	1.24

It is the composition of a glass rich in lime, very analogous to our common glass, colored yellowish green by iron oxide.

We know from analysis the composition of the several materials that go into the preparation of *kun-houng*. Scherzer gives us the proportions in which one mixes them; but there remains one unknown that prevents us from finding the composition of the mixture; this is the amount of white glaze in milk of *yeou-ko* and the amount of milk of lime that one adds to the mixture of the five other ingredients.

Fortunately the Scherzer shipment contained the materials necessary for a precise study of the red glaze; he sent some glazed vases all ready to be fired, some *kun-houng* glaze already mixed in water, and some pieces of red which had run off the foot of the vase during firing in the Chinese furnace. I have analysed these three red glazes of which two were raw and the other fired; this has allowed the determination of the material which volatilized during reduction firing; as one sees, it is only lead that disappears to any extent.

Analysis of the raw *Kun-houng* glaze, in water suspension, gives the following results: the wet material is alkaline to litmus, it contains traces of chloride and sulfate; the action of acid releases carbon dioxide. Ordinary reactions reveal: silica, fluoride, tin, copper, lead, iron, manganese, calcium, magnesium, potassium and sodium; in other words, all of the elements which we have found in the materials that the Chinese said went into the manufacture of the red glaze.

Analysis of this glaze gives:

KUN-HOUNG GLAZE BATCH COMPOSITION

Silica	61.56%
Fluoride	1.75
Lead Oxide	12.71
Copper Oxide	0.60
Alumina	4.37
Iron Oxide	0.85
Manganese Oxide	0.25
Lime	7.43
Magnesia	1.65
Potash	5.82
Soda	2.86
Carbon Dioxide	0.80

On the other hand, one has taken from the Chinese vase (covered with raw glaze) the amount needed to make a single analysis, using hydrofluoric acid.

One has, by this technique, ignored the fluoride, carbonate, and silicate results; but the results obtained for the other components are enough to establish the identical nature of these two glazes, and to be able to conclude that the red is applied to the vases as it ought to be, without the addition of any material other than that which had been found in the water suspension of glaze.

We have, however, analysed some fragments of fused glaze which had been collected in a Chinese furnace in the form of thick drops collected at the foot of vases on their supports; one finds in the red glaze the same elements (minus fluorine) that appeared in the *kun-houng* in the following percentages:

FUSED RED GLAZE ANALYSIS

Silica	70.18%
Alumina	6.57
Iron Oxide	0.91
Lime	8.00
Magnesia	1.65
Manganese Oxide	0.15
Lead Oxide	3.89
Copper Oxide	0.54
Potash	4.79
Soda	2.71
Tin Oxide	trace

In comparing the results of the analyses of the red before and after firing, one sees that during firing a large part of the lead and a small part of the copper and alkalies have volatilized, and that the fluoride has been completely eliminated; these facts were easy to foresee, since we know the red develops at a high temperature in a reducing environment.

The results which I obtained for the composition of Chinese red are very different from those published by Ebelmen and Salvetat, but they agree well enough (save perhaps for alumina and lime) with those obtained by Seger. These authors found in Chinese red after firing:

COPPER RED ANALYSES

	Ebelmen & Salvetat	Seger
Silica	73.90%	71.07%
Alumina	6.00	3.24
Iron Oxide	2.10	1.40
Lime	7.30	9.20
Magnesia	—	1.75
Copper Oxide	4.60	0.92
Lead Oxide	—	4.15
Potash	3.00	
KNaO		8.11
Soda	3.10	

The presence of lead, which was not noted in the analysis of Ebelmen and Salvetat, is nevertheless certain in the sample studied by Seger and in the one which I examined; if one considers the large amount of copper found by Ebelmen and Salvetat, one is lead to suppose that for one reason or another, they determined the lead with this metal. The reconstruction of Chinese red that I have made, based on my analysis as well as the work of Seger, shows that the amount (4.6%) of copper indicated by Ebelmen and Salvetat, is much too high to obtain a beautiful deep-colored transparent red!

The observation made in detail on the analysis of Chinese red published by Ebelmen and Salvetat, does not in the least take away the merit of their having been the first to reveal by their work the composition of Chinese red, and of having shown, according to the text of their memoire: "that the color of the red glaze is positively due to cuprous oxide, distributed in the glaze; that this glaze is fired at a very high temperature, which although less than the Sevres high-fire, is perhaps equal to the Chinese high-fire; that the fusibility of the feldspar in this glaze is aided by the varying amounts of lime whose presence we have noted in the Chinese glaze."

Ebelmen and Salvetat confirmed the results of their analyses by reproducing the Chinese red in about 1849 at Sevres; if their samples, preserved in the Museum of National Manufacturers, do not have the brilliance of the beautiful oriental red, they are, nonetheless, the first specimens to be made in Europe of this beautiful high-fired glaze.

YEOU-LI-HOUNG

To *kun-houng* is connected directly the composition of *yeou-li-houng*, or underglaze red, which the Chinese have used so skillfully, and which until now has not been obtainable in a sure way in Europe.

Here is what Scherzer writes on the subject of underglaze copper red, *yeou-li-houng*.

"This composition is applied by brush to the raw body as is cobalt blue; it gives very uneven results, also it is used only for the decoration of small objects, or to give here and there a little relief to the designs of large vases decorated with cobalt blue.

"According to Lin, one takes 3 parts of ground copper filings and 7 parts of powdered plaster. This mixture, after grinding in a porcelain mortar, will be mixed in water and used to paint the greenware. The vases thus decorated are then covered with ordinary white glaze.

"The manufacturer Li gave me a sample of *yeou-li-houng* whose secret is jealously guarded. It was impossible for me to obtain the formula of this preparation into which enter:

Ma-nao—pulverized carnelian
Tong-hoa—pulverized copper filings
Tche-che—slightly ferruginous aluminous earth
Tze-kin-che—ferruginous clay."

This vague information is very different from the other; but since one doesn't find any sulfate in *yeou-li-houng*, that excludes the possibility of the presence of plaster as indicated by Lin; it remains to verify if the manufacturer Li has been sincere in his communication.

If this latter told the truth, the *yeou-li-houng* ought not to effervesce on acid treatment; nevertheless this red underglaze, when treated with hydrochloric acid gave off a large amount of carbon dioxide; nitric acid dissolves about 80% of the material, and the liquor resulting from this treatment contains copper, lead, iron, aluminum, manganese, calcium, magnesium, potassium and sodium. The insoluble part is composed of silicon, aluminum, iron, calcium, copper and volatile and combustible material.

From these results, *yeou-li-houng* appears to be a mixture of: pulverized copper particles, ferruginous clay, and limestone. Thus limestone would replace the pulverized carnelian in the formula given by Li.

Quantitative analysis confirms this estimation.

Silica	12.27%
Alumina	3.11
Iron Oxide	3.32
Copper Oxide	14.03
Lime	34.28
Magnesia	0.40
Potash	0.46
Soda	0.53
Carbon Dioxide	27.14
Water	1.01
Volatiles	2.53

From this analysis and from the preceding, one can deduce by calculation that the red underglaze is composed of about:

UNDERGLAZE RED BATCH COMPOSITION

Copper Filings	25
Red Clay	10
Limestone	65

Such would be the composition of red underglaze, which gives such beautiful results where the firing is favorable to its development. I have made up a glaze from this analysis, and later on I will indicate the results that I have obtained with this substance, which seems to be very difficult to master.

COPPER RED GLAZE SYNTHESES

GEORGES VOGT

COPPER RED

Without going into the composition of the copper red glaze deduced by analysis of the multiplicity of glassy materials used by the Chinese, I have instead introduced two lead glasses melted in advance, one constituting a colorless crystal and the other containing copper oxide, manganese and iron, which makes an olive green enamel after fusion.

The colorless crystal is obtained by melting:

COLORLESS CRYSTAL COMPOSITION

Sand	50%
Litharge	30
Potash	12
Soda Ash	8

One makes the olive green enamel by melting:

OLIVE GREEN ENAMEL COMPOSITION

Above Crystal	91.5%
Cupric Oxide	3.4
Manganese Dioxide	1.0
Magnetite	4.1

These two materials serve to contribute in the red glaze, the lead, the artificial jade, the copper filings, the glass beads and the bottle glass.

A red glaze is prepared by fine grinding a mixture of:

REPLICA COPPER RED GLAZE COMPOSITION

Olive Green Enamel	20
Colorless Crystal	20
Pegmatite	30
Kaolin	4
Quartz Sand	20
Limestone	13
Magnesite	3

which percentages correspond to those found by analyzing *kun-houng*, neglecting only fluoride, which amounts to 1.75%.

Melted in the conditions necessary to the development of red, the glaze cited here gives a beautiful red, identical to *kun-houng* (which in each firing was taken as a trial piece). If, in a badly regulated firing, the reconstructed red gave a greenish yellow, the Chinese glaze took the same coloration.

Scherzer's shipment contained a biscuit-fired vase covered with raw *kun-houng* glaze; this vase was fired to 1300°C in a Perrot furnace at the Sevres laboratory; the melt was perfectly successful and the red obtained was even more pure of tone and more transparent than that covered with the same enamel that had been fired in China.

I am going to describe at length the following way to obtain, in the Perrot furnace, a convenient reducing fire for the development of the red glaze, of celadon and in general of all of the oriental porcelain.

Firing is divided into three periods of one hour: the first hour the flue damper is closed to 3/4, the air inlet to the burner is only opened ½; the second hour one opens the air inlet to 3/5 and to 4/5 during the third hour; and then the damper is opened completely; gas is admitted to the burner at a pressure of 0.018-0.020 (meters?). Under these conditions, when the temperature has been taken to 1250-1300°C, I have consistently obtained good copper reds with the Chinese glaze as well as with that reconstituted from the analysis.

UNDERGLAZE RED

To reconstitute this material from its analysis, I have mixed and ground with care:

REPLICA COPPER RED UNDERGLAZE COMPOSITION

Ferruginous Clay   20%
Limestone   66
Copper (precipitated)   14

This mixture and the *yeou-li-houng* applied on porcelain in the form of brush marks, along with the glaze designated by Scherzer as that used to cover copper underglaze has only rarely given the red tone that it ought to give, even in firing them where the glaze *kun-houng* had been taken to its red color; nevertheless each time that the *yeou-li-houng* became red, it was the same with the reconstituted red; in the unsuccessful firing, the duplicate and the copy have constantly been the same color, sometimes green, sometimes a yellowish green.

Even though I have not been successful in the rapid fire of the gas furnace in knowing the conditions required to develop the underglaze red, the similarity of results obtained with the original and the copy proves the correctness of the analysis that I had of *yeou-li-houng* and that of its reconstitution.

He that loves a rosy cheek,
Or a coral lip admires,
Or from star-like eyes doth seek
Fuel to maintain in his fires;—
As old Time makes these decay,
So his flames must waste away.

Thomas Carew—Disdain Returned

36 ANNOTATED BIBLIOGRAPHY

In addition to the preceding chapters, which contained examples of classical texts, there are also some minor classics which can be referred to in slightly less depth. This chapter will cover the more recent examples of copper red work and will contain short descriptions of them, so that if you have a desire to read them you will have an idea of their contents. Where it seems appropriate, the description of the work will be a little critical, so that you may avoid wasting time looking up articles which are frequently quoted, but which may not be of interest to you.

1. ORIGIN OF COLOR IN COPPER RUBY GLASS - Atmaram (Atma Ram) -
   University of Mysore - 1970.

Atmaram has spent a lot of time working with copper ruby glasses and in this pamphlet—besides giving several compositions for successful glasses—he promotes his thesis that copper ruby glasses are colored by cuprous oxide rather than copper metal. Since I think that copper metal is normally the coloring agent, I disagree with many of his propositions. Because of the length of the paper and because of the amount of work that the author has done in the copper red glass field, it has to be listed, but I find it difficult to concur with his theses.

2. THE PRODUCTION AND CONTROL OF COPPER REDS IN AN OXIDIZING KILN ATMOSPHERE - A. E. Baggs and Edgar Littlefield - J. Am. Cer. Soc., (1932), **15**, p. 265.

These authors report experiments that show the possibility of producing copper red glazes in an oxidizing or neutral kiln atmosphere, through using silicon carbide powder in the glaze batch or in an underglaze slip. I have tried some of these techniques in a gas fired kiln in an oxidation mode, without too much success. Probably the use of an electric kiln would be better for producing these copper reds, because there would be less loss of carbide from the washing of the flames.

3. CONSTITUTION OF COPPER RED GLAZES - S. F. Brown and F. H. Norton -
J. Am. Cer. Soc., (1959), **42**, p. 499.

This paper presents a good technical study of the reactions taking place during the formation of copper red glazes. They used controlled atmospheres, controlled heating conditions and controlled quenching conditions, and altogether used a very scientific approach to the problem of copper red glazes. The only drawback of their work is that it was done on very small pieces in a laboratory test kiln with atmospheres that would be hard to duplicate in commercial size kilns. They give good reasons for the possibility that copper metal is the colorant in copper red glazes. This paper is readily available and is well worth studying because of its careful experimental work.

4. NOTES ON THE SANG DE BOEUF AND THE COPPER RED CHINESE GLAZES - J. N. Collie -
Trans. Brit. Cer. Soc., (1917), **17**, p.379.

This paper is one of the earlier classics on copper red glazes and in it we find that Collie has made very shrewd estimates of what is causing copper red glazes. He is fairly certain that the red color is copper metal by analogy to the copper red colors in glasses. Collie recognizes that the amount of copper in the *sang de boeuf* glazes is very small and that if this amount of copper is oxidized, it is converted to only a faint green color because of the small quantity of copper involved. He also comments about the microscopic appearance of copper reds and the fact that the red does not permeate the whole glaze, but is present in a thin layer. He also remarks that, as tin is necessary to cause coloration in colloidal gold colors, that possibly copper reds are due to the action of ferrous ions or stannous ions, which would cause reduction of cuprous ions to metallic copper.

5. ON THE DEVELOPMENT OF A COPPER RED IN A REDUCING ATMOSPHERE - Louis Franchet -
Trans. Brit. Cer. Soc., (1907), **7**, p.71.

This work is a paper by a practicing French potter reporting to the British Ceramic Society. It is very interesting to hear this account, describing the actions that he observed during the manufacture of copper red glazes. He advocates the use of alkalies and the need for more tin oxide than copper, as well as the benefits of fritting a glaze. He further comments on the necessity of limiting the oxidation firing so that it doesn't burn out the red after it has already been formed. Other than that, it is a good early account of making copper red glazes in a factory.

6. RED GLAZES AND UNDERGLAZE RED BY REDUCTION - C. M. Harder -
J. Am. Cer. Soc., (1936), **19**,p. 26.

Harder describes the type of firings to be found in most art-type kilns today. He lists several different kinds of glazes and has some interesting comments to make. He recommends the use of reduction of a glaze, followed by oxidation at the end of the firing. Also he recognizes that glazes high in lime produce some of the opalescent effects which lead to flambés and purplish glazes. The chief value of this paper is his recommendation that a very uniform gas composition is valuable for copper red formation and that reduction and oxidation must be taking place at the proper time with regard to glaze fusion.

7. CHINESE CERAMIC GLAZES - A. L. Hetherington - Chapter 3, (1948), Los Angeles.

Hetherington does a good job of covering the state of the art of copper red glaze formation at this time. Many of his comments and many of his illustrations are derived directly from Mellor's work of 1936, in the Transactions of the British Ceramic Society. Everyone who reads Hetherington's work should make a point of going back to read Mellor's two articles. It will then be found that almost all of Hetherington's remarks were made previously by Mellor.

8. THE CHEMISTRY OF THE CHINESE COPPER RED GLAZES - J. W. Mellor - Trans. Brit. Cer. Cer. Soc., (1936), **35**, p. 364 & p. 487.

If there were no other reason for characterizing Mellor's work as a classic, the main reason would be for the complete bibliography which he includes at the end of Part I. He gives an excellent list of references from the very earliest times up until the writing of these papers. However, in addition to this he has some other fine points to make. My favorites are the excellent photomicrographs that he supplies, which show some of the basic characteristics of copper red glazes in the ox blood, the peach bloom and the opalescent type. Mellor's explanation for the presence of the green coloration in peach blooms is outstanding. His very careful examination and description of all of the layers found in a cross section of an ox blood glaze are helpful even though one may not agree 100% with his conclusions. He also notes that either tin oxide or ferrous oxide can reduce cuprous oxide to the metal. In addition he comments on the luster-type copper reds, and his section on peach blooms is unsurpassed. All in all, Mellor's work is well worth studying.

9. THE CALCULATION OF TRANSMISSION CURVES OF GLASS STAINED BY COPPER AND SILVER COMPOUNDS - H. Rawson Phys. & Chem. of Glasses, (1965), **6**, p. 81.

This modern work by Rawson is valuable because of its comments about copper reds and yellows in glass and the conclusions that he has drawn from electron micrographs and transmission curves of his stained glasses. Rawson diffused cuprous ions into glass in exchange for sodium ions and noted that the glasses were then stained yellow. When he examined these yellow glasses with the electron microscope, he found no evidence of any particles in the glass. However, when the yellow stained glass was reduced by hydrogen, and was again examined by electron microscopy, he found that very fine particles could be observed in the glass. In the red stained glass he found that the largest of the particles were 300 Angstroms in diameter and that they graded downward from that. The fact that he found no particles in the yellow (cuprous) stained glass intimates that cuprous copper in glass is in solution and that cuprous oxide or silicate would not give a red color.

10. COLORATION OF GLASS BY GOLD, SILVER AND COPPER - S. D. Stookey -
J. Am. Cer. Soc., (1949), **32**, p. 246.

Stookey tackles the problem of whether metals or metal ions are dissolved in glasses. And, although he is dealing mostly with gold, some of his conclusions can be extrapolated to copper. His general conclusion is that metals have to be dissolved in glass in the form of ions, and that their subsequent appearance as neutral atoms and their agglomeration into particles is what causes the coloration in ruby glass. He considers that tin is acting as a reducing agent.

11. COPPER REDS - by Several Authors -
Studio Potter Magazine, (1979), **8**.

Approximately half of this issue of the Studio Potter magazine was devoted to comments by several studio potters on techniques for making copper red glazes and glasses. This series of articles is well worth reading because there are so many practical tips given by the several authors. However, because of the variety of comments made, one may be a little bit confused after reading the whole. One of the best facets of this issue is the large number of glaze recipes which are cited by the authors.

12. RUBY AND RELATED GLASSES - H. J. Tress -
Phys. & Chem. Glasses, (1962), **3**,p. 28.

This is an interesting collection of thoughts by Tress on redox potentials in glass and possible reactions between copper and either the ferric-ferrous couple or the stannic-stannous couple.

13. COLOURED GLASSES - Woldemar Weyl -
Soc. Glass Tech., (1948), London, pp.420-435.

Professor Weyl, like Mellor, has given us an excellent collection of references as well as a very thought provoking section on copper in copper ruby glasses and glazes. While we may not agree with all of his suggestions, he has provided us with a treasury of ideas. No one who is serious abut copper rubies should omit reading this section in Weyl's book.

14. COLLOIDS AND THE ULTRAMICROSCOPE - Richard Zsigmondy -
John Wiley, (1914), New York.

This book is a classic in the realm of colloid chemistry and the comments that Zsigmondy makes in Chapter 17, on Submicroscopic Nuclei in Colorless Ruby Glasses, need to be read by serious students of ruby glasses. His descriptions on the development of color and the development of crystals in ruby glasses are too good to be missed.

37 BIBLIOGRAPHY

Andreson, Laura, COPPER REDS - Studio Potter, (1979), **8**, p. 12.

Atmaram, ORIGIN OF COLOR IN COPPER RUBY GLASS - U. of Mysore, 1970.

Bachman, G. S., Fischer, R. B., & Badger, A. E., OBSERVATION OF GOLD PARTICLES IN GLASS - Glass Industry, (1946), **27**, p. 399.

Baggs, A. E. & Littlefield, E., THE PRODUCTION AND CONTROL OF COPPER REDS IN AN OXIDIZING KILN ATMOSPHERE - J. Am. Cer. Soc., (1932), **15**, p. 265.

Ball, Carlton, COPPER RED GLAZES - Studio Potter, (1979), **8**, p. 38.

Bamford, C. R., THEORETICAL ANALYSIS OF SPECTRAFLOAT GLASS - Phys. & Chem. of Glasses, (1976), **17**, p. 209.

Bancroft, Wilder & Nugent, R., COPPER OXIDE IN THE BORAX BEAD - J. Phys. Chem., (1929), **33**, p. 729.

Beyersdorfer, K., ELECTRON MICROSCOPIC INVESTIGATION OF RUBY GLASSES - Optik, (1949), **5**, p. 557.

Brill, Robert, GLASS AND GLASSMAKING IN ANCIENT MESOPOTAMIA - (1970), The Corning Museum of Glass, pp. 119-122.

Brown, S. F. & Norton, F. H., CONSTITUTION OF COPPER RED GLAZES - J. Am. Cer. Soc., (1959), **42**, p. 499.

Bushell, S. W., ORIENTAL CERAMIC ART - Appleton Co. (1899), N. Y.

Clarke, F. W., DATA OF GEOCHEMISTRY - Dept. of Interior, (1920), Bulletin #695.

Coleman, T., COPPER RED GLAZES - Studio Potter, (1979), **8**, p. 21.

Collie, J. N., NOTES ON SANG DE BOEUF GLAZES - Trans. Brit. Cer. Soc., (1917), **17**, p. 379.

298

Cordt, F. W., SUGGESTIONS FOR THE PRODUCTION OF RED GLAZES - Ceramic Industry, (1933), p. 172.

Dalton, R. H., PHOTOSENSITIVE GLASS ARTICLE - U. S. Patent - #2,422,472.

Doremus, R. H., GLASS SCIENCE - Wiley, (1973), Chapter 4.

Ebell, Paul, COPPER RED COLORATION IN GLASSES - Dingler's Polytechnische Journal, (1874), **213**, p. 53 & 131.

Franchet, Louis, THE DEVELOPMENT OF COPPER RED IN A REDUCING ATMOSPHERE - Trans. Brit. Cer. Soc., (1907), **7**, p. 71.

Fremy & Clemandot, - Ding. Jour., (1846), **94**, p. 465.

Gilard, P. & Dubrul, L., COLORATION OF GLASS BY STAINING - J. Soc. Glass Tech., (1936), **20**, p. 225.

Glasstone, Samuel, THE ELEMENTS OF PHYSICAL CHEMISTRY - Van Nostrand(1949).

Graff, W. A. & Shelley, R. D., METHOD OF COPPER STAINING GLASS U. S. Patent #4,253,861.

Grebanier, J., CHINESE STONEWARE GLAZES - Watson-Guptill, (1975).

Grego, P. & Howell, R. G., GLASS STAINING METHOD - U. S. Patent #3,079,264 and #3,429,742.

HANDBOOK OF CHEMISTRY AND PHYSICS - 46th Edition, Chem. Pub.

Harder, C. M.,RED GLAZES AND UNDERGLAZE RED BY REDUCTION J. Am. Cer. Soc., (1936), **19**, p. 26.

Hautefeuille, Bull. Soc. d'Encouragement, (1861), p. 609.

Hetherington, A. L., CHINESE CERAMIC GLAZES - Commonwealth Press, Los Angeles, (1948).

Hobson, R. L., CHINESE POTTERY AND PORCELAIN - New York, (1915).

Honey, W. B., THE CERAMIC ART OF CHINA - London (1946).

Ivanova, E. A., DIFFUSION OF COPPER ION INTO GLASS - Structure of Glass, (1960), **2**, p. 241.

Kiefer, W., DIFFUSION COLORS IN GLASS - Glas. Ber. (1973), **46**, p. 156.

Kingery, W. D. & Lecron, J. A., OXYGEN MOBILITY IN SILICATE GLASSES - Phys. & Chem. of Glasses, (1960), p. 87.

Kingery, W. D. & Vandiver, P. B., Song Dynasty Glazes - Bull. Am. Cer. Soc., (1983), **62**, p. 1269.

Kring, W. D., COPPER RED GLAZES - Studio Potter, (1979), **8**, p. 8.

Kroeck, W. H., METHOD OF COLORING GLASS - U. S. Patent #2,701,215.

Lauth, C. and Dutailly, G., RESEARCH ON COPPER REDS AND CELADONS - Bull. Soc. Chim., (1888), **49**, p. 596.

Lawrence, W. G., CERAMIC SCIENCE FOR THE POTTER - Chilton, (1972).

Leibig, E. C., COPPER STAINING OF GLASS - U. S. Patents #2,002,900, #2,075,446, and #2,198,733.

Mann, Jean, COPPER REDS ON PORCELAIN - Studio Potter, (1979), **8**, p.23.

Mantell, C. L., TIN - Am. Chem. Soc. Monograph.

Marboe, E. C. & Weyl, W., THE CHEMICAL DEPOSITION OF MIRRORS Glass Industry, (1945), **26**, p. 119.

Maurer, R. D., NUCLEATION AND GROWTH IN A PHOTOSENSITIVE GLASS - J. Appl. Phys., (1958), **29**, p.1.

Medley, M., THE CHINESE POTTER - Phaidon Press, (1976).

Meistring, R., et al., SILVER AND COPPER ION EXCHANGE ON GLASSES - 10th International Congress on Glass, (1974), p. 8-71

Mellor, J. W., THE CHEMISTRY OF THE CHINESE COPPER RED GLAZES - Trans. Brit. Cer. Soc., (1936), **35**, p. 364 & 487.

Mie, G., Ann. Physik., (1908), **25**, p.377.

Muller, Max, Dingler's Jour., (1871), **201**, p.147.

Parmelee, C. W., CERAMIC GLAZES - Cahner, (1973).

Partington, J. R., A TEXTBOOK OF INORGANIC CHEMISTRY - Macmillan, (1944).

Peters, E. & Frischat, G. H., EXCHANGE OF COLORING IONS IN GLASS - Glastech. Ber., (1977), **50**, p. 63.

Peters, E. et al., THE KINETICS OF COPPER ION EXCHANGE IN SILICATE GLASSES - Glastech. Ber., (1980), **53**, p. 162.

Peterson, M. M., METHOD OF COLORING GLASS - U. S. Patent #2,498,003.

Plumer, J. M., TEMMOKU - Idemitsu, (1972).

Ram, Atma, ORIGIN OF COLOR IN COPPER RUBY GLASS - U. of Mysore, (1970).

Rawson, H., TRANSMISSION CURVES OF GLASS STAINED BY COPPER AND SILVER COMPOUNDS - Phys. & Chem of Glasses, (1965), **6**, p. 81.

Rhodes, Daniel, CLAY AND GLAZES FOR THE POTTER - Chilton, (1973).

Schwoerer, Daniel, PRODUCING BRILLIANT COPPER REDS IN GLASS Studio Potter, (1979), **8**, p.16.

Seger, H. A., COLLECTED WRITINGS - Chem. Pub., (1902).

300

Silverman, A., COLLOIDS IN GLASS - Colloidal Chemistry Volume III, J. Alexander, Chem. Catalog, (1931).

Singer, S. S., USING COPPER FOR COLORING GLASS - Cer. Ind., (1951), August, p. 72 and September, p. 69.

Stookey, S. D., COLORATION OF GLASS BY GOLD, SILVER AND COPPER - J. Am. Cer. Soc., (1949), **32**, p.246.

Tichane, R., CHING-TE-CHEN: VIEWS OF A PORCELAIN CITY - NYS IGR, (1983).

Tichane, R., THOSE CELADON BLUES - NYS IGR, (1978).

Tress, H. J., RUBY AND RELATED GLASSES - Phys & Chem. of Glasses, (1962), **3**, p.28.

Tress, H. J., RUBY AND RELATED GLASSES - Glass Tech. (1962), **3**, p.95.

Turkevich, J. et al., THE COLOR OF COLLOIDAL GOLD - J. Coll. Sci. Supp. I, (1954), p.26.

Turner, T., COPPER RED SALT GLAZES - Studio Potter, (1979), **8**, p. 19.

Valenstein, S. G., A HANDBOOK OF CHINESE CERAMICS - MMA, (1975).

Wettlaufer, George, COPPER REDS FOR POTTERS - Studio Potter, (1979), **8**, p.24.

Weyl, W. A., COLOURED GLASSES - London, (1959).

Williams, A. E., NOTES ON THE DEVELOPMENT OF THE RUBY COLOR IN GLASS - Trans. Am. Cer. Soc., (1914), **16**, p.284.

Williams, H. S., METHOD OF STAINING GLASS WITH COPPER HALIDE VAPORS - U. S. Patent #2,428,600.

Wohler, Ann. Chim. Pharm., **45**, p. 134.

Yates, J. A., ELECTRICAL BEHAVIOUR OF BRONZE SPECTRAFLOAT GLASS - Glass Tech., (1974), **15**, p.21.

Zsigmondy, R., COLLOIDS AND THE ULTRAMICROSCOPE - Wiley, (1914).

INDEX

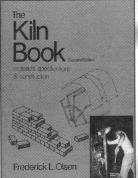

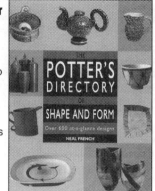

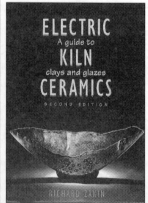